Escape to the Mountain

Escape to
the Mountain

*A Family's Adventures
in the Wilderness*

Marcia Bonta

To Pop, who shared the mountain
with us for a time.

Axios Press
P.O. Box 118
Mount Jackson, VA 22842
888.542.9467   info@axiospress.com

Distributed by NATIONAL BOOK NETWORK.

Library of Congress Cataloging-in-Publication Data

Bonta, Marcia, 1940-
    Escape to the mountain : a family's adventures in the wilderness / Marcia Bonta.
        p. cm.
    Originally published: South Brunswick, NJ : A.S. Barnes and Co., 1980.
    Includes index.
    ISBN-10: 0-498-02365-6 (cloth)
    ISBN-10: 1-60419-002-7 (pbk.)
    ISBN-13: 978-1-60419-002-1

    1. Bonta, Marcia, 1940- 2. Bonta, Bruce. 3. Mountain life—Pennsylvania—Centre County. 4. Wilderness areas—Pennsylvania—Centre County. 5. Natural history—Pennsylvania—Centre County. 6. Centre County (Pa.)—Biography. I. Title.

F157.C3B662 2008
974.8'53—dc22

                                                            2008009562

Contents

Acknowledgments

I COULD NOT HAVE written this book without the help of all the males in my life. First, my father, Harold Myers, who took me hiking over his old home territory near Pottstown, Pennsylvania when I was a girl. He told me of his boyhood, of how he roamed the hills in all seasons of the year, and I vowed that I would raise my children in the mountains of Pennsylvania.

My husband Bruce, whose parents were also displaced Pennsylvanians, agreed with me and we did not stop searching until we found our dream home. Bruce also encouraged me to write this book and was my principal editor, painstakingly working over each sentence with me.

Our three sons were always cooperative subjects, willing to listen and to constructively criticize my efforts at writing. They have appreciated the home we chose for them and reward us by saying they are happiest exploring the woods and fields.

Finally, my father-in-law, Henry G. Bonta, "Pop," who had great faith in my book and who read and corrected my manuscript before I submitted it for publication. Pop died in March, 1978, just a week before this book was accepted by A.S. Barnes and Company.

We love quiet; we suffer the mouse to play; when the woods are rustled by the wind, we fear not.

Indian chief to the
governor of Pennsylvania, 1796

Chapter 1
Discovery

SLOWLY OUR VOLKSWAGON bus ascended the steep mountain road. Five eager faces peered out of the windows. "Gee, we could really go over the edge there," Steve shouted exuberantly as we all stared down the sheer drop to the tumbling mountain stream below.

"Are we going to live up here in the woods?" David asked excitedly. Mark just wriggled in his seat, uncomfortable in his wet diapers.

Bruce kept his eyes straight ahead as he carefully navigated up the deeply rutted dirt road. Finally he turned to me. "Are you sure you have the directions right?"

"Oh yes," I answered confidently, but I was quite relieved when we came at last to a fork in the road.

"The realtor told me to take the left fork over a small wooden bridge," I said, peering down at my scribbled notes. We bumped over the primitive plank bridge and continued climbing. Suddenly, as we emerged from the woods, we could see a wide expanse of fields and a cluster of buildings ahead. Rounding the last curve we passed a small white tenant house. A large bank barn and a tool building were above us to the right, but our eyes were drawn up to a terraced knoll on the left. A large white house with green shutters and stately columns loomed almost level with the tops of the locust and black walnut trees clustered on the lawns below. Framing the scene on the lawn was an old stone springhouse and well. It was the springhouse that sold me. "I don't care what this place looks like inside. Let's buy it!" I exclaimed.

The small white tenant house, later renamed the guesthouse, the first building the Bontas saw as they rounded the last curve of the road.

The next day, when I called the realtor, I was cautious. "We are interested," I said, "but we're a little concerned about the road. Surely a school bus couldn't get up there."

"Well, no, I don't think so," he answered hesitantly, "but I'll call the school authorities and find out."

"Anyway," I continued, "we would like to see the insides of the buildings before we decide." So we set a date for a tour. Unfortunately, the following day began the long Fourth of July weekend, and we had to wait several days to return. The days crept along as we dreamed about our discovery. Already the boys imagined themselves hiking through the woods, and I kept trying to imagine myself navigating that road, especially in wintertime.

Bruce, as usual, exuded confidence. "Don't worry. We'll just solve each problem as we come to it. You want the house, don't you? So we'll buy it."

But we didn't tell the realtor that. We cautioned the boys to button their lips, and this time we took the road in the realtor's four-wheel drive jeep. "Need one of these to get up here in the winter," he commented as we jolted along.

"And I guess I'll need a plow too," Bruce retorted. Inwardly I groaned. Another car! We had enough trouble and expense keeping one repaired. Besides, two cars seemed needlessly extravagant. But I didn't say anything. I let them do the talking and waited to see if the place would hit me just as hard on second sight. It did—and I felt strained as I tried to appear nonchalant.

*The Bonta home in winter, a large,
white house with stately columns.*

We entered the big house by the back kitchen
door. The boys stayed outdoors to explore. The
kitchen was smaller but in far better shape than the
one I had left on our previous farm in Maine. Of
course, it needed work. In fact, every room in the
house but the master bedroom needed work. It had
seen loving care in the past, but during the last few
years the owner, a local businessman, had only lived
there periodically. He had not been able to maintain
it properly. The only furniture in the living room
was an enormous pool table. Ugly stains marked
the dining room walls where the roof leaked. Optimistically I trooped up the winding stairs behind
the realtor. He seemed to be secretly amused about
something.

Perhaps it was the blue and white perfection of the master bedroom, which had been redone a couple years before the previous owner had purchased it. The room had three large windows and a whole wall of closets with louvered doors. I could picture it filled with our hand-stenciled Pennsylvania farm bedroom set and the old pine chest I had refinished. We had always had a blue bedroom and blue and beige furniture to match it. This room, at least, seemed a good omen. The other three bedrooms were more disheartening. The room next to the master bedroom was particularly dark and dingy, with only one window, hideous wallpaper, and a repugnant smell coming from the piles of junk stored in it. Another room was dark because the shutters had been closed to hide the jagged broken windows. It also had dirty dark-brown wallpaper. After seeing the last bedroom, I suddenly started.

"Wait a minute! Where's the bathroom?" I asked.

The secret smile spread. "You'll never guess," he chuckled.

"But this place must have plumbing," I stated.

"Oh, yes! And the bathroom is in the basement."

"Good grief, why?"

"Well, you see, this place has been used as a summer home for many years," he explained. "There is no central heating upstairs either and no insulation or storm windows. Usually they just had a tenant farmer living in the little house as a caretaker."

I was beginning to see some of the problems we were going to have. So did Bruce, and he carefully listed them for the realtor. We would need to buy a second car, since Bruce would have to commute in our bus to his new job at Penn State, twenty-six miles away. Leaking roofs in the shed, tenant house, and main house had to be repaired immediately. We had to heat the upstairs and put in a bathroom. I began to wonder if he was having second thoughts. Gloomily I joined the boys outside, while Bruce and the realtor hashed out the problems.

The boys were busy cramming their mouths with black raspberries which they had discovered growing all over the sagging broken fences. "And there's the old outhouse," Steve pointed out cheerfully. "It has nice wallpaper and three holes—even one for little kids," he added. "It has an electric light, a fan, and an old sign on the door that says 'Kindly flush toilet after each use except when train is in station.' It's really neat!" I went to investigate and found myself in the midst of an enormous old Concord grape vineyard which also supported a thriving black raspberry patch.

Berries are my weakness—I can't get enough of them. Our farm in Maine had had only a few wild blueberries, so I was thrilled by the obvious abundance of berries here. I visualized miles of pies, dozens of cobblers, and uncounted bowls of cream and honey—all filled with berries I had picked in the warm summer sun. "First the springhouse, now berries," I thought. "This place has got to be paradise." When Bruce and the realtor reappeared, though, I was cagey. "Let's see the other buildings," I suggested. So we paraded through the two-car garage, the barn, the tool building, and the rather shabby tenant house. It did have plumbing and wiring of a sort, but that was about all it had. Actually, I was more excited by the purple martin house perched on a high pole out behind the garage. It was centered in the obvious remnants of a large vegetable garden. My gardening blood began to boil. It was obvious that we wouldn't starve here anyway.

Finally, the viewing was over. The boys danced about as Bruce solemnly declared to the realtor that he wished to put a deposit down. "But," I heard him say, "we can't possibly pay the listed price. There are too many things wrong with the place. And we do have to buy a jeep for winter access." At his office in town the realtor drew up a proposed sale agreement with a much lower price on it than that asked for by the seller. Bruce wrote out a check to accompany our offer, and we retreated to suburbia to wait out an agonizing weekend while the realtor went to talk with the owner. At last, on Sunday night, he called with the joyful news that the offer had been accepted. We could close the sale as soon as all the details of mortgage, title, and search could be worked out—maybe in a month or so.

During that waiting period we had plenty of things to keep us occupied. We drove to the town to buy a secondhand jeep, but first we road-tested it on the mountain. "Used to call these jeeps 'kidney killers' when I was a boy," Bruce said encouragingly as we jounced along. "But they sure do ride smoother now."

"I guess so," I murmured unbelievingly as I turned to look down into the ravine, still nervous about the sheer drop-off. "What are we going to do about the school bus," I asked.

"Oh, I'll drop the boys off at school on the way to work," he answered casually.

"But you'll be leaving at 6:45 in the morning," I protested.

"Hope the school opens early," he replied.

"What about getting home?"

"If we buy this jeep, it can be your car," he said grandly, "and you can pick them up at the school every day."

"Oh, boy," I commented flatly.

We did buy the jeep, and I got fond of its ability to drive with the tenacity of a fast bulldozer. But I still had the boys' schooling to consider. We had found that country schools were disastrously uninspiring, so I sighed as I called up the school authorities to register Steve and David. First I had to persuade them to skip each boy one grade because of the private schooling they had received in Maine. Then I had to make certain they could be dropped off at 7 each morning. To my delight, I was granted an interview with a literate and highly innovative administrator. When he saw Steve's and David's records, he promptly agreed to enroll them in the third and first grades.

"Uh . . . do any of your schools start real early?" I asked hopefully.

"Just one begins at 8."

"That's the one they'll have to go to then," I decided and explained our situation. He looked at me as if I were slightly mad.

"You mean you're going to live way up in that place?" he queried.

"Yes, and I don't suppose you could get a school bus up there?"

"Oh no, that would be impossible, but the bus could pick them up and let them off down at the highway," he offered. It occurred to me that the boys could certainly walk across the metal bridge that spans the river, up and over the four main line tracks of Con Rail, and up the mile and a half mountain road to the house. Already I knew in my heart that I was not going to go down the mountain in the winter, even to pick up the boys.

But my good luck was not over. The school administrator continued studying Steve's written evaluations. "I see you are interested in the free school movement," he commented. "We have a small part of the school experimentally enrolled in a nongraded program. Steve is just old enough to qualify." I stared unbelievingly at him. Could we actually get a good education for our boys in this small town? I was thrilled and showed it.

"Please sign him up," I insisted. He looked happy and muttered something about how most parents were opposed to and suspicious of the new program. I left his office in a spirit of good feelings toward the school system.

A few weeks before moving day, we drove up the mountain to show off our find to curious relatives. They were the first of a long list of people who said, "We don't believe this road." But once they reached the property they retracted a bit with, "Well, it is a unique location." Then, "Don't you have any neighbors at all?"

"The realtor doesn't think so," we answered. But we did wonder about that fork in the road just before the little wooden bridge.

Several days later, as we came up the mountain, Bruce said suddenly, "Let's see where that right fork goes," and he swung up the road before I could protest. After a short way we were confronted with two barking dogs. There was another house on the mountain! A woman was hanging clothes on the line, and she came up to greet us when we drove into her yard.

"Hi! We're going to be your new neighbors," Bruce said as he introduced all of us. She seemed pleased and particularly entranced by the boys. "Children on the mountain," she sighed happily. "Just like it was when we were kids." The "we" referred to her invalid brother that lived with her. They asked us to call them Fred and Margaret.

Once it was known that we were buying the Plummer homestead, the realtor began receiving calls from a Mrs. Plumb, the elderly former owner. "I want to meet the Bontas and tell them all about my old home," she requested.

When we stopped at her house in town, she related stories from her youth on the farm, and she even remembered some stories that her father had told her of his boyhood there. Mentioning that Fred and Margaret were also part of the original Plummer family, she told us that the hollow was named after her grandparents, who had been the original settlers on the mountain. With this start Bruce began combing old history and genealogy books, newspapers, deeds, and tax records. Combining the documentary records with the personal narratives remembered by Mrs. Plumb, Fred, and Margaret, we began to get a better feeling for the people who had had the individualism to carve out a farm on the top of the mountain.

The earliest settlers lived in the nearby valleys during the time of the Revolutionary War, though they climbed up the mountain to hunt for deer and turkeys. At least one settler fought a pitched hand-to-hand battle with an Indian on top of the mountain, presumably somewhere near our farm, and that same settler was murdered by a party of Indians that swooped down off the mountain the next year. By 1800, however, the Indians were no longer a threat, and in 1813 an iron forge was established at the bottom of the mountain where the Plummer's Hollow stream empties into the river. The forge company bought vast tracts of land on top of the mountain in order to obtain a large supply of hardwood for conversion into charcoal. In fact, the circular remains of three kilns used for burning the wood into charcoal are still easily visible along the top of the highest ridge. The fifteen-foot-wide holes are considerably filled in with over a century's accumulation of leaves, but because the ridge in that area is very narrow and drops off steeply on both sides, the winter winds have kept the earth around the holes scoured clean of leaves. The blackness of the charcoal layer on the ground is still instantly noticeable. The forge company had built a wagon road up the hollow paralleling the stream so the charcoal could be hauled down to the forge. After a century and a half, it is still our only access road up the mountain.

It was around 1832 that William Plummer went to work at the iron forge. The son of pioneering parents, he had decided to stay in Pennsylvania near the family rather than strike out toward the opening West. Billy, as he was called, was a large, strong, and industrious man. As the years passed he accumulated enough money by 1850 to purchase fifty-five acres of mountain land from the forge company. The following year he began working for the Pennsylvania Railroad, which had just been laid through the valley at the base of the mountain. Sometime in that decade he built a log cabin on his new farm, directly below the knoll where our house now stands. A couple of cows and horses were stabled in a log barn, and a large apple orchard was established above the barn.

He and his wife Catherine had a daughter and eleven sons. The family apparently lived year-round on the farm sometimes and other times spent their winters in their house in the valley. When the War Between the States erupted, five of the oldest boys went off to join the Union forces. One was killed at the siege of Petersburg, but four returned in time to help their parents build a new house to replace the log cabin that had burned to the ground. Thus our tenant house had been built in 1865, entirely crafted by the Plummer boys, with its six-pane sash windows and vertical board and batten siding.

Of course, a houseful of males generated numerous stories. One winter they assembled a large bobsled and went soaring down a steep path through the woods. The sled swerved off the path and hit a tree, and as one of the boys put it in later life, "Plummers were scattered all over the Allegheny Mountains."

According to another local storyteller, "You should never fight a Plummer: if you lick one, there's always a bigger one to lick, and the devil himself can't lick the old man." So Billy and his ten sons strode bigger than life through the old tales.

In 1871 he paid a contractor to build the big white house on top of the knoll, just above the site of the old log cabin. But he and his wife lived only eight years in their new home before they died—she quietly and he violently. On the morning of November 25, 1879, a few months after his wife's death, Billy was at work in the local railroad yard examining the locks and doors of a train standing on a siding. At 4:48 A.M. a freight train going east passed on the outside track, making enough noise to mask the sound of an approaching mail express on the inside track. Billy turned around just in time to be struck by the bumper of the passing engine, and he was killed instantly. So the Plummer family was quickly shorn of its nucleus. All that remained were memories to treasure, a personal estate to settle among the heirs and, in the words of his eulogy, "an excellent farm with valuable improvements upon it."

The heirs sold the farm to one brother, Jacob, in 1881, but his wife disliked the mountain and its isolation. In 1892 another brother, George, purchased the farm as a summer estate. George had gone to Juniata College and became a well-known lawyer in Chicago. The same year he bought the farm he also made a second marriage. His first wife had died several years before. The new wife, Mary, gained national fame as parliamentarian of the General Federation of Women's Clubs. Both she and George looked forward to their summer months away from Chicago at their retreat on "The Mountain," as they always called the place.

When the old barn burned down in 1914, Mary designed a new one patterned after the traditional Pennsylvania barn, with an overhanging forebay on the south side and a bank on the upper northern side leading into the second floor. Her design incorporated a gambrel roof with an unusual added kick over the forebay area. The same year she also designed and built the tool building that sits on the south slope just below the barn. She partitioned off part of the building into a chicken coop and avidly went into raising poultry. An old photo in Fred and Margaret's possession shows her scattering grain to a large flock of turkeys and chickens in front of the barn. Mary laid out extensive grape arbors on the slope below the main house, a large garden near the woods above the house, and numerous berry patches around the garden.

In 1935 George and Mary deeded the farm over to their daughter Phyllis. She and her husband Kenneth Plumb also used it as a summer home away from their year-round residences in Pittsburgh and Cleveland, where Ken was an executive with the U.S. Steel Corporation. They began modernizing the house in 1950, when they finally had an electric line brought up the mountain to the farm. Planning to use the farm as a retirement retreat, they drilled a well and installed modern plumbing, heating, and wiring systems. An architect from the city was commissioned to design two big new sweeping porches on the house. Just as final plans were ready for putting heat and plumbing in the second floor of the house, Ken suddenly died. Phyllis clung tenaciously to the place for eleven more years before advancing age finally forced her to sell it. After 118 years, the homestead passed out of the Plummer family. Shortly after we moved in we decided to name our home Plummcrest in honor of the Plummers and their development of a unique mountaintop farm.

But unlike all the previous owners, we were determined to live there all year long and to learn the changing moods of all the seasons. As we signed the final ownership papers, we knew a little about the mountain and the buildings, and we had a few vague ideas of how we would cope with the problems of the isolated setting we had chosen. But we had much to learn.

Chapter 2
First Year Woes

WE MOVED TO the mountain at the end of August. No large moving van could make it up our incredible road, so Bruce hired some willing teenagers and a truck. As they backed the truck up to the door and started unloading, a major problem developed. The second floor of the house could only be reached by a narrow, winding staircase. Even bureaus wouldn't go up the stairs, let alone our enormous double bed with its seven-foot-high headboard. After surveying the situation, Bruce removed the sashes from one of our bedroom windows, put a ladder against the side of the front porch roof, and hoisted the furniture up with a rope. The teenagers and I stood agape, but Bruce had learned that country living is synonymous with getting by somehow. And to our amazement all our bedroom furniture did make it through the window and into the second floor.

The suburban-bred teenagers stared at the house we had bought. Paint was peeling off the veranda where the roof leaked. Most of the rooms had faded, peeling wallpaper, several bedroom windows were broken or cracked, and many of the floors were hideously painted or covered with old, cracking linoleum. The tool building and the tenant house (which we planned to use as a guest house) were badly in need of paint, and both buildings had roofs that leaked. "Well, good luck," one of them muttered doubtfully as he left. But lost in the euphoria of rolling fields and wooded hilltops, we hardly listened. Even if we had, nothing could have dissuaded us from buying the house. It had lots of land, and that was all that mattered.

As the months passed we constantly reminded ourselves of our love for the land as we struggled with the difficulties of fixing up an old house. Some of the problems could be remedied with money, and luckily we had a little left from the sale of our Maine property. We immediately became acquainted with that most exasperating of American creatures, the contractor. Even before we bought the house, we had asked him to come up for estimates on the leaking roofs, the upstairs heating, and the need for a bathroom somewhere else besides the basement. "Easy enough," he said, waving his hands, making suggestions, and giving a reasonable estimate. Bruce and I smiled happily at each other when he agreed to begin work immediately after we moved in. For once we would pay someone else to do our work.

Ah, what innocents we were! As September faded into October, the roofs still leaked and the upstairs grew frigid. Worst of all, that midnight trip to the bathroom down two flights of steep stairs was hazardous. "Oh, well! At least we don't have to use the outhouse," I said with relief. In the meantime, I spent most mornings on the phone talking to the contractor's secretary, who seemed to be sympathetic. To our relief, the roofing workers finally arrived, but not before the ceiling of the guest house kitchen caved in one rainy day. In a few days our home and outbuildings had new roofs, but by then it was November. Several suburban relatives were expected for Christmas, and we just had to have heat and an upstairs bathroom by then. That was what we told the contractor each day when we desperately called his office.

In the meantime we piled our beds high with blankets, feather ticks, and sleeping bags. Mark slept in his crib with his clothes on under three sets of pajamas and a heavy sweater. We had neither storm doors nor windows, the house was not insulated in any way, and the frigid winds whistled through all the cracks.

Despite our pleas to the contractor, we had neither heat nor a bathroom by Christmas. What we did have was the most devastating flu imaginable. Fifteen days before Christmas we collapsed one by one before the onslaught. Lying in cold bedrooms we shivered and heaved and tried to muster the strength to get down those two flights of stairs to the bathroom. Bruce and the boys dominated the buckets and bathroom at first, but one cold night I awoke very sick indeed. Slowly and painfully I crept down the stairs, stopping to rest every few minutes. At last I made it to the bathroom, and just in time, but that climb back upstairs was interminable. I kept stopping to sleep on the cold stairs because I nearly passed out.

Just as we were recovering, the workers finally arrived to begin the second floor bathroom. Even while we lay sick in bed, they trooped cheerfully up and down the stairs. But although we felt better, the powerful flu germ still lurked in the house. Between Christmas and New Year's, three different sets of guests came and went, taking the flu germ with them. One guest passed out on the cement basement floor and, with poetic justice, those cheerful workers also were struck. "If only it had been the contractor," we muttered vengefully!

He continued on—hale, hearty, and promising— but still there was no heat upstairs. Then came the coldest day of the winter. The thermometer registered ten degrees below zero, and the wind whipped through our house at fifty miles an hour. It was then that Bruce decided to give up on the contractor and begin the long job of installing heating ducts to the second floor himself. After six weeks of sawing and hammering, mess, and confusion, he finished the job, and we were warm upstairs at last.

Whenever we grew frustrated with the progress of indoor work, we went outside to observe the wildlife on the mountain. We frequently saw white-tailed deer, cottontail rabbits, and red squirrels that first winter, and we often surprised opossums scurrying along the road. Eagerly we hung up a bird feeder on the back porch, and it was instantly discovered by the dark-eyed juncos. Rapidly the word spread to the tufted titmice, black-capped chickadees, white-breasted nuthatches, and a pair of downy woodpeckers. By January the evening grosbeaks, wintering goldfinches, tree sparrows, cardinals, and white-throated sparrows had joined the throng of regulars at the feeder. All this free entertainment kept Mark shrieking with delight—which frequently scared the birds away. At night the mountain echoed with the eerie calls of the screech owls and the reverberating hoots of the great horned owls.

The weather, though, was the source of most of our amazement, and sometimes we wondered if the elements were being particularly vengeful toward us. The day before Thanksgiving, we were surprised by a ten-inch snowfall. That weekend we had a marvelous time sledding down our huge, hilly lawn before the normal rain and fog of late autumn returned to the mountain. On into December it rained, and Christmas was very brown and balmy. January, too, began deceptively warm, but at last, in the middle of the month, real winter weather finally arrived. By the time February stormed in, I was able to haul out my Maine snowshoes, and Bruce began to learn the art of plowing a rocky mountain road. Although he had plowed a path wide enough for our jeep, he had made a bad blunder. Our thousand-gallon fuel tank was almost empty by Valentine's Day, and the path was not wide enough for the oil truck to get up the mountain. So for one long day Bruce plowed down the road, each time getting nearer to the edge of the steep mountainside as he precariously pushed the tons of packed snow down the slope. After ten trips he was satisfied enough to call the fuel company. "Could you please try again?" he begged. We had only one day's worth of fuel left and no fireplaces to use even in an emergency. They promised to try the next morning, and we waited in real trepidation. Hours of silence passed, and then we heard a low, labored roar. Slowly the oil truck advanced, and finally rounded the last curve. We cheered as he came up the driveway. It had taken him an hour and a half to make it up our road, and he had almost given it up several times.

Three days later it began to snow hard. It fell thickly and quietly throughout the night and the following day. The snow was deep, but Bruce easily plowed down the road as we drove into town to load up on groceries. On the way back up the mountain, the wind began to blow, and small drifts started forming across the road near the bottom of the hollow.

But we innocently went off to sleep that night, secure in the belief that the hollow was so protected from the wind that drifting was impossible. Shutters slammed against the house as the wind screamed over the mountaintop. By morning the snow had stopped, and the sky was bright blue, but still the wind blew. After a hearty breakfast of pancakes, Bruce went blithely out to plow the road. The drifts along the driveway were enormous and packed solid. The jeep and plow could not budge them. Still undaunted, Bruce grabbed a shovel and began digging. Hour after hour he worked, far into the afternoon, believing that if only he could clear the 600 feet of road down to the guest house, the protected hollow would be free of drifts.

As the afternoon waned, I bundled up against the ten-degree temperature and coursing winds, strapped on my snowshoes, and headed down the road to look things over. On and on I went, up and down colossal drifts, past the guest house, past the corral, and past the little wooden bridge. Over a quarter of a mile from the house the drifts finally petered out. By then I was in the deepest part of the hollow, which indeed protected the road from drifting.

Sadly I went back to report to Bruce. Being snowed in did not worry me—but the cost of being bulldozed out did. When Bruce called the bulldozer operator, he discovered that our snowfall had been the biggest blizzard in ten years. Twenty-two inches had fallen— dairy farmers in the valley were snowed in, schools were closed, and many people were in line ahead of us to be bulldozed out.

The next day was gray and damp, but I was determined to snowshoe down to the railroad tracks. In the middle section of the hollow I removed my snowshoes

The author snowshoes through the
woods after the big blizzard.

and walked, but as I neared the bottom of the mountain, five-foot drifts rippled and curved across the road, higher even than the drifts around the house. I could hear a train on the tracks below, but the big slippery drifts falling straight down into the ravine blocked my way. Slowly I turned to plod back up the mountain, moving quietly through the silent woods. The stream had ice along its edges and high banks of snow on each side, but still it flowed along, a rippling, open passage through the virgin snow.

The following day our mountain remained quiet and untouched. Only the feathery tracks of ruffed grouse and the patter prints of field mice marred the white covering. After Bruce broke a snowshoe trail to the far field, I easily followed his tracks, although I did break my own trail up to the top of the first field. Each step in the softening snow was a heavy effort—but I just had to see the view. The nearest mountains were in a deep purple cloud shadow and the distant ridges were light blue and white. On the horizon I could see Nittany Mountain.

When we weren't snowshoeing we were wearing a trail over the lawn with our sleds or watching the birds at the feeder. Never had we had such a carefree time, closed off from the business of humanity, without radio or television, the only tracks our own or the wild creatures. But on the fourth day our serenity was shattered as the bulldozer came clattering up the road. Even for such a huge machine, the going was difficult. Still, it rescued us. The question was, from what had we been rescued, the beauty of isolation? Reluctantly the boys went off to school the next morning, and Bruce went back to work. Mark and I were left alone in our white world.

Spring flitted in and out during March, filled with blustery winds, snow flurries, and occasional warm balmy days. The day of the vernal equinox was particularly lovely, and the first eastern phoebe came winging in, flicking his tail and singing his monotonous song. I was lost in the wonder of a mountain spring. Geese swept over each night, bluebirds lined up on the telephone wire, flocks of robins hopped over the lawn, and the crows cawed from dawn till sunset in the lengthening light.

In the midst of a sudden temperature drop near the end of the month, snow flurries began to fall thickly, blown about by the strong winds. As I sat inside, gloomy over the apparent return of winter, I suddenly heard a familiar cry above the wind. I ran out into the blowing snow to find our front yard covered with killdeers. Some took alarm and fled to the fields, but the swirling air was filled with their wild cries. Excitedly I watched them search for the first emerging insects, calling their vociferous "kil-dee" to each other as they moved about. For just a few hours I heard and saw enough killdeers to keep me content, but then they whirled off, heading on toward their nesting sites in the valley fields.

April was a wonderful time. We saw our first wild turkey on Sapsucker Ridge, the guest house woodchuck paraded up and down the walk, and the place was filled with cottontail rabbits. Deer grazed peacefully in the field; sometimes we counted twenty in a single herd. All the wild animals seemed bold and unafraid of us. Driving up the road one day, I noticed a strange bird walking along ahead of us. "Is that a chicken?" I asked Bruce. It certainly walked like a chicken, bobbing its head and looking very tame, but its coloring was peculiar. To my amazement, it turned out to be a male ruffed grouse. I had never seen one clearly before—only as an exploding blur in the woods. But this time, despite a roaring jeep and shouting boys, the grouse fluttered leisurely off the road and went stalking slowly into the woods.

Not only the animals and birds enjoyed the new season. Milk snakes and garter snakes uncurled in the warm, still places, and the wildflowers began to appear. First the trailing arbutus bloomed along the paths, and then the coltsfoot emerged down by the stream. Clumps of blue and white hepatica grew in company with tiny white violets and delicate rue anemones on the eroded bank along the road. Our yard was a haze of yellow forsythia, yellow daffodils, and the pale rose of emerging red maple leaves. Between rain storms we walked, explored, identified, and waited impatiently to plant our first Pennsylvania garden. In the meantime we feasted on winter cress and dandelion greens, and we watched the new rhubarb come up from its fall-planted bed.

May arrived with a few clear days, and we managed to plug some peas into the wet ground. But mostly it just rained and rained. Desperate now, we planted despite the wet ground. We set out blueberry bushes, and one heroic day we put in 110 strawberry plants. Next came the digging of a monumental fifty-foot ditch for the asparagus. Near the end of the month we planted the warm weather crops, interspersing the flowers and herbs among the vegetables in an effort to repel bugs. May went by in a haze of garden work, wildflower hikes, and bird observations. We lived every nice day outdoors. By Memorial Day the ground had at last dried out, and we were actually beginning to look for rain.

During the month of June we had more rain than we had ever seen before. At the height of the laurel display on June 10 we were granted one perfect day to admire the sight—then the clouds dropped over us once again. We watched in frustration as the garden turned into a muddy lake and choked up with weeds.

On June 20 the rain turned into a torrent. Two days later Bruce mentioned that the Little Juniata River at the bottom of our mountain had been rising rapidly. "Call the police about 3 P.M. to see if the bridge is still passable," he requested as he dashed out the door and headed for work. Secretly I felt he was being overanxious.

By early afternoon the boys were getting restless. "Let's go downtown to the public library," I suggested.

Enthusiastically they put on their boots and rain-coats, and we raced out through the pounding rain to the jeep. As I started down, I was amazed at the two streams that coursed along the car tracks. By the time I reached our little wooden bridge at the fork, it looked like a river was running down the road ahead of our car. When I saw the height and ferocity of our little mountain stream surging beneath the bridge, I became uneasy. Maybe Bruce hadn't been exaggerating after all. But confident that the jeep could see us through almost anything, I gingerly crossed the bridge and continued on down the mountain. Suddenly a thought flashed through my mind—of course I can get down, but maybe I'll have trouble getting back up again. To the distress of the boys, I decided to back the jeep up the slippery flooded mountain road a quarter of a mile to our house.

As I entered the door, still shaking from my ordeal, the phone rang. It was Bruce. "According to the radio, there's bad flooding all over Pennsylvania. Please call the police and find out about our bridge." Feeling rather foolish, I hesitantly dialed and a very harassed man answered. "How is the bridge over the Little Juniata?" I asked.

"All bridges across the river are closed," he said abruptly.

"But how can my husband get home from State College?"

"No chance, lady, all roads from State College have been sealed off."

In despair, I tried to call Bruce back, but the telephone refused to work. Thoroughly alarmed and desperate to contact him before he started a fruitless journey home, I donned a poncho and boots and ran the half mile to our neighbor's house through the streaming roaring water. I met her at the fork in the stream, where she stood calmly poking at the clogged debris. "Margaret, we're sealed off," I shouted above the noise of the water. "All the highways are flooded and our bridge is impassable." Since she listens to the radio almost as infrequently as I do, she was surprised but not alarmed. Somewhat calmed by her matter-of-fact attitude, I followed her quietly into her house. Her phone, too, didn't work, and I anxiously ran back home.

"Daddy called," Steve reported. "He said he is coming home, but he won't take any chances."

"He'll never make it," I protested. The boys lined up solemnly at the windows, confident that Daddy would do the impossible. Meanwhile, I prepared for the inevitable power break that the high winds would bring. An hour later Steve shouted, "Here comes Daddy!"

"I don't believe it," I answered, but above the howling wind and rain I heard the sound of our bus swinging jauntily up the drive.

"How did you get here?" I exclaimed happily.

"I took Route 550 down through Stormstown, forded several small streams, and gunned it over the big bridge. The river is just inches below the floor of the bridge," he added casually. "Then as I crossed the tracks and approached the woods I could see a two-foot wall of water ahead where our stream is roaring across the road. Without thinking, I tromped on it and slammed into the stream. The bus bucked, hesitated, filled with steam, and barely lurched through to the other side. The culvert pipes under the road must be plugged. With the incredible force of the water, the road will be cut in half in a couple hours." He added that many of the crossdrains coming up the mountain were clogged, and if he didn't act quickly the road would wash away in several places.

After a short rest, Bruce went out into the hurricane to try to open up the clogged drains and save the road. I continued dinner preparations, optimistically hoping that the power would not go off. Just as I began heating up the skillet, the lights blinked out. Feeling frustrated, I hurriedly sent Steven down the road to find Bruce with the message that he should come back and fire up the Coleman stove so I could finish dinner. Somehow I wasn't thinking clearly when I sent him out into that terrible storm. I had supposed that Bruce would be just a short way down the road. Steve was only eight then, but very big for his age, and I had great faith in his capabilities outdoors. However, I had forgotten that he couldn't swim, and when an hour had passed without his return, I became desperately worried. I had visions of him being swept away in the flood waters. Almost hysterical with worry, I paced around, berating myself for sending him out in such weather.

Then a small sodden figure in a bright yellow raincoat came trudging up the road. "Where is your father?" I shouted.

"I couldn't find him," he said. "I found the bus at the big pull-off a mile down the road, and I looked and called, but I couldn't find Daddy." He went on to explain how he had cautiously tramped down and back, avoiding the rushing water. He was quietly proud of his own part in the emergency.

I still had a nagging worry about Bruce's absence, but shoving my fears aside, I served up a cold meal and waited. At dusk Bruce finally came back—weary and wet—but with some of the drains unclogged and the road in better shape to withstand the storm. He had not heard Steve's calls because he had been up in the woods searching for rocks to rebuild a badly washed out retaining wall. We went to bed by candlelight thankful that the frantic day had ended.

The next day it was still raining, though not as hard. With no electricity, I struggled to fry eggs on the Coleman stove, which was out on the back porch perched precariously on our rickety night table. It was cool, damp, and dark inside, so we hitched our chairs close to the windows for light to read by. Finally, in mid-afternoon, we all began to grow restless. Imagining that the skies were lightening, we set off in the bus to see how the big bridge and river fared. We bounced and jostled down the washed road, parking at the big pull-off. Clad in boots and raincoats, we walked down toward the bottom of the road. Our stream was now a roaring river. Every gully down the mountainside streamed with rushing water. When we reached the edge of the woods, I was amazed at the power of the water sweeping through a five-foot deep gash in our road. Carefully we threaded our way around the curve of the stream and crossed it on the remnants of an old planked bridge that had been more sensibly built to withstand flood waters. The stream rushed on through a deep gully and under the railroad tracks. For once the tracks were totally silent—not a train moved through. As we walked down the steep slope of the railroad bed, I was amazed to see our stream flowing swiftly across the county road where another culvert was blocked. Bruce gingerly waded back and forth across the stream, carrying one boy at a time. I held back fearfully, but finally I grasped his hand and also made it across.

At last I could clearly see the Little Juniata River surging over the state highway and sloshing across the floor of the large metal bridge. I watched numbly as the river slammed broken trees and debris against the side of the bridge. Spectators stood silently on high land across from us, watching the bridge, the water, and us. Most of the railing boards had been smashed, and it was a miracle that the bridge still held. We also watched, willing the bridge to withstand the terrible power of the water. "But all those people over there are probably hoping to see it break loose," Bruce commented. We soberly remembered that the bridge had gone out, back in the flood of 1936, and it had been many months before it had been rebuilt. If the bridge went, our only link with town would be the railroad tracks and our own two feet for transportation.

Finally, we abandoned our hopeful vigil and decided to hike along the tracks toward town. Already the flood waters had retreated from the stores along the main street, though they were closed and dark on that Friday afternoon. Only a dingy bar was open—people drinking, singing, and lurching out from its dark depths—and I wondered how many of the patrons had lost all their possessions in the flood. Then a patrol car stopped beside us as a policeman growled "Everyone off the streets now—there's a curfew in effect!"

"At 4 P.M.? There must be looting going on to cause such a thing," I commented unbelievingly to Bruce. Later we discovered that my guess had been correct. Every flood-damaged city in Pennsylvania had been plagued by looters, and the National Guard had been called out to stop them. It was disquieting to see tanks patroling the streets, so we hastened back to the railroad tracks and went out of the town.

The walk back along the tracks seemed unutterably long and wearisome. To our left was the sewage treatment plant, which the flood had made inoperable. The Little Juniata beyond was an open sewer, flinging toilet paper into tree branches and making the air smell vile. I longed for the pure air of our mountaintop and a good clean shower from the pristine water of our well. The drizzly rain had turned into a downpour, and we walked along in muffled, gray, stinking silence. We only glanced over to see that the metal bridge still held; then we plunged eagerly back into our woods, with its roaring streams and tumbling waterfalls. Struck again by its awesome beauty and sweet air, we were thankful that we lived on a mountain. Later that evening the lights flashed back on. We bathed and read and ate and finally slept.

The following day it was still raining, but Bruce had to find a way for us to get out. The flood waters had receded and the metal bridge had held, but our own road was completely washed out at the bottom of the mountain. Bruce loaded the bus with a pile of oak planks that had been left in our barn, hauled them down the road, cleared the former roadway at the edge of the woods, and rebuilt the top of the old plank bridge. After working on it all day, we finally had a way out into the flood-ravaged world. At last we learned the extent of the disaster to the river valleys of Pennsylvania. Such lovely fertile areas those valleys are, and yet, when the rivers rise to reclaim their own, puny buildings collapse like matchsticks before the powerful waters.

The last two months of our first year were almost anticlimactic. But still, nature seemed to be doing her best to discourage us or, perhaps to discover if we were sturdy enough to live on the mountain.

In July the earth dried out at last, and we actually had a heat wave. It lasted persistently for nine days—

scorching sun, little breeze, and breathless nights—but the garden grew amazingly. We worked outdoors in the morning and evening, and in the afternoons we wrote, read, or did projects in our cool basement. Meals were simple and cold; we drank lots of liquids, took salt tablets, and waited for the cool weather to return to our mountain.

When it did, it brought no rain. In fact, we went from flood to drought conditions, and the garden, which had finally begun to look prosperous, started to sag by August. We knew our well was not deep enough for irrigating, so I reaped only enough vegetables to eat and none at all for our big new freezer in the basement. In addition, all the early crops had been nibbled to the ground by voracious cottontails. We had no peas at all and precious little lettuce and chard. Then they began on the beans and carrots. The drought and the cottontails joined forces with a horde of Japanese beetles to finish the destruction of the garden that summer, and all of our garden talk seemed to begin with "next year we will."

As if in recompense for all our setbacks, nature produced bounteous wild crops with which we filled the freezer. We stuffed ourselves with black raspberries, blackberries, and blueberries, and still I had dozens of quarts to freeze. Day lilies flourished in the grape arbor, and their sumptuous buds helped to supplement our vegetable diet. Our own cultivated blueberries had long since been demolished by the cottontails, and the strawberries had been choked by the pestiferous bindweed that invaded the garden.

By September our first year was finished. We had survived the contractor, the blizzard, the flood, the rabbits, and the drought. Our progress both inside and out had been very slow, but we took it all philosophically. Our first year in Maine had been just as disheartening. It takes awhile to get a real grip on a new country home. And though we made many mistakes and had more reverses than advances, we could always step outside, look at the sweeping fields and distant woods, and think how lucky we were to live in such a beautiful place. We could take ourselves off for a walk and, after a few minutes along the paths, our hearts would lighten as we began to make new plans for the many years ahead of us.

Chapter 3
Rambling over Plummcrest

SEVERAL YEARS PASSED, and we spent our time learning as much about Plummcrest as we could by observation and hiking. Gradually we began to develop a little knowledge of all the varied habitats we found on our 140 acres. We learned what to expect of the old grape trellises in the spring, when to look for trailing arbutus on the trails, and what flowers grew in the fields and woods. As we talked about these places we began putting our own names to them. And each year Plummcrest became more uniquely our own bit of land.

We never ceased to marvel at the miracle of the grape tangles. The old broken down trellises meander back and forth along the slope below the back porch, and the poles lie sagging and broken under the huge gnarled vines. Burdock infests the few paths through the area, masses of day lilies carpet the ground with a splendid show of deep orange and green, and giant staghorn sumacs thrust their red fruits high above the maze. Enormous blackberry briers tear at anyone who tries to penetrate the thicket, while numerous wild rose bushes scattered over the slope manage to display their pink and white blossoms each summer despite the competing vegetation.

Every year we vowed to clean up the wild tangle, repair the trellises, and leave just the correctly pruned grape vines. But we find ourselves confused and hopelessly outnumbered by all the fruitful wildings that have intruded among the vines. Large, beautiful elderberry bushes provide white blossoms and deep purple berries which I use for our favorite jelly. The area around the old outhouse at the upper edge of the slope yields an enormous crop of black raspberries. And near the bottom of the slope an old gnarled apple tree looms high above the tangle. During our first autumn on the mountain the old tree produced several dozen large yellow apples that had a wonderfully sweet taste. But since then there has been no crop; only the grapevines that twine up through the lower branches of the tree bear fruit.

The apple tree serves as a lookout perch for all kinds of birds. Evening grosbeaks always land in its branches before they sail into the feeder, and cardinals flee there if they are startled while foraging on the ground. The main trunk of the tree is thick, branching into two heavy limbs that support the growth of all the smaller branches. Both limbs are lifeless near the top, and a yellow-bellied sapsucker has riddled the one limb and stripped off its bark.

Sometimes it seems as if all the woodpeckers on the mountain have to come and explore those two dead limbs. Downy and hairy woodpeckers frequently scoot up one limb or the other, and one winter an immature red-headed woodpecker included the old tree as part of his imperious domain. But the most spectacular visitors to the apple tree came one morning as we sat in the kitchen eating breakfast. We suddenly noticed two large birds swoop out of the woods and land on an oak tree at the edge of the clearing. We rushed to the windows to watch. It was our first good view of pileated woodpeckers, and we were very excited. Then one of the huge birds flew into the old apple tree, hammered on the largest limb for a few minutes, and finally swooped up and over the house. The second pileated woodpecker also landed on the old tree and spent fifteen minutes searching for insects before flying off.

The old tree and the surrounding tangles also provide food and shelter for the smaller songbirds. Juncos, chickadees, tree sparrows, titmice, and all the other regulars dash up to the porch to snatch seeds from the feeder—but the slightest movement at the window sends them fleeing back to the safety of the grapevines. Red squirrels and cottontail rabbits also use the thickets for shelter. One winter an opossum denned in the thickest part of the tangles; another winter a hen pheasant took refuge there, and she found enough food to last her until spring.

With the approach of spring the first signs of life begin to appear on the ground beneath the vines as thousands of lime-green day lily shoots poke up along the slope. Then one day we notice that the large buds on the grapevines have opened into tiny, soft, rose-edged leaves. But though the flowers, grass, and tree leaves grow amazingly fast during April and May, the grape leaves take forever to develop.

At last, in early June, the grape leaves are the right size and tenderness for eating. They became a favorite delicacy in our home when we discovered the Greek dish dolmades—grape leaves wrapped around a filling of ground beef, brown rice, mint leaves, parsley, and onions and simmered in a sauce of beef stock and tomato paste. In the middle of June we can begin to harvest the flower buds of the day lilies, which I serve to the family either boiled or sautéed.

But the Concord grapes themselves are always extremely slow in developing. By August the bunches are full size but still hard and green. Sometime in late September, when the nights grow cool, they are finally just right. Each morning I fill baskets with them, and for weeks Mark and I sit on the back porch in the sunlight, stripping grapes from the clusters and dropping them into an enormous pot. Suddenly the harvesting is over. Autumn wanes and the grape vines sag, as they once again shelter the wintering birds. Juncos and sparrows flock back and twitter in the trellises, a cardinal perches on a sagging wire, and a winter wren investigates a fallen pole. As winter settles over the mountain, most of the land seems cold and lifeless. But the wildlife continues to find food, shelter, and warmth in the south-facing tangles below our back porch.

On the veranda side of the house the lawn stretches over to the driveway. Just beyond the driveway the first field slopes gradually up to the base of Sapsucker Ridge. It is a long, narrow field of thirty-seven acres, shaped very much like an old skeleton key. It was reclaimed from an apple orchard twenty years ago, and for a while the former owner was able to persuade a local farmer to bring his haying equipment up the mountain. For several years we were unsuccessful in getting anyone to cut the field. Each spring the honey locusts and blackberry bushes crept further away from the woods, while late in the summer a sea of goldenrod filled the field with waves of burnished color. The boys played "fox and rabbit" in the tall grass, and the deer grazed peacefully at its edges.

Most of the first field is too steep for cultivated farming. But it does have the virtue of getting the earliest and warmest beams of sunlight in spring. There the first large purple violets appear, and along the

*The view from the top of the first field looks down
at the barn below and the mountains
that stretch off to the horizon.*

edge of the field next to the stream, the earliest yellow coltsfoot emerges. We hold our late winter and early spring picnics on its warm slopes, and we often go to the top of the field for March sunbaths. Most of the berries we harvest in the hot summer sun grow along the edges of the first field. The large, plump black raspberries ripen first in mid-July. Two weeks later the huge juicy blackberries are ready, and I easily pick 80 quarts each summer.

Whenever the weather is warm I sit on the veranda to read or write, turning myself to face the wide sweep of the field. One warm and balmy January afternoon as I sat basking in the sunlight, unable to believe the springlike weather in winter, two deer suddenly emerged from the woods and leaped grace-fully along the edge of the field. They slowed to a walk, ears pricked and white tails high and then paused and looked straight at me. I remained motionless as they moved off unhurriedly. On another warm day a few months later I watched a woodchuck emerge from its hole on the warm slope and forage around in the early spring grass.

At the top of the first field there is an old road that has been cut into the side of the ridge. It winds a half mile through the woods and abruptly ends at the far field. Most of my walks take me to this old overgrown hollow at the far end of our property. It is a peaceful, remote place that has long been abandoned to golden-rod and blackberries, small locust trees, and red maple saplings. Wild grape tangles festoon one end, and on another side it slopes abruptly up to an oak woods. The oldest oak trees on the property—several-hun-dred-year-old giants—form the third border, and the fourth edge blurs into woods. Often in the early spring I have startled large herds of grazing deer, too numer-ous to count, before they leap off.

The far field has a magical feel to it. Just thinking about its quiet existence often keeps me calm, even if I can't always go there when I wish. I have picked berries in summer and seen the last leaves of autumn flutter down. I don't expect to see other people there, and I never have. Sometimes I can hear a train whistle in the valley, but otherwise it is utterly still.

Once I went walking to the far field on a foggy, drizzly day. About halfway along the road I walked right into a very thick cloud. It was a startling experience—I felt almost as if I would be swallowed up and absorbed forever. But then our dog Fritz came streaking up, and the air of unreality diminished.

In the cloud, the woods were motionless and without color, and the sloping hollow of the far field was a faint outline. I sat on my favorite flat rock trying to "feel" the cloud and the reaction of the far field to it. A nuthatch broke the eerie stillness with a businesslike call as it searched for insects. Gradually the outlines of trees and slopes grew more distinct. But the cloud never left the far field while I watched and waited. Evidently it had found a hole to snuggle down into, and it was settling in for the night. I had to climb up through the cloud to continue my walk homeward.

While the far field is my own private place, the trails that crisscross Laurel Ridge are constantly being explored by the boys. The first June we lived on the mountain, on a clear, cool, breezy day, the boys and I had taken a picnic lunch to the top of the first field. Surrounded by tall new grasses, we peered out through the curtain of green to see the sweeping view of distant mountains in their summer dress. Finishing our picnic, we started home down the trail along the ridge. The laurel bushes bloomed in unbelievable splendor, stretching away like pink and white clouds banked high along both sides of the trail as far as our eyes could see. The boys were just as enchanted as I was. "Let's call this the Laurel Ridge Trail," Steve declared, expressing for all of us the wonder of such a beautiful sight. Henceforth the trail and ridge took the name of its most conspicuous bush.

For our daily walks Mark and I usually take a portion of the Laurel Ridge Trail together. We wind up past the farm dump to the top of the ridge and turn left, back to the Sinking Valley overlook at the powerline right-of-way. After a short rest Mark makes the decision to take the Short Way Trail back or the longer way via the Guest House Trail. When he was just two years old we started the almost daily ritual of going up the mountain, and we still take that trail more often than any other. It has been Mark's learning walkway, where he first found trailing arbutus and admired the pink lady's slippers in the spring. He has felt the soft moss that carpets the trail and discovered the British soldier moss that grows on the powerline right-of-way.

One early autumn day, when he was almost four, we went up the mountain as usual. Mark danced along, his eyes sparkling, full of noisy questions. At first we noticed the newly blooming flowers—clusters of white wood asters and late-flowering thoroughwort—and we bent down to examine the minute pale blue flowers of Indian tobacco. Then we discovered the fallen yellow blossoms of the smooth false foxglove. "And look, Mommy, those dried-up brown things are dead Indian pipes," Mark exclaimed. Excitedly, he started to look for the remains of other dead flowers. He quickly found the tired-looking leaves of the lady's slippers and the shiny green trailing arbutus leaves.

His attention remained fixed on the forest floor, and I was amazed at his sharp-eyed observations. He saw myriads of small mushrooms and tiny, unripe wintergreen berries. But he was really thrilled when he discovered a plump green acorn, complete with its little brown cap. He searched around for more, and soon his hands were filled with them. For the third autumn in a row he began his collection of acorns. Somehow their size, shape, and abundance hold an eternal fascination for him that I cannot entirely understand.

He stopped to examine a dead tree, touching its decaying wood and watching it crumble to the ground in a powdery, red dust. He paused patiently to learn about the sassafras tree, and he instantly grasped the difference between the three-fingered leaves, mitten leaves, and plain leaves. The only thing he could not conquer was the pronunciation of sassafras.

"We're here, we're here," he shouted as we stepped into the sunlight of the powerline right-of-way. Crickets chirped, butterflies flitted along, and Mark went exploring—over to a mossy place where he carefully laid his acorns and through the blueberry tangle where he pounced on some ripe berries. Then a shriek of delighted discovery: "Turtle egg shells, Mommy, I found some!" He came running to show me the rubbery white remains of turtle eggs he had noticed beneath an electric pole.

Clutching the shells in his hands, Mark sat down with me on a log and gazed at the Sinking Valley view with its distant blue mountains and neat farmhouses. When we were still, the butterflies came close—yellow, white, black, and orange—all attracted by the goldenrod. Thistle seeds sailed by on the wind, and two wood pewees perched silently on a nearby oak tree. "Isn't it a pretty day," Mark whispered, subdued by all he was seeing.

But he soon leaped to his feet, eager to be off and running. He stopped frequently to run his hands along the soft moss-covered trail, and twice he spotted a fluffy yellow caterpillar crawling over the lime-green moss. He bent to examine some bright red leaves that had already fallen to the ground. Then he noticed that the witch hazel leaves were partly yellow. Autumn was fast approaching.

As we started down the mountain Mark suddenly became impatient with observation. He began running, climbing fallen tree limbs, and shouting with joy. He paused before a huge old stump with a hole at its base. It was a gremlin's house, Bruce once had told him, and he still remembered. He peered into the hole and wondered, "Do gremlins really live there? Where are they? Will they eat me?" All questions were asked with mischievous glee. He wanted to believe, but his almost four-year-old mind protested such foolishness. Then he was off again—a little boy with a great love of life.

There is a shorter trail that goes only halfway to the top of the ridge before circling back to the house. Because I must get up very early on weekdays to get Bruce and the older boys off and Mark sleeps in much later, I quickly formed the habit of taking an early morning walk along the Short-Circuit Trail. Often I startle deer as I walk quietly along. One morning in the early blue light of dawn I went tramping out into six inches of new snow. Off in the woods I saw the movement of a solitary, shadowy figure. A doe was browsing peacefully, and I paused quietly to watch. She saw me, but she only bounced off when I resumed my walk. I often have noticed that in the early morning the deer seem less alarmed by me.

Each small walk on the Short-Circuit Trail is a different experience. For several days one autumn I startled pileated woodpeckers along the trial. They always flew overhead in loud protest at my intrusion. Gradually, though, they began to ignore me, and I frequently was able to watch them land on trees or utility poles and hammer huge holes in their search for carpenter ants.

On a crisp, frosty, winter's day, I walked up past the dump and suddenly noticed the ground littered with fresh wood chips. A rotted tree trunk a couple feet taller than I was filled with fresh new woodpecker holes. One hole was at eye level, and I tried to peer in. A downy woodpecker popped his head out and startled me. I stepped back, averting my face, and tapped on the trunk next to the hole. Out flew the woodpecker, landing high up in a nearby tree without a sound. The rest of that winter, almost every time I took my pre-dawn walk along the Short-Circuit Trail, the little woodpecker popped out of his hole in the dead tree stump as I quietly passed by.

Despite the wildlife I frequently see along the Short-Circuit Trail, I cherish most the peace of dawn, the half hour of untroubled walking which stimulates me to do mundane chores when I get home. A walk on the trail is my own therapy for problems, my recipe for tranquility.

Both the Laurel Ridge Trail and the Short-Circuit Trail are bisected by the powerline right-of-way. Way back in 1907, when electric service came to the town, the power company decided to build a transmission line over the mountain. The powerline right-of-way was constructed over Sapsucker Ridge, down across the middle of the first field, and on up over Laurel Ridge, neatly dividing the farm in half.

Before we purchased our home we hiked along the right-of-way, and we were amazed at the great variety of shrubs, small trees, and ferns that grew there. Many of the shrubs growing all over the dry moss-covered ground were low and stunted, such as the scrub oaks and scrub chestnut oaks. Blueberry bushes looked prosperous, and we foresaw a large crop. There were numerous luxuriant laurel bushes scattered throughout thick beds of ferns. But they all indicated an infertile soil, and the growth very much resembled the rejuvenation of a burned-over area. Several handsome red maple trees stretched almost to the electric lines, and we wondered what the power company would do about it.

Two weeks later we moved in. Eagerly we began exploring the trails, but to our dismay we noticed a strong chemical odor as we neared the right-of-way. There before us lay utter devastation. In order to kill the threatening trees, the power company had heavily sprayed the entire area and every living thing was shriveled, brown, and dead. The right-of-way now formed a long, dark, and smelly blight across our land.

For several months the odor was heavy and extremely unpleasant. We hurried through the area, holding our breath and averting our eyes from the disaster. But over the winter months the smell began to fade to just a lingering remembrance. The following spring we witnessed a small miracle: not everything was totally dead. From the silvered twigs of gaunt blueberry bushes a few small leaves emerged, and at the bases of some of the dead scrub oaks a few new trees had sprouted.

Since the devastation was difficult to forget, we rejoiced each time we discovered a new plant. Large blue violets bloomed, pokeweed sent up new shoots, and the right-of-way became a living portion of our property once again. We found ourselves going there to gaze at the Sinking Valley view, to rest on the small mossy plots, or to sit quietly on a silvered moldering log. When summer came the boys even found some blueberries. During the autumn we sat on the log and watched the hawks soaring majestically along the ridge, heading south for the winter.

The second year after the spraying the right-of-way seemed fully recovered from its ordeal. That spring it showed signs of life long before the surrounding woods and fields did. In the warm sun, blackberry bushes leafed out and blossomed, blueberry bushes sported bell-like flowers, and the scattered laurel bushes bloomed more beautifully than those in the woods. Even a few mountain azaleas flamed pink against the new green undergrowth. Slowly the ferns uncurled— waist-high dark green bracken and feathery yellow-green New York ferns. Along with the blueberries and scrub oaks, the ferns almost completely blanketed the right-of-way. Only a few bare patches of earth and the silvered skeletons of dead trees remained as monuments to the spraying.

That summer the thick cover once again offered refuge for cottontail rabbits and other small animals. The blueberry and blackberry bushes prospered, and we competed with the numerous birds in harvesting the crops. The ground-loving towhees considered the right-of-way prime nesting land; their calls could be heard from early spring until late fall. By autumn the wild turkeys, ruffed grouse, squirrels, and deer were feeding on the sweet new crop of scrub oak acorns. As winter approached the white-throated sparrows and golden-crowned kinglets found ideal brushy places to rest and forage during the cold months. And in late winter the deer fed on the evergreen aromatic sweet fern scattered amidst the dried brown bracken.

The powerline right-of-way continues to be an interesting part of our property, though we realize that some day the electric company may once more attempt to kill all the new growth. But even if they do spray, it will again create only a temporary blight on the mountain. As René Dubos says in his book, *A God Within*, "Destruction always results in a different creation."

Forming a formidable barrier along the northwest edge of our property, Sapsucker Ridge guards the farm from the worst of the storms, winds, and clouds that sweep down off Pennsylvania's Allegheny Plateau. When the wind blows particularly hard out of the west, the mountain seems to shudder from the violent roaring along the crest of the ridge and the whole farm nestles gratefully in its lee. On a drizzly, rainy day, as the heavy cloud masses pile up against the other side of Sapsucker Ridge, small clouds frequently lap over, spilling, swirling, and sliding slowly down into the first field. On other stormy days the wind rises sharply, and storm clouds whirl rapidly down off the ridge toward the house. Suddenly it gets very dark. The rain slashes with great force against the windows, and I can hear the tumult of rushing water sloshing out of the drainpipes and thundering through the ditches. Just as suddenly as they come, the clouds are gone, the rain eases, and the darkness lifts.

When storms, winds, and clouds are not beating over the mountain, Sapsucker Ridge is one of our favorite places to wander. The ridge is not only the highest part of our farm, but it is also the most rugged. Frequently

I clamber over the crest and down a few yards on the other side to one of the steep open rock slides—large fields of huge boulders broken off from the former spine of the mountain and slowly creeping toward the valley below. The view from the rock slides is worth the climb, however—towns, highways, railroad tracks, and developments strung out along the valley, but all dwarfed to insignificance by the Allegheny Mountains beyond. The boys love to go to the rock slides with me, but they are more interested in collecting rocks than in admiring the view. In fact, every little boy that comes to visit is quickly hustled away to the rock slides to hunt for specimens. In the summer months, however, the rock slides are off bounds. Most of the copperheads seen on the mountain in recent years have been on Sapsucker Ridge, and the rock slides are ideal den areas for them.

My favorite part of the ridge is the section between the top of the first field and the far field. The underbrush is sparse, and a number of large fallen trees provide quiet places to sit and watch the numerous birds flitting about. Steve particularly has spent a lot of time there observing the wildlife. One year, to his delight, he discovered a pair of yellow-bellied sapsuckers nesting on the ridge, and he promptly named the ridge after them. Wild turkeys frequently roost in that part of the ridge, and once I startled a flock of six hens out of a tangle of underbrush. They flew up into the nearby treetops and paused for a few moments, but as I drew closer they took off in all directions. In the spring this section of the ridge is carpeted with mayapples and bellworts. Throughout the year two tiny ponds in a slight hollow provide watering places for all the animals and birds.

At the edge of the far field Sapsucker Ridge slopes quite steeply up to a high knob that marks the end of our property, more than a mile from the house. But while it is the end of our land, it is not the end of our hiking area. The mountain continues on through miles of forest, broken occasionally by rock slides, old hunting camps, and small roads that snake up and over, tenuously connecting the valleys on either side. We wander for many miles without seeing anyone, and in reality we have much more than only our own acres to explore. But no matter how often we hike on the mountain, making new discoveries it will take us a lifetime to know Plummcrest fully.

Chapter 4
Winter Solitude

WINTER BEGINS ON the mountain early in December. During the long nights hard winds often roar over Sapsucker Ridge, bringing snow and sleet from the northwest. But the days are frequently still, gloomy-gray, and punctuated with freezing fog and rain. The build-up of snow and ice in our north-facing hollow closes our road to all but four wheel drive vehicles, and it is then that I settle down to the quiet pursuits of winter.

Since Bruce has to take the jeep to work each day, I see little of the world beyond our mountain from one week to the next. Occasionally, however, he takes me down to shop in town, and sometimes we even travel as far as the city, sixteen miles away. The highway to the city parallels our mountain, but how different the scenery is in the valley. The mountain looms gray and clear against the sky, with scattered rock slides standing out against the naked hardwood trees. But once we focus our eyes on the highway, the illusion of beauty is destroyed. Auto junkyards, large billboards, jammed trailer parks, and rows of commercial establishments crowd along its edges. I am so accustomed to the beauty of the mountain that all the ugliness makes a real impact on me. While they seem to be necessary facets of civilization, to me they are symbols of our cluttered, confused, thing-oriented society. I realize the boys need some of the goods that the city provides—such as hiking boots and heavy coats for the deepening winter—but still I resent the necessity of leaving the mountain to pursue those things. The mountain with its sweeping fields and forests, abundant wildlife, and changeable weather represents the natural environment that controls my moods, my activities, and my life.

As ice storm follows ice storm, Steve and David become adept at their daily climb up the mountain from school. I greet them with cocoa and cookies, relieved that they are home at last. When we first moved here we carefully went over the instructions: don't stop on the bridge, don't cross the railroad tracks if you see a train coming, never run across the tracks, and never accept rides from anyone but a neighbor. Still, they were only seven and five years old, and I did worry, especially when well-meaning people would exclaim, "You mean you let those little boys walk up the mountain alone?"

Well, what else could I do? For three months of the
year I couldn't get out by car, and Mark was just a baby,
too small to walk down and up the mountain each day
with me. So I convinced myself that our boys were
gaining self-confidence and independence, and gradually I stopped worrying when they were late. Usually
it was because they stopped to explore or play games.
Sometimes they watched deer drinking in the stream,
and often they had a new bird to report. In the fall, on
beautiful days, they even varied their route by hiking
up to the ridge, a much longer and pathless way.

But one day in mid-December of our second year
they dragged home very late in the midst of an ice
storm. Some of my confidence in them ebbed away
when Steve told their story: "David was walking along
the top of the bank at the edge of the road. I told him
not to, but he did anyway. Then he tripped and slid
all the way down into the stream. He was able to get
out of the stream, but he could not get back up the
steep icy slope to the road. I knew I couldn't leave
him there—he might have frozen to death." So Steve
eased his way down the 75-foot slope, carefully cutting a trail to where David was stranded, and they
slowly crawled and clawed their way back up to the
road. David was soaked, but they forced themselves to
hurry the remaining mile up to the house. Relieved at
Steve's good sense, we added a few more instructions:
don't walk along the bank when it is slippery, and stay
together in bad weather.

During the ice storms, Mark and I are often imprisoned in the house, forced to watch through the windows as the trees and bushes take on a silvery casement of ice. The misty air makes our world white and silver. The birds flock to the feeder looking wet and bedraggled but moving with considerable energy. All their natural food has a brittle, cold covering, and they depend on our seeds for survival. Olive-green wintering goldfinches puff themselves up into feathery balls. Evening grosbeaks arrive in large numbers. Tree sparrows fly at each other in their gluttonous haste, all the while tinkling like Christmas bells.

The storms bring in stray birds—they come once and never again, and I wonder where they have been and where they are going. I hate to label a bird as unknown, but occasionally one appears that does not look like anything in the bird books. During one icy day I glanced out to see a large bird sitting in the middle of the feeder. Its black and white spotted belly was enormously fat, its back was brown, and its beak was very long. We guessed at juvenile starling, but we didn't really know. Our visitor became known as "that funny-looking bird we couldn't identify."

Sometimes, too, I give a common identification to an uncommon bird. On a cold December day I was surprised to see a song sparrow foraging near the feeder. Usually they have all gone South long before winter. But Steven also was watching the birds. "Mom, that's no song sparrow; that's a female purple finch," he declared. To the unobservant eye, the small streaked bird would have passed for some kind of sparrow, but Steve carefully pointed out the forked tail and dark markings about the eye. At once the little bird took on new interest for me. Her flashy mate was far easier to identify, and I knew him well. Now she also became a familiar sight.

After weeks of snow and ice storms, we sometimes have a perfect day. The air clears, it is brisk and invigorating, and the boys prance, yell, dash, hike, and run all day long. They come inside for brief resting moments but are soon out again to celebrate the return of the sun. "Oh, I love this day!" David exclaims, expressing all of our feelings. How good it is to see three sets of reddened cheeks and smell three air-freshened bodies as they race in, flushed from running, to stoke up on treats of fruit and nuts.

Mostly, though, December seems to be made up of rain, sleet, snow, clouds, and cold. But luckily much of the month is devoted to Christmas preparations, for the holiday season begins here as soon as Thanksgiving has ended. The first task is the preparation of our annual Christmas letter. We carefully examine our brief list, adding some names and subtracting those where our relationship has become insincere or distant. Then I draft a summary of the year's events, Bruce rewrites it, and finally we sit down together to make it as accurate, entertaining, and literate as we can. Once the letter receives its final polish, Bruce types it, has it photocopied, and inserts it into the Christmas cards along with my handwritten notes to each friend or relative. We have found, in return, that our caring seems to generate many responses—our most precious gifts each Christmas are the letters we receive along with the token cards.

Christmas shopping is a task I begin in June, mail ordering books and records and watching the current interests of the boys in order to get ideas for presents. They rarely make any requests, and it is up to me to figure out appropriate gifts. By Thanksgiving most of my shopping is finished. I dislike the crowds and canned music of the holidays and the awful feeling of rush and commercialism. I prefer to spend that precious magical Christmas month in quiet preparations at home.

Our Christmas is made up of traditions that began during the first years of our marriage. And each year the boys will not allow us to forget even one of them. "When will you make the gingerbread men, Mommy?" they ask almost daily until I finally roll out the little brown men. The boys help me with the decorating, using icing to make each gingerbread man slightly different from the others: sad ones, happy ones, Santa Clauses, and all kinds of other fantastic little men. The less successful creations are eaten, but the best ones are saved to hang on the tree. The rest of the month the boys make gifts, design Christmas cards, write poems, and plan the Christmas Eve program.

Two weeks before Christmas I finish up the hand-made presents and embark on baking cookies. After many years of trying new recipes, the list has stabilized at eleven different kinds, and I now refrain from baking any more new ones. Two of the cookies are baked for Christmas tree ornaments, and the other nine are for eating. There are nut butterballs and penuche drops, pressed fancy cookies and fruit balls, and "Hello Dolly" bars and marshmallow squares. Then I labor over the pinwheels, the bird's nest cookies, and the brownies. With great ceremony, Bruce brings the Christmas cookie plate down from the attic, and I carefully arrange all the cookies on it. From that moment until well after New Year's, the boys and Bruce have a cookie feast. Right before Christmas the boys decorate an old lard can, fill it with cookies, and deliver it to our neighbors Margaret and Fred.

Usually, while I work on a few simple candy recipes, the boys fill dates with peanuts and roll them in sugar. We take a couple of attractive jars, cover the tops with foil and ribbon, and pile in the candy and dates as presents for their teachers. This is a rather painful job, because the boys really covet that candy, and there isn't much left once the jars are filled.

My final baking effort is directed toward Christmas morning, when there is just too much magic competing with empty stomachs. On Christmas Eve I make the fanciest coffee cake I can and have it ready for the morning to serve up with juice and cheese omelets.

Generally this ruse entices the boys away from their gifts before they faint from hunger and excitement.

During all the flurry in the kitchen, Bruce begins preparations for his annual wreath-making. He and David track through the woods looking for fallen hemlock and white pine branches and suitable pine cones. They tote them all home and drag them into the dining room, where Bruce patiently cuts hundreds of tiny sprigs. He wires them to a heavy circular cable which he has fashioned as a base. Once the greens are attached he adds pine cones and colored balls. The wreath is always very beautiful and lasts for weeks on our door. Very few people see it since we have few visitors during the winter, but it is enough that we have one on our door for our own enjoyment. That simple decoration seems a tribute to the beauty around us.

Getting a Christmas tree is quite a production. Since we have no small evergreens on our property, we have to drive to a tree farm twelve miles away. We wait until a day or two before Christmas and make it a family outing so that all may render their opinions on the most suitable specimen. We spend hours tramping around in the mud, slush, and sometimes snow, agonizing over the best possible tree. In the process of hiking over every inch of the tree farm, we discover bird's nests, pine cones, and lovely mosses among the trees. We have a nine-foot ceiling in our living room, so we finally choose a large tree, either a balsam or a Scotch pine, and bear it triumphantly home.

We begin decorating the tree before supper on Christmas Eve. David makes long paper chains, while the rest of us thread strings of popcorn and cranberries to twine through the branches. All the fancy cookies must be hung along with a variety of handmade ornaments we have fashioned through the years—painted walnut shells, frosted pine cones, eggshell Santa Clauses, and Steve's first angel. Mark contributes great numbers of bells made with egg cartons and crayons. When the tree is at last covered, Bruce wonders whether it isn't a little too crowded and junky. But the boys stand back, exclaiming over each ornament, because to their eyes it is absolutely beautiful—and we agree that it is certainly unique.

By then the boys find it almost too difficult to eat even the simple supper I have prepared. As soon as we have finished, I light a candle for each window in the living room and place several more on the end tables and the old parlor organ. In the flickering candle glow we begin our celebration of Christmas. The boys present the Christmas show they have been writing and rehearsing for several weeks. Then we listen to their grandma recite "Twas the Night Before Christmas" on a record she had cut for us when Steve was a baby. All the lighthearted holiday songs are sung—"Jingle Bells," "Rudolf," "Jolly Old St. Nicholas," and others.

At last we settle into the serious contemplation of Christmas. We bring out a worn copy of the King James version of the Bible and read once again the old stories of shepherds, wise men, and a Christ child. Finally we sing all the beautiful old carols, ending with "Silent Night," and then the magic is over as we blow out the candles. The boys eat a snack, hang their stockings, and hurry up the stairs.

We follow them a few hours later, eager to get some rest and knowing that they will be up long before dawn. One year we were awakened at 2 A.M. by Steve and David tiptoeing downstairs. "Let them be," Bruce advised. "They'll soon be back to bed," and off he went to sleep. I dozed intermittently, vaguely aware that they were still downstairs. Finally, at 4 A.M. I yelled at them to get back to bed, determined to sleep some more. My mistake had been in filling their stockings so well. They were honorable enough not to open wrapped presents, but the unwrapped stocking gifts were too tempting to resist.

Christmas morning is always hubbub and joy as we take turns opening and admiring our presents. Mark's toys are played with first, but soon new records must be listened to, books read, puzzles arranged, and models put together. After a huge Christmas dinner I usually manage to slip out for a peaceful walk. Whatever the weather—sunny and warm, foggy and cold, or even snowy—the mountain seems particularly hushed and serene on Christmas. Inevitably I climb to the top of the first field to see the spectacular view of forests and farmlands stretching off into the distance. As I continue on to my sanctuary at the far field I watch for deer, birds, and other wildlife in the woods. Finally, heading back toward the house along my favorite path, Laurel Ridge Trail, I can't help contemplating the many joys and blessings of the Christmas season.

Once we tuck away the Christmas decorations, shortly after the first of January, winter stretches before us in an unbroken line. There are no holidays to distract us, so we turn toward the outdoors for our recreation. Freezing rain alternates with snow, allowing hours of superb sledding down our sloping lawn and road. The skim of ice that covers the ground makes walking difficult, but the sleds move along at terrific speeds. Turning at the bottom of the steepest slope on the lawn is tricky, and Steve brags each time he misses the drainage ditch. Mark and I don't risk the turn—we take the straight gentle incline from the pear tree, going just fast enough to be exciting.

David, though, is the indefatigable sledder. He plods up and down for hours, trying the road as well as the lawn. I remember when he was three years old in Maine. We had a nice hill in our backyard, and David plugged up and down in the intensely cold, whipping wind, dragging the small toboggan. Since the hill was wide and clear of obstacles, he didn't have to guide. He just plunked himself on the toboggan, gripped the sides with his small, mittened hands, and slid blissfully down the hill. Now he bellyflops with authority on the large sled and steers the runners with practiced agility. It is David who stomps down paths in new storms, who musters his brothers out each snowy day, and who continues sledding long after the others have given up.

On moonlit nights, after the boys are tucked into bed, Bruce and I often slip outside for some sledding. The air is cold and crisp on our faces as we whip down the hill, and it catches in our lungs as we labor back up with the sleds. But we go on and on for hours, captivated by the silence, the white glow of moonshine on snow, and the glitter of Orion in the sky just above the black bulk of Laurel Ridge. Finally we take one last run and rest peacefully on our sleds at the bottom, listening to a great-horned owl calling from the top of the first field. At last we gather the strength to drag the sleds back up to the veranda. The house seems too warm and stuffy when we step inside, but the cocoa I make is a welcome comfort to cradle in our cold hands.

After long days of cold and sledding the weather suddenly turns warmer. In fact, every winter in Pennsylvania we can count on a January thaw to lighten our winter-frozen spirits. The date varies from year to year, but that momentary thaw never disappoints us. The thermometer soars above the freezing point, and the silence of winter is interrupted by the drip, drip, drip of melting icicles. The ground is mushy underfoot; the air is soft and warm.

Even the birds are reactivated. They not only eat, but they sing and call more vigorously than they have for many months. The nuthatches "yank-yank" as they travel headfirst down the tree trunks searching for insects. Echoes of the hammering woodpeckers reverberate throughout the woods. Chickadees perch on the twigs of bridal wreath and attempt a chirp rather than the usual "dee-dee-dee." The tufted titmice call their melodious, "peter, peter," and the crows, who have been away during the cold, "caw" across the fields.

On such days Mark and I cannot stay within the suddenly suffocating walls of our home. We must go out to bask in the sun on a warm hillside and watch the jet trails crisscrossing in the bright blue sky above us. "Is it still winter?" Mark asks as we discuss the possibility of a picnic. Without wool hat or mittens, he cannot understand this change in the weather. He answers his own question. "It must be winter; there is still some snow in the woods." But he is pleased to be able to play on the porch with his trucks and build houses with scrap lumber.

Later I treat him to a winter picnic. I fill the thermos with hot cocoa and prepare the usual sandwiches, fruit, and cookies. Then we debate—where shall we go? Finally we decide to go down the road to eat beside the frozen stream. An uprooted double tree makes a splendid seat, and I tuck the cocoa between the two trunks, nestled in the cooling snow. As we eat we watch the movements of the water beneath the skim of ice that covers a small pool in the stream. Our neighbor drives by, looking slightly puzzled at our mad insistence on having a picnic, but we wave cheerily at her. Finishing our lunch, we reluctantly leave the shining stream and filtered sunlight.

On another warm day we choose the top of the first field for our picnic. After we have eaten we make pillows of our jackets and sprawl out in the beaten down, dried out hay. Lying joyously in the sunlight, we listen to the silence and doze a bit. Suddenly we sit up, just in time to see two deer parade by, slightly below the crest of the hill. They are startled to see our heads pop up, and they run off in confusion. We are slightly drugged by the sunlight, our reactions are slow, and we can only stare after the retreating forms. Eventually we walk home, knowing that it is only a January thaw and not the advent of spring.

But the most wonderful part about the January thaw is the promise it contains. Chickadees can be heard singing "fee-bee," their loud, cheerful mating call, and occasionally the cardinals will render a short song. The days are growing longer, encouraging the flower buds on trees and bushes to swell just a bit. Early insects buzz in the warmth of the sun's rays. In a month or so winter will be fading away as spring approaches. It won't happen all at once, because spring will retreat many times before it finally arrives. But until that definite day, it is nice to have a January thaw as a promise.

All too soon the glorious warmth is gone, and the sun is swallowed up in a sky of pewter gray. Breathless and still the world waits. A solitary flake flutters

The Bontas' road, which is a
white wonderland in winter.

down, then another. In a few minutes the air is filled
with thickly falling fluff, as if a giant in the sky had
suddenly opened a hundred million feather pillows
and spilled them over us. Very quickly we are shut-
tered in on the mountain, cut off from any contact
with the outside world and content to let nature show
us the beauty of a snowfall.

The sere brown earth is gently covered with a
counterpane of white. Every weed head is gloriously
adorned with a white crown. As the snow falls more
thickly, Sapsucker Ridge becomes a silver smear in
the distance.

The birds are very busy during a snowstorm because
their supply of natural food is being rapidly covered
up. They whirl in and out of the feeders and tap eagerly
around on the back porch, looking for spilled seed.

Usually all the regulars—tree sparrows, juncos, nut-hatches, and chickadees—throng about.

As the snow silently piles up, I pull on my boots. A couple of common redpolls buzz companionably with a flock of tree sparrows. Usually these striking, sparrowlike birds, the males with their strawberry-colored breasts and heads, are able to find plenty of wild food to eat. Being residents of the Arctic, they like the cold and are not very shy toward people. Soon I discover a flock of about thirty redpolls out behind the barn. As they surround me, some come close enough to touch, yet they never seem concerned by my presence. Ignoring me, they flutter from one weed head to another. Congregating on a weed, they bend it beneath their collective weight as they strip it of seeds.

Our road has become a white wonderland. The stream still flows through snow-covered banks, and the hemlock branches hang low and heavy over the road. One touch and a cascade of snow covers me, trickling wetly down my neck. In the shrouded woods no creature moves and no sound is heard except the muffled movement of my feet through the six inches of heavy snow. Nature is at peace.

The day after a snowstorm, when it has warmed up and the wind is still, we set out to discover the identities and habits of the wildlife on the mountain. Using Olaus Murie's excellent book, *A Guide to Animal Tracks*, we follow the trails the animals use, learn the habitats they prefer, and sometimes even track them to their dens.

One day we heard rumors that a black bear had been sighted right beyond the far field. Since there was fresh snow on the ground, Bruce and Steve set off to see if they could find bear tracks in that vicinity. Thoroughly combing the area, they finally located the tracks of a very large dog. I remembered a wild dog pack I had seen near there, running silently and swiftly in pursuit of a deer. Their leader was a large black dog. Could that have been the "bear" someone had glimpsed?

Gray foxes are often reported on the mountain. Steve swears he saw one during a hike, but to my regret I have not been as lucky. Imagine my joy when I discovered the small, single-line track of a fox in the woods linking the two fields. The habitat there is very suitable for gray foxes since they often have their dens in rock piles. And in that woods, just over the crest of the mountain, there are several very large rock slides overlooking the town. But as frequently as we take our visitors there to show them the magnificent view, we have never seen the gray fox in person near his rock slide home.

One winter, while tramping quietly along, I saw a sudden movement on the trail ahead. A small animal flashed dark brown against the snow as it moved quickly and quietly over the trunk of a fallen tree and twisted through the underbrush. I carefully examined the tracks and concluded that I had had a glimpse of a long-tailed weasel.

From tracks in the snow we have learned where the ruffed grouse take cover and the places where the deer drink from the stream. We can find squirrel holes and rabbit retreats. Sometimes we can reenact the death of a mouse: a lacy trace of tracks, the feathery prints of an owl's wings, and a drop of blood. Whenever there is a fresh snowfall we all go out to look for more answers to the mysteries of nature surrounding us.

Even when there is no snow on the ground we can still make new discoveries, because in winter the woods are always open and inviting. No thick green canopy of leaves hides the animals and birds. From my window I can glance across at the sloping mountainside and watch a cottontail or deer browse peacefully.

At a distance all the gnarled trees, shorn of their leaves, look identical. But as I examine them closely, I can distinguish the silvery smooth trunk of the American beech from the furrowed darker chestnut oaks. The evergreen shrubs stand out distinctly from the naked trees; suddenly we discover rhododendron that we never noticed in the lushness of summer's green. The numerous laurel bushes shimmer in the sunlight of a winter's day. Occasional hemlocks or white pines can be seen in bright contrast to gray-brown tree trunks. And along the ridges the grotesquely shaped jack pines loom above the forest.

Our paths are luxuriously covered with a great variety of mosses; shiny evergreen leaves of trailing arbutus sprawl over the mossy bed. In summer this green richness is obscured by small, many-leaved blueberry bushes, but now only a few scrubby silvered twigs are seen. The brown carpet of fallen leaves makes a beautiful backdrop for the red wintergreen berries and the deep green Christmas ferns.

The woods are so open with their secrets that when I walk the ridges I can follow the dim lines of distant mountains. There is no need to go to a special open overlook to see the view. When I was first learning my way around our land, I found it much easier to understand our relationship to the nearby mountains and valleys in the wintertime.

For birdwatchers winter can be a rewarding time. The variety of birds is very limited, but their activities are easy to observe. Many times I have watched the downy woodpeckers as they move busily up and down the tree trunks, making the quiet woods ring with their resonant hammering. The most spectacular woodpeckers on the mountain are the crow-sized pileated woodpeckers with their large red crests, their sledgehammer bills, and their loud flicker-like calls. Every winter there seem to be more of them. The first year I had only a glimpse of them, but as time went on they appeared to grow less wary of us. Occasionally they came to the edge of the woods by the stream, and often I saw one occupying a pole on the powerline right-of-way. There was one pole on each ridge riddled with their huge three-foot cavities, and I rather suspected that the pole on Sapsucker Ridge was a winter home. One day I was walking up the right-of-way when I heard a pileated racket in the woods. Suddenly one swooped out, landed on a pole, and went right into the large hole in its side. Usually, whenever I startle a pileated it flies off from whatever tree it is clinging to, calling loudly—but this fellow had settled in to stay. Generally these elusive birds carve out their nests in the dead standing trunks of deciduous trees. Pileated means crested, but other names for this bird are far more interesting. According to Arthur Cleveland Bent's Life Histories of North America Woodpeckers, terms such as "log-cock," "stump breaker," "cock-of-the-woods," "laughing woodpecker," and "johnny-cock" were widely used homespun names. In Pennsylvania's nearby Juniata Valley, the name "cluck-clock" was often preferred.

No matter how frequently we see them in winter, we always stop to watch the handsome black and white creatures as they pound large splinters of wood out of the oak trees. No doubt they are attempting to rid the trees of carpenter ants, their favorite food. Many times pileated woodpeckers save trees from being killed by large infestations of these ants.

The trees of our mountain should be amply protected from all kinds of insect invasions during the winter. If we look closely we also can see the elusive brown creepers as they spiral up the trunks searching for insects and eggs. They work so quietly that they look very much like a part of the bark they are carefully examining. The golden-crowned kinglets, too, are busy foraging for insects in the trees. Their tiny "zeep" calls seem to echo in the winter peace. No matter how gray and dreary the weather, I can always find an active flock darting about.

In England during the winter bird-watchers compete with each other in collecting and identifying birds' nests. Sometimes the remains of infertile or cracked eggs are found in a nest, making identification of its former occupants somewhat easier. But usually nest identification is a precise science that involves careful examination of dimensions, location, distance from the ground, kind of tree or bush in which it was built, surrounding environment, and materials used in construction.

Our far field is filled with small nests in the six-foot high red maple saplings. Carefully examining one, I find that it is made of woven maple leaves, weed heads, and grasses. The inside is softly lined with pine needles. But that is as far as my research goes. I cannot identify its owners, although I am able to appreciate the beauty and intricacy of its construction. I think I shall leave identification to the patient care of the British.

By February winter seems a permanent condition. Amidst the many gray bleak days an occasional radiant one surfaces. As the sun rises over Laurel Ridge it first lightens Sapsucker Ridge into a brilliant rosy red. Gradually the sunlight moves down the mountainside and across the fields, pink-tingeing all the dead brown grasses that lay heaped over the ground. Then through the trees I see the sun fully up, with ice crystals sifting through the strong rays. At last the house and porch and sloping lawn are warm. We run to the windows to look at that brilliant miracle, the winter sunshine, and our eyes blink at the unaccustomed radiance.

On a cold clear day the view from the top of the first field is worth the chilly climb. The mountains are deeply blue and stretch to the horizon. Even Nittany Mountain is visible. The boys and I admire the sight but quickly scramble down the hill because the wind blows coldly. As we walk briskly along David suddenly stoops to scoop up the tiny, gray, frozen body of a smoky shrew. Steve cradles it in his glove and takes it home to sketch and study. "How soft his fur is," he tells me.

Steve always seems to have a special affinity for little creatures. One February day he was outside poking around the drainage ditch when suddenly a shrew popped up nearby. As Steve watched, the shrew leaped down into the water, swam to the other side, and disappeared into a well-concealed hole. After waiting to see if the shrew would reappear, he drifted over to investigate the grape tangles. A mouse leaped in front of him and scurried into a hole. Steve sat down and patiently watched as the mouse emerged and began scurrying about the grape arbor in its search for food.

Every winter we have new creatures that come to spend the season with us. One year was opossum winter. Another year we remember fondly as the winter of the red-headed woodpecker. Actually the woodpecker was a brown-headed juvenile when he first joined the feeder regulars in October. He quickly established his position as bully over the smaller birds. Swooping down to the feeder with a flourish, he scattered everything but a determined red squirrel who sat confidently shoving pawfuls of seeds into his mouth. The red-headed woodpecker looked insulted. He began jabbing at the squirrel while it continued complacently eating. When that didn't work, he fanned out his wings threateningly. Finally he launched an all-out attack. A brief battle ensued before the squirrel leaped from the feeder and retreated to the grape tangle. Nonchalantly it climbed a pole and sat stiffly with its tail curled over its back. It waited until the woodpecker had flown off before starting back toward the feeder. Zoom—the woodpecker dive-bombed it from the air, crying his loud, ratchety call. Completely demoralized, the squirrel fled.

After that it was total war, or at least the woodpecker thought so. No red squirrel was safe from his attacks. Any squirrel caught climbing up the three balm of Gilead trees would instantly be set upon by the red-headed woodpecker, because he considered them all his private domain. He also dominated the black walnut trees around the yard, and he attacked any squirrel found in the vicinity of the feeder or back porch.

I admired his spunk and labeled him a "he" even though male and female red-heads have identical plumages. His whole manner and stance was that of a teenage bully. Like most bullies, when he was defied by a red squirrel he would look nonplussed and just a trifle crushed. For a few seconds his confidence would crumble—and then he would reassert himself at the expense of the smaller birds.

He lived in a former squirrel hole in the biggest balm of Gilead, or balsam poplar, tree. On winter days his alarm calls echoed over the yard. Sometimes I looked up and couldn't see anything that might be annoying him. He just seemed to enjoy his own noise. Although his head began to change color, gradually assuming its bright red adult plumage, his actions remained bullylike. By early February the physical change was almost complete—mostly red with just a few streaks of brown—but mentally he would always be the same: quarrelsome, overbearing, and threatening to all except his own species.

According to Bent, red-headed woodpeckers are known to be very compassionate to their fellows, comforting and caring for the injured or sick in their midst. They also enjoy each other's company, and they usually migrate south in large groups. But if the crop of acorns and beechnuts is plentiful, many remain in the north throughout the winter. Since I had never seen any breeding red-headed woodpeckers on the mountain, I assumed that he was migrating south when he discovered our yard with its squirrel-holed trees filled with acorns.

By the end of February he sported a perfect red head as he flashed handsomely about the yard. But in early

March we missed him during several blustery, stormy days. Could he have gone off somewhere else to settle and raise a family, we wondered? A few days later Steve discovered his body lying in the window box of the guest house, an apparent casualty of the March winds. He must have been dashed against the window and killed. I went down to view his crumpled body—his handsome black and white feathers were a disheveled dirty gray color, and the proud red feathers poked ludicrously up from his battered head. The blustering bully was dead, and the red squirrels seemed to know it. They dominated the bird feeder once again and ran freely up and down the balm of Gilead trees. I missed his rattling calls, his self-assertive airs, and the color he added to my winter days.

It seemed ironic that the wind had killed the red-headed woodpecker, since he had survived an unusual number of ice storms that winter. The thermometer would hover at 31 degrees above zero for days on end before, inevitably, we would get still more freezing rain. I always took Mark walking as soon as the ice storms ended. We both were entranced by the fragile beauty of the ice-encrusted world. Ordinary weeds glistened and glittered in the sunlight; the laurel bushes shone with a transparent gleam. One day Mark made a fascinating discovery. Somehow he slipped the icy coating off a laurel leaf and held in his hands a perfect cast of it. Even the central vein left its imprint down the middle. It looked like a fine piece of Steuben glass. Doing some experimenting, I found that I, too, could remove a cast if I slipped a fingernail between ice and leaf. There was a tiny bit of suction between the two, but with a little care the cast always came off perfectly. Mark was thrilled by his discovery. He wanted to take it home to show his brothers. "It will melt," I protested. He looked at me unbelievingly. "Open your hand," I suggested. When he did, he discovered that the cast had already begun to dissolve. But he never tired of collecting them and admiring their ephemeral beauty. He soon learned to remove even the tiny casts from the wintergreen leaves.

Occasionally that winter we had small snowstorms that lasted only a few hours. The thermometer would still be hovering at freezing rain temperature, but miraculously it would snow instead—large, feather-pillow flakes that would quickly accumulate into an inch or two on the ground. One day Mark and I went out in the midst of such a snowfall. As we entered the woods we were both awestruck by the thick white fluff clinging to and accentuating every tree and bush. The few pine trees looked lovely, but for once the hardwood trees were even more beautiful. Every branch and twig, large and small, had two inches of snow piled upon it. The small blueberry bushes were totally encased in fluff, looking like miniature snow sculptures. "That one looks like a giant turkey track," Mark declared, pointing down to one tiny bush. The laurel bushes were topped with heavy piles of snow that bent down their elastic branches. The silence of the woods was frequently broken by a soft plop as one of the laurel branches flicked off its burden of snow and emerged shiny green again. Those few branches were the only green accents in a magical white world.

Mark and our new puppy Bobbin bounced along in this wonderland. Every snow-covered bush made a miniature fluffy hideout. They went from one intriguing place to the next, Mark poking and peering and Bobbin sniffing and snooping—two youngsters in a newly minted world. Just as we arrived home the snow stopped. In a few hours the branches lost their snowy covering, and we could only describe to the rest of the family how the woods had looked all festooned in white.

Gradually, as Mark grew older he expanded his walking distance, and we began to take longer treks. As we covered new territory, he made discoveries that established certain landmarks in his mind. One trail, for instance, had an enormous old log on it that was always covered with puffballs. What child—or adult even—can resist squeezing their puffy shapes and sending a powder of spores into the air? Neither of us could pass the trunk without squeezing a few. Mark always alerted me as we came near. "There's the puffball log," he would shout. Mark spotted a rotted but still standing tree along Laurel Ridge Trail that sported an excellent collection of shelf fungi. Mark always paused to admire their shapes and to feel the leathery specimens. "Feels like bread," he commented.

"Well, maybe, very stale bread," I agreed. He developed a real eye for fungi of all kinds. The orange ones particularly attract him, but any bit of color catches his attention and admiration.

Walking down the road one February day he exclaimed ecstatically about all the smooth silvery trees. "What are they?" he queried. To his child's eye, the naked American beech trees were beautiful. He was intrigued by the colors and shapes of all the various hardwood trees with their strangely twisted branches, irregular bark, or rotted trunks filled with holes. I remember one fall day when all the leaves had fallen from the trees. I was prepared to give Mark a talk about the bareness of winter, but as we walked toward the woods, he suddenly stopped and looked up at the bare branches with joy on his face. "Why do the trees look so silvery and beautiful?" he asked.

"The leaves have all died and fallen off the trees," I explained.

"But now I can see all the branches," he added happily. I was amazed that his sense of beauty appreciated the spare as well as the bountiful. Throughout the winter he kept pointing out new sights that he always called "just beautiful."

I don't always take Mark with me for walks, especially on the weekends when Bruce is home. Those days are mine for solitary roaming, and I am always disappointed if the weather is miserable. One cold damp day in mid-February I almost convinced myself to stay home and listen to the Saturday afternoon opera on the radio. They were presenting *La Bohème*, a favorite of mine, and I had just been ecstatically borne through the first act. But the temptation to seclude myself at the far field was too great, and I bundled up. Shopping downtown in the morning had been a dismal, raw experience—wouldn't walking on the mountain be even worse? Resolutely I marched out into the cold grayness, but a couple of minutes of exertion warmed me pleasantly—the weather no longer mattered. When I reached the far field I was comfortable enough to rest at the base of a tree for a half hour. Crows flapped blackly across the sky. A hawk sailed into a large tree at the edge of the field, shook his tail feathers, and rested for a time. The gray day made it impossible for me to identify him even though I watched carefully as he finally flew off across the field. Eventually the cold ground drove me up and away from my sanctuary, but I was glad that I had forced myself to go walking.

As winter draws to a close on the mountain the crows begin to caw more vociferously, the wintering songbirds start polishing their pipes, and the starlings come up from the valley to mimic in the balm of Gilead trees. A final light powder of snow falls and effectively covers an icy glaze. The boys sled enthusiastically, knowing that this may be the last time till next year. They whoop and holler, their cheeks redden, their heads sweat, and they come in with soaking wet dungarees. A Pennsylvania winter is a small boy's paradise: just enough snow to have fun, but not too much to make the going difficult. There is lots of slippy ice to make the sleds whiz along and not much bitter cold weather. They can zip about without snow pants; they can prance and slide all over the lawn. They can tramp through the woods following animal tracks and clamber over the rock slides, searching for treasure. Most of all, they can look out the windows after a snowstorm and enjoy the beauty of the coated trees and slanting sunlight. Nothing escapes their eager eyes. Spring is almost here, but winter on the mountain is always a delight.

Chapter 5
Fellow Inhabitants

SOMETIMES WE LIVE closer to nature than we like to. Our home is actually invaded by the small creatures that live about us. The red squirrels which occupy our walls all year-round have apparently always built their nests there. They clatter up and down the attic steps and occasionally scamper across the basement floor. One autumn they discovered my open shelves of jams and jellies—I found tops and chewed paraffin scattered all over the shelves and floor. Sweeping up the mess and moving the untouched jelly to closed cabinets, I muttered angrily about their invasion of our home. Most years the squirrels gather huge caches of black walnuts from the many trees in our yard, and they store them in the walls of the house. As we sit in the living room, we often hear them rolling the heavy nuts across the ceiling.

But squirrels are not the only invaders. Our first winter on the mountain I began to notice tiny teeth marks on the apples stored under the outside cellar door. One day when I went to gather some apples, I surprised a large-eyed, large-eared little creature with white underparts that scampered away through a small crack in the door. It was an exquisite white-footed mouse. Townspeople rarely see this mouse, because it prefers brushy cover and a woodland habitat. Not wishing to trap the beguiling creature, we went into action to save the apples. A heavy piece of plywood was fitted over the cardboard apple box. Now we could relax and "suffer the mouse to play," as the old Pennsylvania Indian chief had said.

Another time I discovered a strange little animal trapped in a bucket in the basement, dashing about in a frenzy, trying to get out. Steven identified it as a short-tail shrew. We learned from *Mammals of Pennsylvania* that shrews are the most common mammals found in the state, but they are rarely seen because they are elusive nocturnal animals. It was 4½ inches long from snout to tip of tail, and it seemed to have no eyes at all. Actually, its eyes are no larger than small dots. According to the book, their keen sense of smell and tiny ears, hidden in their fur, guide them to food. As an experiment, we put some canned cat food in the bucket. It sniffed about for a moment, rushed over, and quickly consumed it. Shrews require from one-half to three times their own body weight in food every 24 hours, and they die of starvation in one or two days if they don't eat. After drawing and studying it, Steve released it in the grape arbor, where it darted away, no doubt desperately searching for more food to keep alive.

Shortly after we moved here we found a heavy mesh screen covering the drain in the concrete basement floor. When we questioned the former owners, they told us that a copperhead had come up through the drainpipe one day. I didn't protest even though I was quite certain that they had seen a harmless milk snake. I remembered the old Italian belief that a milk snake in the basement is a lucky omen for the owners.

Red squirrels, mice, shrews, and snakes all may live down in the cellar and sometimes even up in the house. If they bother us they are gently discouraged. But if they merely look fierce—like the large, hairy wolf spider who lives under the sink in the basement—we allow them to attend to their business unmolested.

One of the few creatures I fear having in my house is a rat.

They cause much destruction in an old farmhouse, and they can be vicious if startled. I read Albert Camus's book *The Plague* years ago which reinforced my hatred and I associate their presence with filth and disease.

Returning from a week's vacation late one summer, I bent down in the kitchen to pick up the wastebasket.

Tucked back in the corner on an outside wall was an enormous hole chewed through the baseboard. In a panic, I called Bruce. "Just a squirrel hole," he said— but I didn't believe it.

Nothing happened in the next few months, and gradually I forgot about the hole. Then in early November we began to hear loud rustlings in the kitchen as soon as we settled into the living room for the evening. Several times Bruce sneaked out and turned on the light. Nothing. Then one night he yelled, "There's a rat. Get the broom!" He should have known better than to ask for help from me. I pulled my feet up under me on the couch and just trembled. The rat popped over the sink top and disappeared.

A few days later we were returning from supper at my sister's. As we entered the dining room we heard a series of scurryings. Bruce and Steve rushed to the kitchen, and I ran back outside. With lots of yelling, they went racing through the dining room and down the basement stairs in hot pursuit of the rat. It escaped into an opening near the bathroom sink which Bruce and Steve promptly plugged up.

By this time I was getting very nervous. I never went into the kitchen alone at night. And, of course, we baited large rat traps. Every evening we heard the rustlings, but they never touched the traps. Then one morning I discovered a sprung trap and blood all over the floor. No rat, but we figured we had gotten the creature.

A few mornings later, I went down to fix breakfast in the winter darkness. As I turned on the light, something zipped over the back of the sink. Well, maybe a mouse, I hoped, and went over to the stove to fry the eggs. I turned around to get a spatula just as a head popped up behind the sink and then went back down. My nervous chirps brought Bruce into the kitchen, freshly shaved and suited for work. "There's something under the sink," I faltered. He flung the doors open and rattled the newspapers, but nothing was there. Then I opened the silverware drawer. Nestled in a corner, staring up at me, was the largest gray rat I had ever seen. I screamed and backpeddled into the dining room as the rat jumped out of the drawer and ran after me. Bruce intercepted it with a swift kick, rolling it several yards across the kitchen floor. Instantly the rat scrambled up and streaked out through the hole in the baseboard. The boys came running down because I had a case of hysterics in the dining room. I had a difficult time choking down my breakfast. All I could think of was Bruce's impending business trip to Denver and my being left with a houseful of aggressive rats. "We've got to do something before you leave," I implored, still shaking from the experience. He promptly went down to the basement, mixed up some patching plaster, and filled up the hole in the baseboard.

On the other side of the kitchen, Bruce had been working for several weeks at removing an old door and installing a new window in its place. Beneath the window he had patched in a piece of plaster-board but had not yet finished smoothing off the taping or putting on the new baseboard. So the next morning we found several large holes chewed in the bottom of the new plasterboard. Since the traps simply weren't working, I went out and bought some rat poison. The following morning all of the poison-baited boxes were empty. Bruce quickly cut some scrap lumber for temporary baseboards, and then he left to catch his plane.

A few days later there was a smell in the basement. Each day it became stronger. At first I thought the boys' "invented" mixtures were a bit smellier than usual. Since I have a keen nose, I went sniffing around, trying to track it down. But it was so potent and all-pervasive that I couldn't trace its origin. The whole basement reeked.

By the time Bruce returned from Denver, the basement was almost uninhabitable. But we insisted on playing our nightly round of Ping-Pong despite the odor. Luckily Bruce hit the ball that skittered into the clutter under the cellar stairs. As he groped for the ball, he suddenly said, "Here's what caused the smell. There's a dead rat lying next to the croquet set. Funny you never saw it."

"Just lucky," I said, and I shivered as he took the rotting carcass away. Now, whenever we play Ping-Pong, I let Bruce retrieve the ball from under the stairs—I take no chances.

The familiar house mouse plays frequently in every room. One night I sat in the living room quietly knitting. Something flashed down my arm and into the knitting basket. I dumped the basket over, and out scurried a mouse. They haunt the bedrooms, too. Several times we have been awakened by gnawing at our bedroom door. A mouse wants to get out. Bruce sleepily opens the door, and the gnawing stops.

When Steve began collecting dead insects and butterflies, he kept them in open cases on his bureau. One morning he found the whole collection consumed. Only the pins were left. Another time one of the boys must have surreptitiously eaten a cookie in the living room, because when I straightened out the slipcover on our chair, I found holes chewed through it.

Our guests find these invasions a little hard to take, especially in Steve's room, which doubles as our guest room. In the corner of the room is the door leading to the attic. Steve quickly got used to the red squirrels scratching at the door at night. Our guests never have. One lady awoke to the sound of rustling in the room. She switched on the light and saw a mouse nibbling at a dried flower arrangement. It darted down the hall and into the new bathroom, where presumably there should be no escape holes for mice. Apparently there were, although we never found them.

I suppose if I were willing to have a cat in the house we might avoid the rodent invasion. But generally I have been unlucky in my dealings with cats, even though I like them and they seem to like me.

The first year we were married we owned a cat that was almost perfect. He was a black male we named Bongo. It was my first experience with cats, though Bruce had been raised with them. Bongo had lots of personality. He bounced and jumped and cuddled and practically tore our first Christmas tree apart. Then he began scratching up the furniture. So Bruce went out into the Pennsylvania woods and brought back an enormous old log which he installed in the living room as a combination coffee table and scratching post. It worked, and we all lived happily together for six more months. Then Bongo grew up and set out on his mating adventures. One night he didn't return.

For several years we lived in apartments in the Washington, D.C., area, and they were not suitable places for cats to live, according to Bruce. When we moved to Maine, I began agitating for another cat, confident that all cats would be like Bongo. He had been housebroken in one session! This time we chose a beautiful long-haired black-and-white female kitten from a large litter. Steve named her Katey. We picked her for her looks, an unfortunate mistake. In addition, we took her from the mother cat much too soon, for she didn't know how to catch mice or lick herself clean. She became increasingly filthy and impossible to housebreak. Doggedly I threw water over her, trying to get her wet enough so she would start licking her fur. Finally, clumsily, she began, although she never became an immaculate cat.

As the long Maine winter set in, David was just learning to crawl. Katey, it developed, had a wild, erratic disposition, and every time David tried to crawl, she attacked his face with her claws. She spent the long winter in the basement. Finally we had her spayed, which seemed to calm her disposition.

She liked being outside, and she usually bounded along with us on walks. I remember a particularly beautiful hike on Thanksgiving day, just over a year after we had gotten her. She bounced over the thin snow cover with us, up the hill, through the fields, down the woods to the lake, and finally back to the house—an exhausted and happy little cat. A couple of nights later she disappeared forever—probably killed by the same fisher, we guessed, that had invaded our neighbor's shed a few weeks before and torn all their cats apart. Fishers don't like competing predators in their range, and they are known for killing cats. But I failed to see how our inept little Katey could have threatened it.

"No more cats!" I vowed. All cats were not like our exemplary Bongo, I had discovered. Cat-lovers sought to persuade me otherwise. "Oh, Katey was just unusual," they said. "Why almost every cat is easy to housebreak, and most are natural hunters. Cats are very clean creatures, too."

"Uh huh," I nodded, but I held firm, especially when I discovered I was pregnant again. I had no intention of keeping another cat down in the basement while my new baby learned to crawl.

Matters stood still for several years. Sometimes I looked nostalgically back to Bongo. I even remembered the beautiful but dumb Katey with fondness. But I made no active effort to secure another cat, even when we moved back to Pennsylvania and it became obvious that rodents made free use of our mountaintop home. Then Jellicle entered our lives.

On the first night of frost one autumn, the stars shone brightly in the cold still evening. Wrapped in my enormous old chenille bathrobe, I was curled up on the love seat reading. It was Bruce's night to work, so I was deep into a novel in an effort to stay awake until he came home. I was aroused by the rattling of our dog Fritz's pan on the back porch. Probably just a squirrel or chipmunk, I reasoned, because they are always poking about for tidbits. I burrowed down deeper into my bathrobe, reluctant to get up. Another rattle whetted my curiosity. I arose to check, and I switched on the porch light just as a cat darted away. By sheer coincidence I had some cat food in the cupboard, so I put it out in a dish. In an instant the cat reappeared and ate as if starved. She consumed two helpings and a saucer of milk as well. I refilled the saucer but placed it inside on the kitchen floor. Holding the door opened, I waited. Slowly, cautiously, she inched into the room, and I quietly closed the door behind her. In one hour she was fed, tamed, and seated on my lap, purring and cleaning herself. She looked very much like Bongo—a black cat with white markings. She also was extraordinarily affectionate and fastidiously clean. She never struck out at anyone with her claws; she preferred rubbing noses with everybody, from small children to adults.

We named her Jellicle after T. S. Eliot's "Song of the Jellicles." She was a small cat and, wonder of wonders, she could catch mice. She hunted all night and most of the day, coming in only to eat ravenously or warm up for a time. Despite being partially blind in one eye, she swept our house clean of mice, stalking the foundations and coming up with at least one victim a day.

Winter was coming on, though, and she liked her comforts. Optimistically, I put a litter box in the basement and introduced her to it. She was totally disinterested. She took to hiding upstairs and leaving odoriferous packages all over the hall. We spanked her and put her out time after time. When she forsook the hall and adopted David's quilt as her bathroom, I gave up. We relegated her to the barn, letting her in the house only for short supervised periods. When we forgot, she left a mess for us to clean up. I consulted the cat experts, and they all said that she was too old to change her ways—so that was that.

In January she went into heat. She rubbed herself against table legs and mewed and cried for days, but no male found her—our home was too isolated. We decided not to spay her. If she did have kittens sometime, it would be an interesting experience for the boys, we thought. There would not be the usual problem of finding homes for the kittens because with our big unused barn they would have a fine place to live.

In the meantime, word had spread among our city relatives that we were accepting cats again, and when we went visiting to New Jersey in mid-April, we were offered two city-bred cats. Both were male, but they were spayed, I was assured. While I demurred, the boys begged, and finally I agreed to take the best of the two cats. In fact, his supersize intrigued me. With his tiger coloring he looked like his father had been a bobcat. So we took him home as a playmate for Jellicle.

His former owners had called him Soo-Loo, but Bruce thought that sounded too delicate for such an enormous cat. Again we turned to T. S. Eliot for help in naming him. This time we discovered that tiger cats were known as "Gumbie" cats, so Gumbie became his name. With summer coming on we restricted Gumbie and Jellicle to a milk diet, hoping that they would catch prodigious numbers of rodents. Jellicle worked in a fury, constantly dragging a mouse or mole about in her mouth, but the spoiled overweight Gumbie spent his time whining for food around the back door. I hardened my heart, and after a few weeks he began to catch on. He slimmed down into a sleek, quick cat, stalking through bushes and behind buildings in pursuit of prey. However, he seemed a cat without emotion, very aloof and really difficult to get attached to.

Once I watched a duel between Gumbie and a feisty little chipmunk. Gumbie crossed the backyard with the chipmunk hanging limply from his mouth. While I like chipmunks, they had been feasting on my strawberries, so I tried not to feel sorry for the beautiful striped creature. Gumbie set it down and stretched out beside it. The chipmunk leaped around but did not run off. Instead, it sat up on its hind paws and began batting at its adversary with its forepaws, looking like an enraged miniature boxer. Gumbie batted back, seeming to enjoy the sparring. As I watched, the chipmunk continued fearlessly boxing, all the while adroitly manuveuring Gumbie over toward the roots of the balm of Gilead tree. Suddenly it disappeared into its hole. The cat actually looked puzzled as he peered about, searching and sniffing around the roots, wondering where his victim had gone. Though he always cruelly played around with his prey, Gumbie undoubtedly would have killed the chipmunk and eaten it sooner or later. Jellicle, on the other hand, always made a swift kill. She hunted, pounced, killed, and consumed without any cruel reinfinements.

Sometime in early summer she at last found a mate. Gumbie, despite his impotence, had given it a try several times, but her true mate was an elusive white cat we occasionally saw about the barnyard. By late July she bulged grotesquely and swayed as she walked. She rested often, rubbing her head against my cheek, purring affectionately. Looking as uncomfortable as any small woman, nine months pregnant, she still shined herself and frequently begged for milk.

Jellicle had her kittens the first week in August. We found her curled up in a feed trough in the barn, set upon by four blind nursing kittens. One was black and white, another was tiger striped, and the other two were tricolored—orange, black, and white. Each day we went down to admire them, congratulating Jellicle on her wise choice of a nesting site and her lovely kittens. But for the first few weeks we did not attempt to handle the kittens—we wanted to give her a chance to learn that she could trust us with them.

In twenty days they opened their eyes and began moving around on shaky legs, squeaking occasionally. But even during an awful heat wave, they sought the warmth and darkness of their nest. Jellicle loved to nurse, lying still and composed as the kittens pressed all over her, searching for a nipple. One nursed upside down, his little paws pushing against the air. They were a wriggling mass, constantly digging their sharp claws into Jellicle, yet she never seemed to mind.

By September they were attempting to clamber out of the nest. And Jellicle earned some respite, because they frequently were more interested in exploring than in nursing. We would be watching their endeavors, Jellicle would come back from the hunt, and they would ignore her.

Gumbie adopted a reserved, grandfatherly approach to all of them. Aloof but respected seemed to be his attitude. He also became the arch enemy of a small, red, female dog hanging around the place. Our dog, Fritz welcomed her presence, but Gumbie attacked her whenever she ventured on the grounds. She screeched and howled while Gumbie pressed his advantage; but back she would come again, and Gumbie would be after her in a second. Besides attacking the stray, he entertained himself by playing with katydids. One morning he was on the back step watching one jump. Hesitantly he tapped it with his paw. "Cheep! Cheep!" went the katydid. It became a great game. Gumbie tapped, and katydid cheeped twice. Bruce and I were intrigued, and we went out to tap it. Silence: no reaction at all. Then Gumbie tapped—"cheep, cheep" went katydid.

So the warm autumn weeks passed. Proudly Jellicle brought her kittens up to the house, and they tumbled all over the veranda and back porch. We named them all according to their colors, and each boy adopted one kitten as his own. Mark spent hours each day down in the barn, playing and talking to them, especially drawn to the shy tricolored one. I felt partial toward the black-and-white kitten with his pushed-in pugilist nose, but we all acknowledged that the tiger was the brightest and most curious of the lot. Steve particularly loved him.

Whenever we went outside they would try to slip in. Sitting on the steps or lounge chairs, I would be quickly covered by snuffling, nuzzling, licking little kittens. Then Jellicle would come mewing, and they would all leap off to nurse. Sometimes, when the boys brought them inside, she would mew at the door with a mouse for them. But I noticed she made no effort to teach them to hunt. In fact, she began to abandon them to our care. By our infinite attempts to be gentle with the kittens, we had caused her to lose her instincts for the safety of her litter.

Then tragedy struck. One evening, as usual, I put the dog dish down for Fritz on the back porch. Suddenly all four kittens swarmed about. I grabbed up the black-and-white one and shooed away the tricolors as Fritz made a low growl. I must have turned around for an instant, because the tiger somehow slipped past. The next thing I knew, Fritz snapped, and the tiger was writhing on his back on the porch steps. I screamed for Bruce as the other kittens began mobbing the dish. We quickly scooped them up and tossed them into the house while Fritz continued eating.

"I think Fritz hurt the tiger," I cried to Bruce, and I went back inside, leaving him to investigate. He came in a second later with a sick look on his face. "Fritz crushed his head, his eyes are popping out, and blood is gushing from his mouth. I must put him out of his misery," he said sadly as he went upstairs to get the rifle.

The boys and I stood horror-struck. David began to sob, and Steve maligned Fritz. "Why, Mommy, why?" the boys cried as the single shot was fired.

"Because they bothered him while he was eating," I replied. Jellicle had known better but had not trained her kittens to also stay away from the dog's dish. So Fritz had struck at the tiger kitten—that beautiful loving creature—the greatest explorer and the boldest of the four. His aggression had ended his life. That day I had spent lots of time fondling the tiger, and Fritz had pushed in jealously several times. Perhaps he remembered that when he lashed out so violently at the small creature. In any event, he ended the beauty and joy of tiger's small life in an instant of anger.

"I will never, ever forget the tiger. He was so beautiful," Steve sobbed. And we heavy-heartedly turned our attention to the three remaining kittens as they frolicked all over the house, unaware that one sibling was gone. Jellicle somehow knew, because the next morning the kittens were down around the barn again. But from then on I fed Fritz in the kitchen.

During the summer I had fed Gumbie and Jellicle on the elevated front porch where Fritz was not able to disturb them. To my distress, shortly after the tiger's death, Jellicle brought her kittens back up to the house and taught them to leap up on the porch to share in the bowl of milk. The bowl became the center of an incredible mob scene twice a day—kittens and cats pushing and shoving each other as they fought for the milk. Jellicle was beginning to wean the kittens, and she threatened to attack them if they came near her. She was particularly harsh toward the black-and-white male, but he nearly always had first try at the dead rodents she dragged in. The tricolors got the remainders, if any.

Then I tried a new feeding tactic, designed to lure the kittens back down to the barn. We put their dish in a trough, again to avoid Fritz's interference, and twice a day Steve filled it with milk. As November advanced Jellicle made no attempt to teach the kittens to hunt. And Steve reported that they appeared to be defecating in the same trough where they ate and slept. But mostly they hung around the house, trying to get in, refusing absolutely to be barn cats.

Late in November, Gumbie disappeared. I had heard coon hunters in the woods that night, and I assumed that he had been attacked and killed by the coon hounds. We never found a trace of him. Two days later Mark's tricolor was gone. We surmised that an owl must have caught her. The boys took the losses philosophically and cuddled the three remaining cats. But when Steve discovered the body of the second tricolor in the barn a week later, I began to suspect that disease, rather than predators, might be the cause.

Now only Jellicle and the black and white kitten were left. Both moped about apathetically, and Jellicle made no attempts to teach her remaining offspring to hunt. The little kitten cried mournfully, and Jellicle hissed whenever he came near her. The next morning I watched her chewing on a garter snake in the unseasonably warm sunshine. That was the last time I saw her.

With her disappearance I was almost certain that, despite their robust appearance, all the cats and kittens had been sick. I called the vet and was told that it had probably been distemper, although they had not shown any of the usual symptoms. The diagnosis came too late for all of them: the black-and-white kitten died on the porch the next morning.

After the deaths of the cats we still had Fritz, our beloved grayish-brown and white seven-year-old mongrel. He was wonderful with the boys, though he made an impressive watchdog—all forty pounds of barking fury whenever a stranger came near. When we were having our bathroom put in that first year, Fritz always had difficulty allowing the various workmen to come into the house. Only my strong assurances that everything was all right would calm him enough to let them enter. One afternoon as the workmen were leaving, Bruce and I told them that we would be going into the city the next morning but that they should feel free to come in by themselves if we weren't here. However, we had not counted on Fritz. The carpenter arrived at 9 A.M., but the dog would not let him across the lawn. About 9:30 the big, burly electrician arrived in his truck and was quite amused by his timid friend. "No dog has ever stopped me—I'll show you how to get in," he said, and started boldly toward the house. As he explained to us when we got home at 11:30 and found the men still in the truck, "That dog stayed between me and the house—he laid his ears back and made this low growl.

Clearly it was either him or me. Understand, I could have easily kicked him out of the way, but I knew you wouldn't have wanted me to hurt him."

Fritz never allowed me to go walking without him, and sometimes I was annoyed when he scared off the wildlife. Mostly, though, I loved his exuberant joy in life. He was a healthy, happy dog—king of 140 acres— never tied but always sticking close to home anyway. Only twice during his life on the mountain was he gone overnight.

He did like to chase deer when he went walking with me, but the deer soon discovered that he was a humbug. Two deer would leap in front of me heading west: several minutes later Fritz would appear, panting and barking, sniff around furiously, then head east. Occasionally he would practically stumble over one (he was very near-sighted), and I would have to call him back. He would always come obligingly, because he really had no idea what to do in those situations. One winter he discovered a doe trapped in deep snow up on the side of Sapsucker Ridge. Hearing his frantic, persistent barking, we strapped on our snowshoes to go up and investigate. Despite the barking, Fritz had not tried to harm the deer. When we called him away, she slowly wallowed up the ridge and disappeared.

He was the same way with rabbits—lots of frantic barking, plenty of bumbling about, but never a catch. About the only creatures he was really interested in killing were the woodchucks. When he cornered one of them, I just could not seem to call him off. He appeared to have an inbred hatred toward them.

Fritz barely tolerated having the cats around, but he did enjoy the company of the little red stray dog which Gumbie had always terrorized. We, too, had tried to drive her away, which made her very cautious, and she came to frolic with Fritz only at night or while we were gone. We knew she was still nearby because she impolitely defecated on the lawns, the road, and the trails.

Then, in early January, came several weeks of freezing rain. Day after day the thermometer stuck at 30 degrees as the ice coating built up on the six-inch snow cover. We could not even venture outside the house without falling. Fritz stayed indoors, snoozing except for necessary but brief forays outside. Then one cold miserable evening he did not whine to come back in after he had eaten his dinner. When we went out to call him, he did not answer. "Must be a female in heat in the valley," Bruce commented as we went off to bed.

For three more days the sleet and rain continued—and Fritz did not return. We began to get worried. He had never been away for so long. On the fourth day there was a thaw, and Mark and I tracked Fritz through the slushy snow. We discovered that he had, indeed, gone down into the valley. I called our nearest neighbors, I advertised in the newspaper and on the radio, and I notified the constable and the dog pound. No one had the dog. Each day we all grew more despondent.

On the seventh day one of our neighbors called to ask if he had come back. "No," I said sadly, "but Mark and I tracked him over the ridge, heading for Sinking Valley." There was a long pause.

"Maybe I shouldn't tell you this," she said.

"Go ahead," I answered wearily.

"There's a farmer down there that shoots any dog that crosses his property. He doesn't care who the dog belongs to or whether it is valuable. Lots of people have lost good dogs."

So I had to accept the fact that Fritz was dead. The farmer she had mentioned did not live far from us. It seemed all too likely that Fritz had wandered over to his property that dreadful rainy night and been shot. I only hoped that death had been instantaneous. He had paid dearly for the freedom we had given him. At least we could take comfort in the fact that the seven years of his life had been happy and carefree. But, as Steve said sadly, "Walks won't be the same without Fritz." No, and neither would be my life on the mountain, I thought. Fritz had been my friend and protector. With him at my side I had been able to face hunters and curiosity seekers. Now my natural friendliness would be guarded, because with Fritz's death some of my tranquility was shattered.

That evening, when I went out to the compost heap, I seemed to hear a howling sound coming from the barn. It was windy, warm, and very clear, and at first I thought the noise was a combination of the wind and the boys carrying on in the house. Then the sound became louder and more insistent, and I hurried down to investigate. Next to the barn door a small black puppy with white paws and a red chest sat back on his haunches howling. I spoke quietly to him, and he stopped to watch me. At this point Steve came racing down and scooped the puppy into his arms. The puppy didn't object; he snuggled against Steven's jacket, his big, dark eyes carefully watching us.

We took him up to the house to show David and Mark. Then we fixed up a box with rags and gave him some milk. He lapped it up and settled down quietly. He let all the boys hold him, showing no fear or aggression. We knew, of course, that his mother was the little red stray, and we assumed his father had been our Fritz. In some miraculous way the little male pup had been sent to replace his father—or so it seemed to us.

The next morning I went out to hang up clothes. More howls came from the barn. I ran down and discovered another male pup, looking much like the first one, but he did not have his brother's calm, trusting disposition. As I attempted to pick him up, he tried to nip me. Then he scuttled behind some boards and peered distrustfully out at me. So I went back to the porch, gathered up the first pup, and brought him back down to the barn. They seemed pleased to be reunited.

The boys and I paid periodic visits to the barn, trying to find the puppies' nest, but we were unsuccessful. The friendly pup always came running out to be petted, his tail wagging furiously, while his brother streaked behind the huge wooden feed bin. Finally Steve shoved the feed bin out, and there sat a third puppy. He had very short black hair and brown and white markings around his face. "He looks like a beagle," David shouted happily. Then they began naming the puppies.

The shy puppy was called Frisky—"because it sounds almost like Fritzie," Steve sighed wistfully. The newest find was labeled Snoopy, after Charlie Brown's famous beagle.

And the friendliest puppy had the best name of all: "Bobbin," Steve pronounced, "because his tail wags so hard."

Occasionally we glimpsed the red stray trotting away from the barn after nursing her puppies, and sometimes we found the remains of rabbits she had dragged in to supplement the pups' milk diet. Clever, resourceful, and dedicated, she labored day and night for her pups. "Are you sure there aren't any more?" our neighbor asked.

"Oh no! There can't be," I replied confidently, as I sent Steve down to feed them.

A few minutes later he returned laughing. "I just surprised the stray nursing four puppies," he said.

The next day the barn was empty. The mother had moved her puppies away, and for a couple of days we could not find them. Then, late one afternoon as I was walking down the road, I saw the pups tumbling about outside an abandoned woodchuck hole in the bank above the stream. For several days the boys stopped to play with Bobbin, who remained the friendliest of the litter. And I began receiving incredible pressure from Steve. "Please, Mom, can't we keep Bobbin?" Finally I agreed, and he scooped him up and brought him home to his old box in a corner of the kitchen. Bobbin ravenously consumed the milk, bread, and meat we fed him, and he was fairly good about using the newspapers in the corner of the room. He had grown since we first discovered him. His reddish-brown legs had lengthened and were finished off with white paws. His black tail, which curved up over his back, had the barest bit of a white tip, like a paintbrush. He was mostly black with silken long hair and a white bib. His eyes were dark and watchful, but not suspicious. He wanted to play with everyone by spinning around, dancing, and leaping up, his tail wagging furiously.

It took him a week to forget his mother and siblings. During the day he was happy playing with the boys, but at night he cried and howled. The noise was so loud that we had to move him to the basement. Still he persisted. No one else was bothered by the noise, but my stomach clutched up just as it had when the boys were infants. At first I tried every way to pacify him. I gave him water and food, spoke sharply, and put him firmly in his box, but still the howls continued. Just like a baby, I decided, and began ignoring him. Gradually each night the protests grew less vociferous. Coupled with Bobbin's noise all night long was the continual barking of the red stray. One of her pups was gone, and she knew it.

After a week she accepted her loss, and Bobbin was completely adjusted. Mark and I took him walking up the powerline trail one cold snowy day. He bounded along, a joyful puppy following Mark's explorations through the tunnels made by the snow-laden laurel bushes and poking his head curiously in the secret places Mark discovered behind fallen logs. Mark clambered over and Bobbin squeezed under—small boot prints followed by small paw prints. Both young ones came home to rest from their exertion, with Bobbin stretching out on the dining room rug and Mark retreating to the peace and warmth of his bedroom.

The barn remained a pleasant, remembered sanctuary for Bobbin. Whenever he could he raced down to sniff around the places where he and his siblings had slept and played. He chewed the bones left there by

Mark, the author, and David, with Bobbin.

his mother, and he never came back when I called. But then Steve would come home from school. Standing out on the veranda, he would holler, "Here Bobbin!" The puppy would burst out of the barn with joy on his face and come dashing across the road, but a fence blocked his straight path toward Steve. Each time he puzzled his way around it, sniffing, looking for holes, and finally circling out to the edge. Then he leaped across the ditch, covered the last yards in a second, and wriggled into Steven's arms.

In a month's time Bobbin grew rapidly. The boys still kept a watch on the woodchuck hole, but they rarely got even a glimpse of the puppies. Occasionally we heard the red stray barking at night, so we assumed that all was well with her. Then one day in early March, the family appeared again at the barn. We were shocked at their appearance. Frisky, who had been larger than Bobbin, was now considerably smaller. Snoopy, too, was small and emaciated looking. But the most pitiful of all was the black runt of the litter. He could scarcely move, yet even when we fed his brothers he stayed hidden and frightened. Only when they had fed and I had moved away would he venture out to take the scraps. We never heard or saw the red stray again, and we could only assume that she had been killed.

Frisky and Snoopy quickly lost their shyness, joining Bobbin and Mark in the walks all over the mountain. We dubbed Mark the "Pied Piper of Puppydom," because wherever he went a bevy of pups trailed at his heels. A little food had changed the pups from lethargic drooping creatures into bouncing curious bits of irrepressible goodwill. Only the runt, whom we named Spooky, stayed off by himself in the darkest corners of the barn. I began to feel that malnutrition had affected his mental development.

I started feeding the puppies on the veranda in an effort to entice Spooky out of his hiding place. It took him a day to venture up, but if we even approached the windows he would flee. When Steve caught him one day, he was so frightened that he defecated all over Steve and refused to be comforted by petting. He made no sound. He just huddled piteously, his great dark eyes luminous with fear. The other pups tumbled and sparred with each other, but Spooky stayed off by himself, only occasionally sniffing at his brothers. They seemed to tolerate him, but he was never a playfellow.

As I tried to tame him, he grew even more terrified. He began howling most of the night, and his eyes had a strange, haunted look. After a month he had not improved at all; rather, he seemed to regress. We really believed he was mentally deranged as a result of his early starvation, and he seemed unable to be a pet for anyone. So Bruce took him to a veterinarian to be put to sleep. But I will never forget the terror always present in his dark eyes.

I decided to give Frisky and Snoopy away to good homes. We were sorry to see them go, but we had the best of the experience—all their young puppy-hood filled with discovery, boundless joy, and tumbling play. Mark's love for them had made them all wonderful pets for children. One day a teacher and his two children came to take Snoopy. For once the puppy was sober and passive. Somehow he sensed that something was happening to him. We gently lifted him into a rag-lined box and put him into their car. We were glad to see him placed in a good home but sad to have him leave us and his brothers. "We will still call him Snoopy—that is a good name," the father declared. A few days later my sister took Frisky, so we could see him whenever we wished. Once again we were left with only the joyous ebullient Bobbin.

We had been amazed to find that all the pups in the litter were male. Most unusual, we thought. Then Bruce's parents came up from their winter home in Georgia. After watching Bobbin for awhile, Bruce's mother, who was born and raised on a farm, said quietly, "You know, I rather think that Bobbin is a female."

"Oh no, he can't be," I protested, picking him up and displaying his underside.

"Well, you see," she explained carefully, "the genitalia all looks the same at first. It's the placement that counts."

She was right, of course, and Bruce and I had to take a good deal of ribbing from friends who wondered why country people couldn't tell the difference between males and females. Frisky was the male pup, and we had no idea what Snoopy really was.

Once we realized that Bobbin was a female, her charming ways seemed subtly feminine as she burrowed her way even more deeply into our affections. No longer did she seem merely a replacement for Fritz. She was her own self: beautiful, winsome, and happy. Unlike him, she was a very quiet dog that never barked at anyone, friend or stranger. Whenever Steve called, she came running, adoration on her expressive face. Dog and boy had become inseparable friends.

Chapter 6
Mountain Spring

MARCH CREEPS SOFTLY in—warm, hazy, and blue-skied. Slowly I put winter thoughts behind me; my attention is focused on the coming of spring. Gone are the memories of cold winter days—spring is here and it will last forever. The boys come home from school, amazingly cheerful—"Because spring has come, and there is so much to do," David rejoices. Shorn of hateful boots at last, with a chance to wear light jackets, they throw off the heavy shackles of winter.

Mark is freer than any of us. He roams the woods and fields all day, coming inside only under protest for lunch. He is much happier when we have a picnic— "Then I don't have to come in at all," he declares. I hear his happy voice as he sings all over the mountain, roaming confidently and unafraid. His badge of identity, his symbol of freedom, are his shoe boots. He can pull them on by himself and go marching out into the sunshine. He can tramp through the watery ditches, play by the small stream, and squish through the sucking mud without any worries about wet feet.

March and mud season arrive together. The ground thaws and refreezes through weeks of intermittent snowfalls and heavy rain storms. Mark sneaks in to change his clothes several times a day—a muddy, wet, and happy little boy. Boys and mud make a splendid mix. And what boy can resist stamping through puddles? Not mine, surely. I meet them at the door as often as possible, because I would like to keep most of the mud outside where it belongs. Occasionally, though, it trails in on careless feet. Usually the door has a pile of muddy clothes next to it, and the washing machine works overtime. So do I, scrubbing floors, hanging out clothes, and washing dirty hands and faces. But I am so happy to see spring arrive that I clean up without complaining.

I find it very interesting that some of the earliest signs of spring are black, certainly not a color that poets associate with the season. But even back in mid-February, when I hear the cawing of the first crows, I know that spring has begun for me. Not many people would call the crows' noise beautiful, but I really enjoy listening to their constant calling as they range over the fields or complain in the balm of Gilead trees in our yard. Crows do not migrate, but they do seem to leave the mountain during the harshest winter months. They have been universally disliked by farmers because of their fondness for corn, but they do eat enormous amounts of harmful insects such as grasshoppers, beetles, and grubs.

The next blackbird to arrive for a brief visit is the much maligned starling. In 1890 some misguided people, determined to populate the United States with all the birds mentioned by Shakespeare, released sixty European starlings in New York's Central Park. Ever since these aggressive birds have been multiplying to fantastic proportions, crowding out bluebirds and swallows from their nesting sites and evading numerous extermination attempts. I have always been amused by their slightly off-key mimicry of other birds, and during our dreary years in Washington, D.C., the starlings were often the only birds we saw. Although year-round residents of towns, most of them spend only a few weeks in early spring in the vicinity of our house. I am really sorry that they usually do not nest here in greater numbers because they devour huge amounts of Japanese beetles, a very prolific pest around our gardens.

Shortly after the starlings wheel in, the first true migrating birds appear. "Okalee," the male red-winged blackbirds call from the tops of the black walnut trees. On and on, through wind, rain, and cold, they buzz

in early morning and again at sunset. Near the end of
March they are joined by the females. One year the
females arrived in a large flock which filled the yard
with an incredible cacophony of buzzing. About eighty
females occupied the tops of two trees, evidently resting
from their travels. Their sound drowned out all other
bird songs—the morning shook with their monotonous calls. Two pileated woodpeckers quietly fled the
noisy yard as I scanned with binoculars. One robin sat
among the black mass of sound, unheard but easily spotted with its orange breast gleaming in the new sunshine.
The pups were in a huddle down by the lilac bushes.
Looking at their dumbfounded faces, I was certain that
they, too, were overwhelmed by the sheer sound of the
blackbirds. Jubilantly the dogs rushed up to greet me,
ready to go for a walk and probably as eager to escape
from the noise as I was. The sound followed us as we
walked along, but nearing home again we noticed a
sudden silence. The yard was empty of females when
we returned, and my ears were grateful for the peace. I
could hear the single phoebe, the brilliant cardinal, and
the one singing male red-winged blackbird. But that
female migration would be a signal for the males to leave
our upland fields and seek their proper watery environment where they would establish suitable territories for
their courtship and nesting.

Another blackbird, the common grackle, is rarely
seen on the mountain because it prefers extensive cornfields for food. But one March evening Steve watched

about 300 fly overhead. Despite the damage they do to ripening grain, they compensate by cramming themselves full of crop-destroying insects and plump field mice. And their beautiful, iridescent coats reflect many shades of purple in the early spring sunlight.

Steve's favorite black arrival is a bird of prey. Usually in late March, as we sit at the top of the first field having a picnic, we see a couple of black forms drifting over the ridge. "Mom, the turkey vultures are back," Steve joyously proclaims. Most people are not charmed by turkey vultures—also called buzzards—because they prey on carrion rather than living animals. When I was a child, I felt a shiver of fear whenever I saw the black creatures. But with a son that thinks they are beautiful, I have to admit I have changed my opinion. I enjoy watching them as they soar gracefully above the ridge, and I know how valuable they are in cleaning up the landscape.

It is the bluebirds, though, who bring the first flashes of brilliant color to the mountain each spring. Unfortunately, these beautiful sky-blue birds are becoming rare. The use of pesticides in orchards, the loss of preferred nesting sites in wooden fence posts, and fierce nesting competition from the imported starlings and English sparrows have greatly reduced their numbers. Some experts predict the extinction of the bluebird by the end of the century.

What a pity that would be! These gentle birds, long symbols of love and happiness, are also valuable consumers of cutworms and grasshoppers. But most of all, they are among the earliest and brightest signs of spring. One March a bluebird returned right in the midst of a snowstorm. Gripping the branch of a locust tree with his feathers blowing, he was buffeted by the snow and wind. We wondered how he had ever found his way through such a fierce storm.

The robins also seem to come back too early. The ground is still frozen and the earthworms remain buried below the frost line, but the searching robins content themselves with the scant bits of insect life they can pick up. Edwin Way Teale, in his book *North with the Spring*, states that they move north as the average daily temperature reaches 35 degrees. Sitting at breakfast, Mark spots a flock of robins ranging over the lawn. "They are so big and bright," he comments. I wonder if his admiration, like mine, is based on a desire to see a new and different bird after so many months of the feeder regulars.

Not that the regulars are untouched by the new spring warmth. The male cardinal sits high in a black walnut tree each morning, singing his brilliant song, his deep red coat a striking contrast to the blue sky. Which is more beautiful, the color or the sound? I debate with myself as I stand watching and listening.

The downy woodpeckers begin tapping more enthusiastically as March progresses. One bright warm day I discovered a male downy making reedy echoes on a slender forsythia stem that bent over precariously from his weight. Another year, on the first day of spring, an excited female downy caught her foot in the suet bag hanging from the feeder. As I tried to get near to help her, she flapped wildly and propelled herself into the feeder, showering seeds over me. I have very slow reflexes, and I knew that I would be unable to grab her with one hand and free her with the other. So I decided to wait until Steve came home from school. In the meantime I settled down a little distance from the tangled bird and kept an eye on her. She attempted to loosen herself by flapping her wings and flipping her body into the feeder. She would flap and flip furiously for a few seconds and then rest and try again. Finally she just hung quiescent while other birds came and went, ignorant of her plight. A couple of times the male downy landed on a porch post near her, seemingly concerned, but she would flail her wings, and he would zip off to the old apple tree. I was unable to tell whether he understood that she was caught or was just frightened off by her frantic actions. After her two hours of imprisonment Steve came up the road and was all eager action when I showed him the problem. One lightning lunge, and he held her firmly in his hand. She immediately relaxed, watching with her intent yellow-black eyes as I snipped away at the netting that encased her foot. Gently we tugged and eased off the imprisoning material. Then Steve opened his hand, and she flew over to the apple tree with a slight lurch. She began to climb up the trunk immediately, her foot apparently recovered from its tangled ordeal.

The lovely days continue as I marvel over the new month. Was ever March so benign, so beautiful, so fragrant, so incredibly warm? I wonder each year. As I bask in the glowing sun I am serenaded by the newly arrived male song sparrows caroling from the bridal wreath bushes and the grape tangles. They continue their singing all through March because they need at least a month's courtship before they actually begin mating. And while the female broods the eggs, her mate continues his serenade. Once I found a perfectly cupped nest in a Maine meadow, a gem of minute perfection guarded by a sitting female song sparrow. She flew off only at the last minute, almost directly beneath my feet. I had not seen her or the nest until she moved, so well did she blend with the field grasses.

Slightly behind the other March arrivals, about the tenth of the month, the male phoebe makes his appearance. By then March is showing her lionlike tendencies, and the phoebe comes back on the coldest day, his tail flicking as he balances on the electric line. I have to look for his appearance because he is silent for a few weeks before he begins his monotonous song. Once he starts, however, nothing stops him—neither heat nor cold nor rain nor sleet. When his mate arrives, they chase about in all kinds of inclement weather. Perhaps they need those few precious weeks of joyous freedom, because once they begin rearing a family, they work without cessation to raise three sets of nestlings.

In fact, none of the songbirds begin nesting during March. There is simply not enough food available. We are more likely to see starving birds and animals in March than back during the bitter cold winter months. The seed-eating birds are most dependent on the feeder; most of their natural food has been consumed. The new arrivals—song sparrows and robins—also will venture near to see what is available.

The feeder becomes a magnet for honeybees on warm days. They swarm into the feeder in a buzzing, menacing mass, and we all stay away from the back porch. So do the birds—I watch them as they approach, notice the bees, and whirl off again. For a while I didn't know what attracted them, and I was definitely unnerved by the singing throng. Then I read that the husks of the seeds look like pollen to the bees. Learning this, I was less intimidated by them. At least I knew what they wanted and why they came to the feeder.

One day in late March a beautiful sunrise had turned Sapsucker Ridge a flaming red color and I set off eagerly with the three tumbling pups. As I walked past the garden I scanned the first field just below the ridge, looking for deer. A reddish-colored animal was trotting across the field—a wild dog, I thought—but nevertheless I focused my binoculars on the slow-moving form. I couldn't believe it—a magnificent red fox with a long, flowing, white-tipped tail was busily hunting for food. He was totally unaware of my presence and that of the questing pups. I watched motionless from the path, but when my binoculars steamed up, I lost him. After they cleared I set out across the field to search, not really expecting to see him again. Surely he would spot us and flee. Then I saw a movement further up the field. The red fox was quite intent on hunting, making small graceful pounces as he moved along. Even with the binoculars, I was too far away to see if he caught any mice, and unfortunately my lenses continued steaming up. Occasionally he glanced in our direction, but either he did not see us or did not care. I watched him for about fifteen minutes, his burnished red coat shining in the sunlight, until he suddenly looked quite purposely toward me. Then he turned and trotted off into the woods of Sapsucker Ridge.

The following dawn it was cold again, with a penetrating wind that rattled the dead weeds like old clacking bones. Our mountain had been turned into a shrieking demon by the wind, which shattered trees and spattered limbs like rain. In spite of this, I found myself dashing through the swaying woods in an attempt to reach the far field without being hit by a falling branch. But once I reached the field, I sat in perfect peace in a grove of locust saplings. It was as still as the eye of a hurricane as I basked in the sun, watching the scudding clouds and listening to the roaring of the wind on all sides. The clarity of the air made the field, and especially the dried goldenrod, glimmer in the sunlight.

As I was dozing there peacefully I suddenly felt a small movement in the locust sapling next to me. Slowly I opened my eyes and turned my head to watch. A golden-crowned kinglet was darting about in the branches near the ground, almost close enough to touch. I could plainly see his golden crown and diminutive gray and white body. Quickly he flitted on to another grove, but for just a few minutes I had been magically close to the vibrant creature.

Finally, sun-soaked and rested, I wound my way quietly back along the road amidst the rocking trees. An animal ran across just ahead of me and popped into a prominent hole at the side of the road. It was a large woodchuck—the first one I saw that spring. Usually I spot at least one woodchuck at or near the far field in March, several weeks before the guest-house woodchuck appears. Both the sheltered field and road warm up very quickly.

Toward the end of the month the silence of the evening is broken by the "peent, peent" call of the woodcock. Normally we are unable to find the birds, so well do they blend with the brown grasses. But one March we were very lucky. It had been cold and cloudy all day—not very inspiring weather for any of us. Just at dusk Steve heard the call of a woodcock close by. "I'm going out to find him," he announced. A few minutes later he came racing in, terribly excited. "I saw him, Mom. He was up in the garden. He just flew up into his mating flight. Come on." I went barreling up to the garden. There sat the woodcock, loudly peenting, just a few yards away.

"Go get my binoculars and bring Dad," I whispered. A few minutes later they both joined me. We could clearly see the woodcock's long bill and the slight inflation of his wings every time he called. Suddenly he soared up into the sky, circling higher and higher and making us dizzy as we tried to follow his flight. He almost stopped, fluttered his wings like a bat, and then let out a marvelous trill of music. He plummeted down into the first field and began peenting again. After a few minutes he repeated his breathtaking flight, but he landed in the same spot in the garden where we had first seen him. The next flight culminated in a drop into the field. He appeared to be alternating between the two locations, totally unconcerned by our excited, and not very quiet, presence. He was still performing when we were forced inside by darkness. Because woodcocks like earthworms, they feed at night when their favorite food is most active. A series of holes in the ground will mark the places where they hunt. They, too, follow the thawing ground northward just as the robins do, taking up at dusk the task the robins have abandoned for the night.

But despite the many lovely days and the encouraging green signs of spring, March usually ends with cold rainy weather that changes to sleet and snow. As the sleet comes down, coating the lawn and roofs, the song sparrows carol on: "Hip! Hip! Hurrah! Spring is here!"

April is a celebration of all the many shades of green. Reddish green tulip tips poke above the brown earth at the edge of the lawn, and dark green wild onions have grown several inches high along the borders of the woods. Herds of deer graze in our fields at dawn and sunset, feeding on the first grasses that have penetrated the thick matting of dried hay. The moss-covered trails and banks are bright green, freshened up by the soft rains of early spring.

Down the back slope the day lily shoots carpet the grape arbor in chartreuse. One splendid, warm night, when the earth was lit by an orange full moon, Bruce and I stepped outside to listen to the day lilies grow. The slope, with its thousands of day lilies, was filled with tiny popping noises. It seemed as if the earth was straining, heaving, and bursting in a thousand different places from the strong pressure of those spearlike plants.

In the barnyard I hurry to harvest the shiny, dark leaves of winter cress. It makes a mild-tasting cooked green in early April. With a bit of bacon, vinegar, and sugar added to the pot, we really relish this first fresh vegetable of spring. Later in the month the leaves and buds become bitter. We know because we tried the broccoli-like buds one year. They made a gummy, mouth-twisting dish that we all bravely tasted and rejected.

As the winter cress ages our green diet is replenished with dandelion greens. During mild days in mid-April I sit on the lawn patiently cutting thousands of leaves which I fix just as I do the cress. For a couple of weeks we eat them nearly every evening for dinner. All too quickly the first yellow blooms appear, ending the harvest for another year. Luckily we have no neighbors who object to the presence of thousands of dandelions in our lawns. Cutting them all out would be a lifetime occupation. Besides, those little yellow disks against the new green grass are a beautiful sight.

Our lawn is not a golf course. We have neither the time nor money to sow its many acres with grass seed, and when it gets long a large variety of interesting weeds and wild-flowers bloom. Purple violets mingle with the golden dandelions, and stars-of-Bethlehem grow in clumps near the spring house.

Gill-over-the-ground, or ground ivy, a dark green vine imported from Europe, sprawls over the lawn and garden. Its tiny purple flowers bloom very early in April. This vine has been prized since the time of Ancient Greece. A bitter tea made from its fresh leaves is said to dispel the harshest cough. The first spring I was pleased to have such an illustrious and aromatic plant on our property. But by midsummer I was reviling it as I pulled armloads of the tenacious stuff from around each strawberry plant. It grew up and over everything, even the thick piles of hay I had used to mulch the strawberry rows. Once, during a January thaw, I discovered a few tiny blossoms in the tulip bed. They seemed like a special miracle then. And I do enjoy musing over all the fancy names given to this lowly vine. Euell Gibbons, in his book *Stalking the Healthful Herbs*, says that in addition to its quaint common name it is known as Robin-run-in-the-hedge, Lizzie-run-up-the-hedge, haymaids, cat's foot and, because it was used to clarify beer, alehoof and tunhoof. Only the English could have devised so many charming names for such a simple plant.

April showers not only green the earth, they fill up our stream as well. Every spring Mark relearns the joy of running water. Down the road he races, his little legs pumping hard. Then he pauses hopefully. "Mommy, can we stay by the stream? I want to throw stones in the water." I settle on a mossy log to watch as he searches for a stone, tosses it into the flowing water, and screams happily as it makes a big splash. How many times I sat and watched Steve and David throw stones into a Maine lake when they were little fellows. I am particularly charmed by rushing streams as they tumble over and around rocks and stones of all sizes. I like to wade in streams and swim in lakes, but throw stones—never! It is enough for me to watch all my eager, sparkling, laughing little boys as they toss in unending numbers of stones. "You just don't understand, Mommy," they chorus, when I wonder aloud why they enjoy pitching stones into water.

Gradually I am beginning to understand their fascination with the garter snakes that live around the well. On the first sunny April day Mark runs down to look for them. "Snakes are out," he calls, and I go to look at their wriggling bodies as they groggily emerge from their nests. Usually there are between four and six snakes of varying sizes crawling over each other as they wriggle joyously in the new warmth of the sun. When Mark was three years old, he delighted in watching them, and I asked him why. "Because they are beautiful the way they curl up, and because Steve likes them," he answered. As soon as Steve came home from school, Mark begged him to pick one up so he and David could stroke its dry skin. He was willing to watch and talk to them for hours, but neither he nor David, who was then seven, would venture to hold one. They each had a residual fear, or perhaps it was just hesitancy, to actually hold a snake, and they greatly admired Steve's bravery.

The next April all that was changed. Easter was a bright, very warm day, and the snakes were energetic. The boys ran joyfully shirtless and barefoot for the first time that year. "Let's play with the snakes by the well," Steve shouted, and down they ran to see them. That year David was a brave eight and he confidently grasped a snake, holding the back of its head firmly so it could not turn around and nip him. Very soon the snake was tamed, and it twined elegantly around David's arm. Steve picked up another, larger snake.

Steve and Mark playing with a black snake.

Mark carefully watched his brothers as they collected a box and dumped four garter snakes into it. Quickly the snakes derived individual personalities and names. Fierce One was impossible to tame, Scott Snake was large and aggressive, and Cindy Snake was small and female, or so the boys reasoned as they played gently with them. Without any fanfare at all, Mark suddenly picked up the fourth snake. A look of incredulous delight spread across his face as the snake curled up in his hand, its small head with questing red tongue held high. After that, I rarely saw Mark without a snake. His love for them seemed genuine and deep; he appeared to relate to them as fully as he did to the puppies.

His affection for the harmless, gentle garter snakes did not extend to the larger nonpoisonous snakes. When I discovered a long black rat snake stretched motionless in the garden and called the boys, Mark stared in fascination as the snake suddenly curled up, hissed, and rattled his tail threateningly. "Well," Mark said, "I like garter snakes better."

Mark finds April a continual joy. Not only are there snakes for him to play with, but there are numerous emerging flowers and plants to identify. He takes a personal interest in everything that grows, and he delights in showing me the newest opening daffodil or the mint growing beside the spring house. One April he was in a state of anxiety for several days because the trailing arbutus was blooming and incessant rain had kept us from hiking up the mountain to see it. "The trailing arbutus is out, and I can't even see it," he wailed each morning as still more rain fell. Finally, one cold blustery day he insisted on laboring up the trail, pushing against strong winds and stinging ice pellets. He exclaimed in delight over each blossom, considering it his personal property to guard and show off to everyone.

Classified as an evergreen shrub in Grimm's *The Shrubs of Pennsylvania*, the fragrant pink and white blossoms of arbutus are also known as Mayflowers. According to legend, trailing arbutus was the first spring flower the Pilgrims saw after their long winter. Gratefully they named it for the ship that had brought them safely to the New World. We feel very privileged to have the paths along the ridges carpeted with deep green trailing arbutus leaves, because this shrub has become quite rare in many areas. For some reason, people used to enjoy pulling it up by the roots, although it has none of the characteristics of a proper cut flower.

In our family we have never allowed our boys to pick any woodland flowers except the large purple violets. All the others wilt instantly and are dead before they can be put into vases. Instead of bringing the flowers home, we go off into the woods to see each new flower as it emerges. In early April, when the boys come up the road from school, they exclaim happily that the colts-foot is blooming. I always run eagerly down beyond the corral fence near the stream to admire the buttery-yellow discs growing in a bright clump. The blossoms look very much like dandelion only somewhat smaller.

And whereas dandelion leaves appear before the flower, coltsfoot is leafless in the spring. Only a single hairy stem supports the flower; the large, seven-inch leaves grow up in the summer, long after it has wilted.

The eroded bank along the road produces a large variety of acid-loving flowers. The first to appear is the round-lobed hepatica or liverleaf. In mid-April I discover several clumps of the delicate blue flowers growing on their hairy stems, looking frail and lovely on the washed-away brown banks. Then, a few days later, the tiny white blossoms of the rue anemone appear. We return day after day to admire their beauty and to watch eagerly for the later flowers to emerge—orchid-colored fringed polygala, bellworts, white violets, and Canada mayflowers. Those banks hoard all kinds of flower seeds and lacy ferns which gradually add sprinkles of blue, purple, white, and green to the brown earth.

Among my favorite spring wildflowers are the trilliums. On our Maine farm I was thrilled to find large clusters of white trilliums, several individual purple trilliums, and even an occasional painted trillium. But when we moved to Pennsylvania, to my distress I could not find any trilliums on the mountain. Then, one spring day while walking down the road, I spotted a huge clump of purple trilliums blooming next to the stream. Searching carefully about, I found several more in various places beside the road. To my delight, I even found one clump of purple trilliums which had yellow flowers, a rather rare occurrence. John Burroughs, the Hudson River naturalist of the last century, also was quite fond of trilliums, and he used their popular name "wake robin" as the title for his most famous book. As he said in the preface to *Wake Robin*, "This is mainly a book about the Birds. . . . I cast about for a word thoroughly in the atmosphere and spirit of the book, which I hope I have found in Wake-Robin . . . the common name of the White Trillium, which blooms in all our woods, and which marks the arrival of all the birds."

Much as I love the wildflowers, I also am very fond of the cultivated flowers around our home. Early in April the yard is still mostly drab-colored when the forsythia bushes begin to bloom. One warm day they are budding; the next day they are in full flower. If the weather stays cool the blossoms last almost three weeks before the pale green leaves appear. On a bright sunny day the bushes shimmer in the sunlight. Forsythia seems almost miraculous, because it thrives with no care at all. Our first winter the rabbits nibbled a large bush next to the stone wall, and that spring there were very few blossoms on it. Following our usual policy of benign neglect, we let the bush alone. Two springs later the bush was larger and lovelier than it ever had been before.

I must confess that we don't even prune the forsythia bushes, and yet they achieve the most graceful shapes all on their own. The one beside the garage is enormous and grows so fast that I must constantly cut away branches sprawling across the door. Usually I wait until winter to snip off the offenders. One year I cut several sprigs just before Christmas and stuck them in a vase of water, which I placed in a sunny window. By New Year's Day we had a lovely bouquet of forsythia on the dining room table. I believe I could have forsythia all winter long if I industriously kept snipping and forcing. But I would not like to become immune to its beauty by overexposure, so I keep my forcing down to a minimum. It is good to know that whenever winter seems long and unending, I can make the forsythia bloom.

My favorite garden flowers blossom in harmony with the forsythia. The former owner had two long lines of daffodils planted in the backyard, and I have added others in every available space. Our first spring here I was amazed and delighted at the number of daffodils that emerged. Judiciously I picked enough to fill my vases and still leave plenty to brighten the yard. When the pear trees bloomed I mixed the daffodils with white sprigs of pear blossoms.

My love affair with daffodils began years ago when I was only two years old. My parents built a new home and filled their garden with daffodil bulbs. Noticing how pleased they were with the beautiful flowers, I traipsed over the yard, picking the daffodils and carefully placing them in my new red wagon. Satisfied at last with the big bouquet I had gathered, I went in the house to present them to my mother.

To my distress, she was upset. "Did you pick all the daffodils?" she cried.

"Oh no! Mommy. I left one for the garden!" From that time on I have loved the daffodils better than any other flower. But until we moved to the mountain, I never had enough to satisfy me. Perhaps I never will be wholly content until, like Wordsworth, I can see 10,000 at a glance.

During April the bushes and trees of the woods also blossom. First the shadbushes scatter white patches against the naked hillsides. Early settlers noticed that their drooping clusters of white blossoms always bloomed during the runs of shad up the creeks and rivers, hence the name shadbush. An alternate name, Juneberry, refers to the sweet and edible fruits produced in June and eaten by ruffed grouse, deer, opossums, foxes, and knowledgeable country people.

Along the stream the spice bushes are a haze of yellow-green. Their blossoms provide honey bees with an early supply of nectar. So do the white flowers of our pear trees, which hum with bees on any sunny day. The scarlet blossoms of the red maple trees are easy to see against the fine silver color of the trunks and branches. Along the edge of the woods I am particularly enchanted by the long golden catkins of the black birch trees. On a bright breezy day they glitter and shimmer in the spring sunlight.

April is an easy month, because it is too early to plant anything but peas, lettuce, and chard. And the weeding is still manageable. Just a little work around the rhubarb, asparagus, and flower beds keeps them looking neat. Otherwise I spend long hours sitting in the sunshine and watching the birds come back. One day I hear particularly loud calls from the "pileated woodpeckers" before I suddenly realize that the ruckus is too noisy for the pileateds. The yellow-shafted flickers have returned. For days they court and call and do battle with the already resident starlings for proper nesting holes. The hollow dead limbs of the balm of Gilead trees make particularly resonant pounding posts, and they seem unconcerned with my admiring gaze as I watch them storm from one tree to another. All their energies are concentrated on courtship.

Not long after the flickers' arrival I hear another familiar call: "chewink" the male towhee calls as he lands in the grape tangle. Or he sings "drink your tea" to attract a returning female a few days later. Soon we have two mated pairs foraging in the backyard and dozens more up in the woods. As I walk along the trails they scratch through the leaves, searching noisily for insects. I consider towhees to be among the most handsome birds around. The male, with his black, white, and reddish-brown body, seems a brighter, cleaner, and more flashy version of the somewhat drab-colored robin. The female, with her beautiful chestnut back, is as lovely as her mate.

What could be cheerier than their short call and song? Certainly not the long unending string of musical phrases that the brown thrasher renders from the top of every tree on the place. Each year I wonder hopefully when I hear his first song, "could it possibly be a mockingbird?" But no, the bird is reddish-brown with a spotted chest and long tail, and while he sings from dawn until long after sunset without ceasing, he is decently quiet at night. After a week of this I begin to wish that some female would return his ardor. Such persistence should be rewarded.

So the April days are noisy with bird songs. Even the evenings produce new sounds. A long, low drumming on Sapsucker Ridge grows steadily louder—the ruffed grouse are courting again. On another night, a whippoorwill starts his monotonous calling, and down near the stream a couple of spring peepers trill. But I am not content until one evening, late in April when the ridge glows in reflected sunlight, I hear the first musical notes of the wood thrushes. At last I know there is no turning back—spring has really come to the mountain.

May is one of the loveliest months in Pennsylvania. It is also one of the busiest. The spring rains that water the beautiful array of cultivated and wild flowers make the grass grow unbelievably fast. We find ourselves torn between a dozen tasks. At the same time as the lawn needs cutting, we feel compelled to view the wild azaleas in the woods or to watch the phoebes hatch out. May, for us, is a grand balancing act. Somehow we must not miss the wildlife happenings, but we must get the garden planted and weeded. The only time we really rest is when it rains, and then we have the long-neglected indoor chores to attend to.

But is there another month so beautiful as May, filled with the songs of numberless birds, the scent of dozens of bushes and flowers, and the sight of the grandest pageantry of wildflowers? May begins with tulips and lilacs in the garden and violets and wild azaleas in the woods. The ridges are a symphony of soft colors—muted rose, orange-brown, and lime green—accented by the white blossoms of wild cherry trees. At last the tiny, perfectly formed leaves explode from the bursting buds. Very quickly the open vistas of the winter woods fill in with the hazy greens of springtime, and when I go walking I must poke carefully along Sapsucker Ridge, watching for a faded trail that has become enveloped by the emerging green.

The woods are dominated by oak trees, whose new leaves are deep red with burnished golden tips. Of all the oaks the chestnut oak is the most common on our ridges. Each May I examine and marvel over the inch-long downy leaves that have opened. They are a deep coppery-red tone—beautiful miniatures of autumn-colored leaves.

Chestnut oaks, or rock oaks, are an important part of our history. In pioneer times tanners set up their shops near stands of chestnut oaks because their bark, which is very rich in tannin, was used extensively in tanning leather. During the middle of the nineteenth century the wood was used to make railroad ties, and I wonder how many trees from the ridges of the mountain were cut to build the railroad tracks through the gap. Unfortunately we do not have any chestnut oaks left today to equal the size described by Colonel William Byrd in the eighteenth century: "This tree is of terrific height since the trunk alone, to the branches, is fifty or sixty feet tall and four to five feet thick on an average." But these trees still grow tall and stately on the rocky ridges, and they produce the sweetest-tasting acorns each autumn on which the wild turkeys, deer, and red squirrels feast.

Growing among the chestnut oaks are the small sad remnants of the American chestnut tree. Their tiny new leaves are yellowish green, a contrast to the reddish hue of the oaks. Before this century and the importation of the chestnut blight, the American chestnut was one of our most beautiful trees. In springtime the ridges glowed with their large white blossoms, and almost everyone relished their tasty nuts each autumn. But in 1904 a fungus was discovered on the chestnut trees in New York Zoological Park. It was believed to have come into this country on the highly resistant Chinese chestnut trees. With growing horror, people watched as the blight spread rapidly across the country, decimating the great stands of chestnuts throughout the east and midwest. The disease spores were carried by the wind, and nothing could stop them. Even so, each spring the tiny sprouts in our woods produce new bright leaves. In some places those sprouts grow into twenty-foot-tall trees, but inevitably they are struck down by the blight. Perhaps someday one of those sprouts will grow into a mature tree, and from that tree foresters will propagate a new strain of American chestnuts that will be able to resist the blight.

The lovely reddish-golden hues in the spring woods belong to the newly opened leaves of the red maples. These medium-sized trees are among the first to repopulate a cut-over forest, and their saplings make popular browse for deer and rabbits. Sometimes called the swamp or scarlet maple, the red maple can be found in bottomlands as well as mountain ridges. In fact, it is America's most common maple tree, and in every season of the year it displays its red color. Before the leaves begin to emerge, the blossoms are a deep showy red. As the leaves rapidly increase in size they become bright green, but the leaf stalks retain their red color. In autumn the leaves change to a deep winey hue, and during the winter the red buds and twigs of these trees are among the few splashes of color on the mountain.

Looming above all the colorful hardwoods glowing on the ridges are the gaunt, grotesque shapes of the pitch pines. Far below on the forest floor the deep green laurel bushes are surrounded by low bush blueberries. In May the delicate, white, bell-shaped flowers of the blueberries are set amidst pale green leaves with borders of deep red. The pink flames of the wild azaleas contrast to the perfect white and green of the flowering dogwood trees.

Occasional displays of wildflowers are clustered among the green of emerging ferns. My favorite is the pink lady's slipper, or moccasin flower. Each spring we locate all the green shoots that will eventually produce the showy flower. Always there are many more shoots and leaves than actual blossoms. Our first year on the mountain the most impressive display was just a few hundred feet from the guest house in a small clearing in the woods. "How perfect," I thought. "My own small garden of lady's-slippers." But the following year there were only half as many as the first year, and the year after that there were only five. By that time, though, the dump trail was lined with them and was promptly renamed Lady Slipper Trail. On one walk Mark and I counted seventeen flowers along that trail. In some inexplicable way, the flowers had all been relocated. As long as we know there are lady's slippers somewhere in our woods, we don't mind searching for them again each spring. It adds a bit of zest to our spring walks.

Every year we seem to find more fringed polygala, or gaywings. They grow on the banks above the road and on the wooded slope near the end of the Short-Circuit Trail. Fringed polygalas are small, paired, orchid-colored flowers supported by a slender stem which also holds four evergreen leaves. The leaves look much like those of wintergreen, so the plant is often called flowering wintergreen. Despite its small size, it is one of the showiest flowers in the woods, particularly when hundreds of the small blossoms carpet the banks with their pink-purplish color.

Every child I have known has been fascinated by mayapples. From the time the umbrella-like leaves pop magically from the ground, Mark eagerly watches them. He calls them "elves' umbrellas" as he peeks under each one, searching for a flower bud. Not all the leaves harbor a bud, but those that do are anxiously watched. Week after week the umbrellas expand. Then one day a lovely waxy flower blooms from each bud. If one is especially patient, waiting and watching long into July, the flower produces a large, lemonlike berry that children use as missiles and grownups make into jelly. Also called hog apple because its fruit is "eaten by pigs and boys," according to botanist Asa Gray, mayapples are the most common of all the wildflowers that grow in our woods.

Of course violets far outnumber the other spring wildflowers on the mountain if we count all the varieties that grow in the fields as well as the woods. I have not yet sorted out the different shades of purple violets that grow in the fields, but I have noticed that most of the varieties have long stems, large heart-shaped leaves, and good-sized blossoms. However, an almost stemless variety, without the characteristic leaves, grows only in the sandy soil of the far field; tiny white violets grow in the woods along the road; and yellow violets are found solely in the partial clearing around the dump. The yellow and purple violets also have found a place in our garden. I discovered that they were very easy to trans-

The author's favorite wildflower,
the Pink Ladyslipper or Moccasin Flower.

plant, so I dug them up, replanted, and watered them during our first spring on the mountain. Before I knew it they had spread themselves throughout the iris bed and crowded against the transplanted ferns.

We even eat the flowers and leaves of the violets in our tossed salads because of the incredible amounts of vitamin C they contain. I tried cooking the leaves once, but we didn't like them. According to Euell Gibbons, the juice of the flowers can be extracted to make a gelatin dessert, but we found that while it was a beautiful color, the taste was less than memorable. Besides, despite the millions of violets we have, it was still difficult for me to pick all those flowers to make a cupful for extraction. Rather, I now content myself with picking just a few to keep in my small blue and white Delft vase.

So much growing and changing takes place along the road during May that I frequently go off to investigate. I particularly remember a bright lovely day one May when I went for a walk all the way down the road. The light shone through the glimmering new tree leaves and blossoms, and the only sounds I heard were occasional bird calls and the roaring of the brimful stream as it tumbled down through the hollow. I felt totally alone in the universe. It was difficult to believe that a busy highway and railroad lay at the bottom of the road and that the town was a little over a mile away.

Wildflowers were strewn in clumps throughout the woods. The Solomon's seals had unfurled their long leafy stems, but the paired yellow bells had not yet opened. The wild geraniums had just begun to blossom, and the bright, shiny, green leaves of the Canada mayflowers covered the mountainside. White violets, large purple violets, and long-spurred violets grew everywhere, while masses of purple trilliums nodded along the stream. Standing tall above the flowers, glistening with fragile green leaves, were the beech trees. The stately old hemlocks guarding the road provided an acid carpet of dead needles that helped to nourish the abundance of wildflowers.

The rushing stream attracted a Louisiana waterthrush, one of the most interesting members of the warbler family. I stopped to watch this brown bird with a lightly spotted breast as he stood on a log, continually pumping his tail. This "pumping," a peculiar kind of teetering he does, looks similar to the bobbing of a sandpiper and makes him easy to identify. Bent reports in *Life Histories of North American Wood Warblers* that an astute observer named Edgar A. Mearns in 1879 described the habitat of the Louisiana waterthrush as follows: "Its notes cannot be dissociated from the sound of gurgling, rushing waters. . . . Even a casual allusion to this little bird recalls . . . a bright picture of clear mountain streams, with their falls and eddies, their dams of rocks and fallen tree trunks, their level stretches flowing over bright, pebbly bottoms, with mossy banks and rocky ferneries."

As I walked quietly along I glanced up to see four scarlet tanagers sitting silently in four separate trees, their gaudy red and black coats giving a tropical air to the surroundings. They are my favorite birds, but until we moved to the mountain I had only had brief glimpses of them. They prefer heavily leaved treetops, their activities are usually veiled from onlookers, and since their songs sound like hoarse robins, most people dismiss the sounds as being just robins singing slightly off key. But the elusive males are still easy to see in the early days of May while the tree leaves are small.

Many different kinds of ferns were pushing up through the brown duff in the hollow, their fiddle-like heads uncurling in the sunshine. Huge deep green ostrich ferns grew like tropical vegetation in large circular clusters on the stream bank. The ever-green Christmas ferns spilled out of the bank along the road, and sensitive ferns, so-named because they are instantly killed by the first frost, displayed their broad, almost triangular leaves. The interrupted ferns had dark spore cases halfway up the fertile leaves. These spore cases ripen and wither rapidly, leaving interrupted spaces in the leaves from early summer onward. Knee-high bracken with its almost horizontal leaves opened in every available space.

The stream looked so beautiful with its miniature waterfalls and quiet pools that I attempted to walk beside it on my way back up the mountain. At first I was able to go on one side of the stream or the other with relative ease. Then I found my way was blocked by a dense tangle of enormous rhododendron bushes. It was either straight up the slope to the road above or on through the tangle. I chose the latter course. Dead branches cracked across my face and arms as I pushed my way along. Eventually, though, there was nowhere to go but up to the road. Crawling and clawing hand over hand from sapling to sapling, I finally reached the top. After such exertion I was content to climb the road easily up to the house. Although I regretted that my peaceful interlude was ending, I knew that whenever I chose to explore the road there would always be new discoveries awaiting me.

Often, though, I must put aside my desire to explore, because May is the month we plant the garden. Each year we get more ambitious and expand its size. And, of course, every bit of it except the squash must be fenced. Bruce does all the cultivating, while I do the planning and most of the planting. Each year I pore over the garden manuals, attempting to mingle herbs, flowers, and vegetables in companion plantings that will repel insects and disease. As a further precaution against pests, I also rotate my crops each season. As we labor late into the twilight we are liable to hear a whippoor-will on the ridge or an owl hooting in the distance.

Always we are aware of the birds—in the garden or on the porch in sunshine or rain. In May all the most spectacular birds return. Sitting on the porch on a sunlit afternoon, I suddenly notice several deep blue birds flitting around the driveway. The indigo buntings have returned. They fly toward the lawn and the spotted carpet of yellow dandelions. As they cling to the stems, swaying gently in the breeze, they begin to eat the dandelion seeds. Soon they are sharing their feast with a couple of male goldfinches.

A few minutes later I hear a melodic new bird song as an orange and black Baltimore oriole lands on the fence. Singing loudly and with great vigor, he puffs himself up proudly. Then he dips down into the ditch to wash himself off, no doubt feeling dusty from his long trip. Flying back up to the fence, he carefully grooms each feather, and finally, feeling satisfied with his appearance, he flies over to the blossoming old apple tree and begins to sing.

On another day, as I work in the kitchen, a whirring, buzzing little bird comes tapping at the back door. "What is that?" Mark asks as he eats his breakfast.

"A ruby-throated hummingbird," I answer as I run to look closer. In a split second he has zoomed off as far as the apple tree, and with another whoosh he is out of sight.

"He is so little. How does he lay eggs?" Mark wonders.

Two May arrivals that we hear more often than we see are the yellowthroats and the crested flycatchers. The yellowthroats, with their loud "witchedy, witchedy" calls, look like black-masked bandits. I occasionally see them in the grape tangles, on lilac bushes, or perched on the locust branches. Once spotted, even at a distance, their masks make their identity unmistakable. But I am always momentarily stumped by a crested flycatcher, particularly if he is silent—a vague bit of yellow on his belly, mostly all over olive green, some faint wing bars, and a crest. Then I remember to look for a rufous tail. That distinguishes him from all other birds of similar coloring. I know that both yellowthroats and crested flycatchers stay to nest around the house because we hear their calls throughout the summer.

While the birds noisily announce their courtship and mating, the many small mammals conduct themselves quietly and inconspicuously. Usually we are only aware of the fecundity of the creatures about us when we begin seeing the young ones—small inexperienced rabbits, tiny frolicking chipmunks, and bold, hungry red squirrels. One spring was particularly memorable because of the meadow vole nests we discovered. Bruce accidentally dug up one nest while rototilling a piece of the field, but he managed to rescue one young vole. It skittered along actively as the boys attempted to fondle it. Then Bruce fed it some milk, which it seemed to like. But its mouth was so tiny and the medicine dropper so big that we felt it would be better to find another nest for it. Later that afternoon David found an occupied meadow vole nest, and immediately the mother began moving her babies from that nest to another. They looked the same age as the foundling, so he hastened to put it into the old nest. He watched in amazement as the mother came back, grasped the newcomer, and carried it away to the new nest. What was one more mouth to feed?

That spring we found nests in all stages of development. One day Steve brought in a handful of four just-born meadow voles, completely naked, pink, and gray, and "looking like miniature pigs," he said. Meadow voles are more commonly known as field mice, and yet their round little bodies are so unlike the house mouse that I like to distinguish them from those pests. They are very prolific, able to produce their own young at three weeks of age, and have a litter of from two to nine young every month of the green season. So it seemed silly to be concerned about the lives of these small orphans, who would likely be eaten by one of the many creatures that prey on meadow voles. In fact, without a large crop of voles each year, the whole prey-predator balance collapses. The hungry foxes, weasels, owls, and opossums will switch to chicken if they can, an unhappy affair for the farmer. Still, any living animal, no matter how small and common, is a source of wonder to the boys and must be cared for and treated with respect.

As May draws to a close, the peas and lettuce have grown several inches high in the fenced garden. We have had numerous cuttings of asparagus and plentiful rhubarb desserts. Tulips and lilacs have been replaced by the first iris and mock orange. The bright woodland flowers have faded—only the small white Canada mayflowers and false Solomon's seals still bloom. The wildflower pageant has shifted to the open waste places where the showy purple dame's rockets loom above the tall grasses. May is gone and with it a mountain spring.

Chapter 7
Mammal Adventures

WHEN WE FIRST moved in we were excited by the abundance of cottontail rabbits—cute, cuddly, and soft, with twitching noses and powder-puff tails. They loped along the road, hopped through the fields, and lived in every brush pile. The winter snows were littered with tracks, and in early spring we discovered one family residing under the guest house.

Mark was thrilled the first time he saw "Easter bunnies," as he called them, leaping out ahead of us on the trail. But as spring progressed, we began referring to them as the "Plague of the Mountain." One day I went out to see if the crocuses had finally opened. Every crocus had been chomped to the ground and most of the tulips as well. Despite the abundance of owls and hawks, we had a terrific population of rabbits. Among their most deadly and efficient enemies are foxes and, to my distress, we have very few of them on the mountain. Foxes are heavily hunted for their fur and because many local hunters classify them as "varmints." Actually the fox's major sin is killing rabbits, which people prefer to kill for themselves. Therefore, rabbits are cute and cuddly while foxes are vicious, tricky killers.

Rabbits reproduce at a fantastic rate. They breed from February to September, and each female produces a litter of three to six rabbits every twenty-eight days. The young leave the nest in two weeks, mature in three weeks, and start reproducing immediately. By the end of our first year here, we were considering calling in rabbit hunters to reduce the population.

Then we began fencing in our garden. When we, and not the rabbits, began harvesting the first lettuce, chard, and peas, we felt a little more kindly toward them. But they had their revenge: they suddenly developed a taste for the unfenced cucumber shoots and the tomatoes we had just set out. Luckily, we had planted sixty-seven tomato plants, and the rabbits only ate eighteen before they quit. However, they never gave up on the cucumbers, so homemade pickles were deferred for still another year.

My feelings about cottontails were further confused one cold, rainy afternoon in late May when the boys raced in excitedly carrying four baby rabbits. Fritz had discovered a nest in the field which he had torn apart. One spunky baby had squealed loudly in protest, and the boys had eagerly rescued the lot. The bunnies were soaking wet and very hungry, but quite appealing with their wide open brown eyes and soft fur. Despite our overwhelming population of rabbits, I could not turn them out to die.

We had not the slightest idea what to do with them, but Bruce took charge, carefully drying the bunnies off with a towel and tucking them into a grass-lined box which we placed near a heating register. Then he grasped each squirming bunny, carefully pried its mouth open with a medicine dropper, and fed it some warm milk. Two of the bunnies were definitely stronger, and they quickly understood what Bruce was doing. They sucked busily, consuming three droppersful of milk before they were filled. But the two smaller bunnies were far more stubborn, clamping their mouths firmly shut and refusing to cooperate at all. Any milk they received was poured down their throats with no help from them. We managed three feedings before bedtime, and at the last feeding I noticed that one of the smaller rabbits was much colder than its warm siblings. It was listless and almost still.

In the early morning, I was half afraid to look. The little cold one was stretched out stiff in the middle of the box, but the other three were huddled in a warm pile in the corner of the box, bright-eyed and expectant. Since Bruce had to go to work, it was my turn to

David feeds Thumper with a medicine dropper.

force feed them. They felt so little and frail and they wriggled so much that I was afraid of hurting them as I tried to insert the dropper past their tightly closed teeth. Finally, realizing that if I didn't feed them they would die, I grasped their heads firmly with three fingers, carefully jimmied the dropper in past those little teeth, and gently squeezed the milk out. At first most of it got on me and all over the bunnies, but the two stronger ones soon began sucking busily. The smallest one made a comical little protesting face and considered me an instrument of torture.

With three bunnies left, our three boys naturally claimed one a piece. The littlest went to Mark and was called Cottontail. David's was Thumper because it was always kicking out with its back feet. Steve named his aggressive little feeder Cuddly Bunny. I fed them every three hours, allowing the boys to play with them only during feeding time. After three days Thumper and Cuddly Bunny outgrew their small box, so we transferred them to a much larger box where they could hop about and eat the grass, clover, and lettuce we gave them.

But Cottontail stayed huddled in the box no matter how active her brothers might be. She never groomed herself as the others did, and they cleaned her off and tried to warm her. However, she didn't grow, and she refused to suck the milk or eat the greens. On the fourth day she became increasingly passive as I fed her, and she huddled in the box in a sorrowful heap. By nightfall she was listless and still, submitting meekly to the dropper. In a half hour she was dead. I felt heavy hearted, afraid that I had hurt her in some way. She had become a definite, gentle personality to me, and I had so enjoyed the sight of Mark with the littlest bunny cuddled in his hand.

The next day I taught Thumper and Cuddly Bunny to lap up milk from a small plastic lid. They consumed several refills a day and spent all their waking time drinking and eating or hiding under the grass. Once I stopped feeding them with the dropper, they became totally wild, shifting entirely for themselves. After ten days they were escaping from the box constantly, and we were liable to find them anywhere about the house. As children often do, the boys had lost interest, and I was left with tending them. Finally, I gave the boys a choice—should we keep them as pets or release them? Steve decided to gather them up, and he walked off from the house, far, far up into the field, and let them go. They hopped quickly off with never a backward glance. Their world had become warm and green; they would survive as long as most bunnies do in the wild.

Deer seem almost as abundant on the mountain as cottontails, but compared to the rabbits they do very little damage. One autumn some bucks rubbed their antlers on a few young apple trees, and each spring I find their hoof-prints in the wet soil of the garden. Looking over the crop to come, I worry each year, but when the corn is ready the deer never make an appearance.

No matter how often I see the deer, I always stop to admire them. During our Maine years, spotting a deer was a rare occurrence; in fact, we saw just three of them in our five years there. Here in Pennsylvania the woods and fields are filled with them. In the early springtime they graze in the fields like cattle, twenty to thirty in a herd, and before hunting season in late autumn the woods teem with them.

Shortly after we moved in I took the boys walking along the ridge. We weren't being particularly quiet—little boys seldom are—but we did pause on the trail to rest. Suddenly a large buck came leaping down the trail toward us. Evidently he had not caught our scent, and he certainly did not see us. I jumped to my feet and shouted. He veered off into the laurel brush as the boys yelled, "Wow, did you see his antlers?" I had, indeed, and his hoofs as well. After that, seeing deer became so commonplace that we never even mentioned them when we returned from a walk and someone asked, "Did you see anything?" Anything means something different or exciting, and deer fit into neither category.

While we see them constantly as they flee from us, we rarely have a chance to observe them for any length of time. Their fear of the hunter is too great. They seem to sense, though, that they are not hunted in the spring. Certainly they are most visible then. One memorable day in early April, just as the grass had begun to green, I emerged from the woods into the far field in time to see twenty-two deer flee. I sprawled out on a mossy, sunny bank, absorbed some warmth, listened to the robins singing, and then moved languidly on along the wide, leaf-strewn road, headed back toward the first field. Suddenly, I stopped as I noticed silhouettes against the sky on the hillside just ahead. A herd of five deer was peacefully feeding at the top of the first field, and this time I saw them before they saw me. Moving as quietly as I could, I edged closer. The leader abruptly raised his head and turned to stare at me. I froze, and we watched each other for ten minutes without moving. When he resumed his feeding, I slowly moved my binoculars up to my eyes and crept nearer. His head rose, he stared at me, and he finally made up his mind. He went slowly to each of the deer and in some way warned them. As each was alerted, it looked over at me and then lowered its head and continued eating. Apparently the leader would decide whether or not to flee. Undecided still, he watched, grazed, and watched again. I tired first and shifted my feet. In seconds they were gone—I never heard a sound.

During the height of hunting season one year we had a six-inch snowfall. As the storm raged outside, we saw three deer calmly browsing in the sheltered woods, undisturbed by the flakes that clung to their brown coats. We crowded at the windows to watch as the doe and her two fawns moved slowly down to the stream. They stepped lightly across to nibble at the brush on the other side. Finding the gnarled old apple tree, they nudged around, looking for fallen fruit. They wandered back and forth between the tall weeds and the small stream, poking peacefully along, undisturbed by the house above and all the awed faces pressed to the windows. A dreamlike hour went by before they finally moved slowly away, back to the security of the woods.

Dogs are the biggest threat to the deer herds, according to the local hunters, just as foxes are the varmints that kill the rabbits. Chasing dogs are a menace that may be shot on sight, so we always kept Fritz confined to the basement during hunting season. I find myself unable to differentiate between a dog or a person hunting the deer. If the dogs are all as inept as Fritz, a person is certainly more dangerous.

Unfortunately all the Nimrods are not deadly shots. Driving back up the mountain one January afternoon, we saw a large deer grazing quietly beside the stream, seemingly unaware of all our roaring noise. "Look at that deer down there, Bruce! I wonder why he doesn't run off?" I asked. We stopped the jeep and peered down at him. As he turned, ever so slowly and carefully, we suddenly knew why he didn't run. He couldn't: one of his back legs hung uselessly. As we watched, he sank slowly to the ground. He appeared so beautiful and healthy, lying there looking at us, that we could scarcely believe what we had seen. But it was obvious that he was dying a slow, agonizing death.

Quickly we drove on up the mountain and called the game warden. Since a hunter had caused the wound, the official in charge of the hunters should take care of their damage. "Nothing you can do but shoot him," we were told, and he was too busy to come up and do it. So Bruce called our neighbor who called a hunter friend to come and do the job. Later we learned that the deer had been grievously wounded in the rump during hunting season and had been carrying the pain and disability since then. For at least a month he had struggled to survive, but the effort was clearly hopeless. Once dead, even his meat was useless, ruined by the suffering he had endured. We could only reflect on the human-centered life of our mountain, even as isolated as it is. It seems so sad that the wild creatures live in constant fear of us—fleeting glimpses of many of them are all we ever see.

Only occasionally, as in the case of the baby cottontails, do we get a chance to observe the wild creatures more closely. One year our back porch became a feeding place for two opossums. The first visit was more or less an exploratory trip. One night in late October as I tucked the boys into bed, descended the stairs, and walked through the dark dining room, I glanced out the window and immediately noticed a moving form coming up the slope. The silvery hairs of a very large opossum shone in the moonlight. Calling softly for the boys to come down and have a look, I switched on the porch light. The opossum never even noticed. Quietly we watched as it meandered right up to the window. Fritz was dozing along the wall, and to our surprise, the opossum inched up to him, sniffed, and then retreated back down the slope. Fritz never even awoke. The opossum shuffled slowly off looking like a disgruntled old man, casting many backward glances at the house and sleeping dog.

An opossum approaches the back porch,
its ears slightly tattered from the hard winter.

Nearly a month later I heard the rattle of Fritz's pan on the back porch one evening. By the time I groped in the dark and found the light switch, the intruder was gone, crashing off into the underbrush. I called Fritz inside, put more dog chow in the pan, and waited. A half hour later I heard another rattle. Bruce and I crept quietly into the kitchen and switched on the light. A small, young opossum was on the steps, nosing about in its near-sighted way, trying to rediscover the dog pan. It seemed unaware of the light and our presence. Blindly it cast about until it finally found the pan, tilted it on its side, and ate bits of the chow. In its eagerness it tried to climb into the pan, which bounced up to spill the opossum over and out. Undaunted, it continued feeding. Then it backed off slowly toward the grape arbor. "What a homely, stupid character," Bruce commented. Its long, naked, ratlike tail was unattractive, but its young face with its pink snout was almost cute. During the rest of the winter we frequently heard the pan rattle at intervals during the night as the opossums came to feed.

We knew that opossums have dens where they hole up during severe winter weather, since their ears and tails, particularly, suffer from frostbite. We had very little snow that winter, but enough to record the small, handlike tracks of the opossums. We were liable to find them on Laurel Ridge Trail, on the road, or on the lawn—anywhere we went walking. One day Mark and I noticed tracks leading out of the woods. "Come on, Mark," I said, "let's see if we can find out where that fellow lives." We quickly traced its tracks along the road, across the yard, and into the grape tangle. There we found a hole in the hillside which was cluttered with opossum tracks. It was only a hundred feet from our porch, but it was completely protected by a prickly screen of blackberry canes. At least one of our nightly visitors had its den there for the winter.

Usually Fritz seemed deaf to the opossum visits to his dish. But early one January evening I heard a tussling sound on the porch and hurried to investigate. Fritz was pacing possessively around his pan. The small opossum lay in a furry heap to one side. "He's killed the opossum," I shouted. Bruce came running, called Fritz in, and went out to examine the creature. "It's not dead, just playing 'possum," Bruce said as he gently turned it over for me to see. The opossum's mouth was stretched wide in a grotesque, still grimace that was horrifying. As Bruce nudged it a bit, the animal slowly blinked open its eyes. Then Bruce came inside to watch. In a few seconds the opossum stood up, looked about, then slid under the porch railing and meandered down the slope, none the worse for its fright.

The opossums did not always resort to playing dead when they were frightened. Another night I discovered Fritz standing guard over his pan while the opossum hid behind a propped up storm window on the porch. I persuaded Fritz to come in, and then I spoke soothingly to the opossum. Its ears twitched, and it hissed softly—I could have touched it, but I didn't. Its hiss was too intimidating. Once we went inside, it calmly resumed its interrupted dinner.

All through the winter the nocturnal visits continued. But by March the opossums finally were gone, off searching for mates no doubt. With all the new excitement of spring arrivals, we forgot about our winter visitors. Then one night in mid-April we heard a commotion on the porch. We went out to find an opossum crouched in a corner hissing and Fritz excitedly outside the railing trying to squeeze through the slats. We brought him in with a little struggle, and I reassured the opossum, who finally shuffled off. Fritz's dish was empty, but a little later I went outside and found the opossum sniffing hopefully around. I filled the pan with dog chow and heard it banging around almost immediately. Watching at the door, I saw it tip the pan, ravenously pick up a piece of food, quickly swallow it, and snatch another. Its fur looked mangy, and it was terribly hungry. It ate quite a bit before it slowly moved down the slope toward the grape arbor den. That was the last visit we had from an opossum that year, but they certainly had aroused our interest during the long winter months.

The following year an opossum emerged from the windy woods one cold March afternoon. It meandered past the old apple tree and disappeared into the grape tangle. Minutes later Steve reported that it was climbing up the compost heap enclosure. Hunger had driven it to forage in the daytime wherever its keen sense of smell led it. We went out to watch it firmly seated on top of the eggshells, carrot scrapings, and rotten squashes. Since its weak eyes could not warn it, it didn't see us until we were quite close. It fell on its side and spread its mouth into a wide grin, exposing all fifty of its teeth. Its neck was raw, red, and hairless, and there was a bald patch atop its head. We guessed that it had recently been mauled by a dog. A halo of late sunlight encircled the opossum as Steve painstakingly turned it to expose its best side, centered it on the heap, and snapped its picture. Then we left it to a peaceful feast. Even as we looked back, the grin relaxed and it slowly rose to its feet. A half hour later it clambered out and continued its solitary ramblings.

Late in the afternoon two days later Steve came back from the farm dump with the same opossum in his arms. It was playing dead again with its horrible, toothy grin. We wanted to keep it until Bruce came home so he could get some good photographs. Steve put it gently into Mark's wagon where the opossum laid in its death pose for a few more minutes. The puppies clambered around for a good look but did not try to hurt it. Since it was obviously still very hungry, I put some meat scraps and dog chow into the wagon next to it. I noticed its nose begin to twitch as it came out of its act, but it was still more frightened than hungry. As it tried to climb out of the wagon, the puppies came sniffing up, smelling the food, and it immediately began to hang motionless. After a few minutes it retreated back to the wagon and began shaking violently.

Then I could almost see its mood shifting from total fear to just a partial fright. Its naked nose twitched harder, and slowly it eased itself over to the food. Once it began eating it grew bolder, cleaned up the wagon, and climbed down to the ground. As I talked soothingly to it, I spread more food on the ground, forgetting that the puppies, too, were hungry. But to my surprise the three puppies and the solitary opossum ate companionably together. They were still eating when Bruce came home, and when he took his photos, the opossum posed like a veteran. Throughout our dinner we looked out the window and watched the opossum having its meal. At last it finished, gave a hopeful sniff, raised itself up on its four black legs, and carefully plodded away. Its need for food had tamed it more quickly than is usual for a wild animal.

Another common mammal, the woodchuck, causes quite a stir in Pennsylvania during early February. We have not actually seen a woodchuck on groundhog day, although one particularly mild winter Fritz killed one on February 25 as it emerged groggily from its long sleep. The day was sunny and warm, and there was a crusty layer of glistening snow covering the ground. I ambled along examining the abundant and varied animal tracks in the snow, but as I neared the far field I heard Fritz barking frantically. Running quickly to the clearing, I saw him on the sunny slope circling a dark-colored animal. Suddenly he trotted calmly over to me. There was no sign of his opponent. But I followed Fritz's tracks back to the slope and discovered the body of a small woodchuck. I was sorry to see its life ended so abruptly; its early awakening had caused its death.

Any woodchuck that ventures out on February 2 has a paralyzing cold to contend with in these parts. But it is hard to erase the centuries-old celebration of ground-hog day. The traditional festivities have a confusing history stretching back to pagan cultures thousands of years ago. Animals emerging from hibernation marked the festivals of spring, but the custom later became associated with the Christian rite of Candlemas on February 2. When the English brought the ancient custom to the New World, they mistook the American woodchuck for the Old World badger, or groundhog, and the tradition continued with a new animal in a new land.

The newspapers delight in following the predictions of local woodchuck watchers. Will he or won't he see his shadow? For one day in the year woodchucks become important to people. The rest of the time human beings turn their guns against them. It is said that their holes are dangerous to horses in farmers' fields and that they do great damage in gardens. There is a belief that the world would be a better place if all woodchucks were killed off, and many hunters attempt to do so. Back in Maine we had a woodchuck that I could see from my kitchen window. Its den was in plain sight of the road, and so was it much of the time. I enjoyed watching it as it nibbled the tender grass outside its burrow, and it certainly wasn't doing us any harm. It didn't take long, though, for the local woodchuck hunters to get wind of its activities. Cars began to slow down as they passed its burrow. Bruce was outside working one day when a car full of men stopped, terribly eager and helpful.

"Would you let us shoot that woodchuck up there?" they asked pointing over to the field.

"Why, no," Bruce answered. "It's not bothering us, and my wife enjoys watching it from her kitchen window."

There was a long silence and puzzled looks of disbelief. They drove off, their guns lowered. Bruce had spoiled their "fun" for that day.

I will admit that when I lose a tender lettuce crop to a woodchuck I am disturbed—all that grass to eat, and they prefer my lettuce! Once we fenced our garden, the cottontails were foiled, but not the woodchucks. They took measures. They dug holes under the fence, ripped down some pea vines, and cleaned out a second planting of lettuce. Bruce promptly filled in the holes. The next day the holes were bigger than ever. Then he filled the holes with rocks—big ones—and covered them with dirt. No woodchuck was going to outwit him. But of course it did—it just dug new holes. So Bruce pulled out some old snow fencing, laid it on the ground next to the garden fence, and tamped it down with dirt and rocks. The idea was that the woodchuck would have to tunnel under the snow fencing for several feet before it reached the garden fence. Surely that would discourage it. It didn't, although it did delay the woodchuck for several nights. But in the end the animal was victorious. So that summer we reluctantly shared the garden. Luckily it only snacked, and I had planted enough for all of us. A few tender peas and some lettuce leaves kept it content—it did not feel bound to eat everything as the bunnies had done.

During an unusually warm spell one November, I went out to hang up some clothes just as Bruce headed down to the barn. "Say, look at that woodchuck," he called up to me and the boys. A small woodchuck was foraging in the road drain next to the barnyard. It was amazingly unafraid of us as it moved off down the road, under the fence, and across the lawn. To our surprise it made no threatening noises or movements. Previous woodchucks we had come upon had rattled their formidable teeth like castanets. We walked slowly with it as it shuffled down the slope beside the guest house, heading for the corrals. At one point, when we cornered the woodchuck, the animal went from one person to the next, right up to our feet, but it never attempted to bite us.

The next day, coming back from my early morning walk, I encountered the woodchuck again beside the guest house fence. As I stopped to watch it, it circled slowly around a bush, making no attempt to run off. Once it stumbled slightly on the rough incline, but it still kept up the monotonous circling. I walked off as it continued circling, and I never saw it again. It was a small chuck, probably just born that spring and, with Fritz gone, perhaps it had never learned to fear humans. Or possibly it had been sick, although it certainly had not looked it. Later I learned that woodchucks suffer from brain worms, and I suppose that was the reason for the circling woodchuck. But I preferred to believe that it was merely affected with Indian summer fever.

About the time the guest house woodchuck emerges from hibernation each spring, we begin to hear the loud "clunk, clunk" noises of the awakening chipmunks in the woods. The mountain is filled with them. Before I knew they made such a peculiar sound, I would sit on the porch wondering what was making all the noise. Then I saw a chipmunk sitting on a fence post, its little body vibrating—the clunking sound was coming from it. Actually chipmunks are not true hibernators. They store their food for the winter in their burrows and occasionally wake up to eat. But they are certainly not as active as the squirrels, because only on very warm days in late winter are we likely to hear them.

In the summer the chipmunks haunt the back porch, searching for tidbits spilled from the dog's pan. One little fellow was particularly bold. As I stood silently on the steps, it moved past me toward the pan without seeming to notice me. I began making chipping noises, and I scattered sunflower seeds. A few seeds even struck it, but it seemed unable to see them. As it cast blindly around, sniffing, I saw that its right eye was closed. Apparently it found its food by smell. Finally it must have realized my alien presence, because it turned and stumbled away. I never saw that particular chipmunk again. It probably did not live long with such a handicap.

Chipmunks are beautiful creatures, though, even if they do use birdseed to fill their burrows for the winter. They stuff their cheek pouches, rush off to unload, and scurry back for more. This usually goes on throughout the mild days of November. But when a cold spell sets in, the chipmunks are gone for the winter. Unfortunately they are almost instantly replaced by their voracious cousins, the red squirrels, and I spend the rest of the season shooing them with the broom so the birds can have a fighting chance.

Red squirrels cannot be discouraged. They sit in the feeder eating as I rap at the window. I open the door—still they sit. Only when I grab the broom and lunge do they quickly zip up the drainpipe, peering down to see if I have retreated. As soon as I do, they are back. Every morning we battle, though usually I give up before they do. Only during the winter of the red-headed woodpecker did the other birds have an even chance at the feeder.

Besides bullying the birds, the red squirrels also manage to keep the larger gray squirrels away from the house. Despite their superior size, the gray squirrels are utterly cowed by their smaller cousins. Once I saw a gray squirrel creep along the stone wall near the guest house. Suddenly he sat up, his paws folded together across his chest—a sure sign of fright. Finally he moved stealthily on across the lawn and leaped up to perch nervously on the fence post. He kept peering all around, looking like a naughty child who had stolen a cookie. But for once the red squirrels were not nearby, and the gray squirrel sprinted behind the balm of Gilead tree and disappeared. Usually, whenever a gray squirrel ventures across our lawn, a red squirrel will come charging down a black walnut tree, scolding loudly, and chase the gray squirrel off into the woods. I have never seen a gray squirrel meet this challenge.

The mountaintop does not seem to attract some of the most common mammals of Pennsylvania. Perhaps the long climb deters animals just as it does humans. We have seen only one raccoon on the mountain, we have smelled a skunk just once, and only twice have we spotted porcupines. One evening we were driving up the road when we caught up to a galloping porcupine. It was really bounding along for a porcupine, but it refused to get off to the side. Steve was hopping with excitement. He wanted to see the front of the creature but he was a little afraid to approach it. Finally, though, Bruce let him out of the car, and Steve easily caught up with and passed the portly fellow. The porcupine spun around and gave all of us in the following bus a good look at it. Then it turned toward Steve and hurried on again. After several hundred yards it reached a ravine and trundled up out of sight as we watched.

One July evening Bobbin started barking loudly. Steve went tearing out to investigate because Bobbin almost never barked. A few minutes later he came racing back in—"Mom, Dad, there's a porcupine up in a tree." Of course, we all went out to look, with me poking along with barefeet and a kaftan on, the boys in pajamas, and Bruce as usual fully dressed and armed with his camera. The porcupine was high up on the branch of an old apple tree. From the ground it looked like a prickly ball in the gathering dusk, so Bruce started up the tree to get a closer look at the creature. As he neared the porcupine, Bruce kept calling down more precise descriptions—"Wow! The quills look like four-inch syringe needles" and "Look at that tail thrashing." Finally he reported that the porcupine's teeth were bared and clicking furiously as he moved in closer for photographs. We could see very little from our vantage point, but whenever the porcupine moved, we were afraid it would be onto Bruce with all those quills. After Bruce got his pictures, we left the porcupine alone in the tree.

Steve said, when we got back to the house, "You never know what you're going to see around here."

Chapter 8
Endless Summer Days

JUNE FLOUNCES GAILY in—warm, breezy, and clear. But usually the beautiful days are not nearly as plentiful as the humid, overcast, and rainy days. The garden soaks in all the moisture, holding it in reserve against the dry days of July and August. And most of the month the temperature is cool enough to produce bundles of lettuce and Swiss chard and set numerous pods on the pea vines. There is always at least one hot spell when we worry as the young lettuce wilts and the pea vines sag against the fence. Then the rains come, the thermometer drops, and cool weather returns.

Some years in early June the ridge is thick with laurel flowers—every bush glowing white or pale pink against the waxy green leaves. Other years I have to narrow my

appreciation down to the individual beauty of each
blossom, because only occasional bushes have more
than one or two flowers on them. At first I was hesi-
tant to clip even one flowering branch for my vases.
But I discovered during good years that cutting a few
branches from the thousands of bushes was hardly
noticeable on the ridge. And they stay fresh for over a
week, dropping the individual flowers a few at a time.
On a beautiful June day filled with chittering chipmunks and flitting butterflies, Laurel Ridge Trail is a
magical place to walk, hemmed in as it is by the towering bushes. Nothing else seems to matter as I walk
along, lost in the magnificence of a natural garden. Of
all the spectacles the mountain offers, the best is Laurel Ridge in bloom, a most flamboyant greeting to the
summer season.

With June comes summer, filled with flowers and
birds, mammals and insects. Many creatures have their
first families in June—the phoebes hatch out, spotted
juvenile robins hop all over the lawn, and every square
yard of the field holds some kind of mammal's nest—-
cottontails, woodchucks, meadow voles, or shrews.
Some females don't make nests, though. One day Steve
came in yelling to us that he had discovered a female
wolf spider on the lawn beneath the clothesline. We
went out to see this mother who carries first her eggs
and then her babies around with her. Her back was
covered with the little spiderlings, most of them sleeping, but a few crawled over her head or hung on her

legs. What a burden she carried as she moved along, and yet she didn't seem bothered by it.

I was not nearly so intrigued by another creature Steve brought inside one afternoon. Lovingly he caressed a dark brown, 3½-inch-long millipede as it crawled over his arm. He said hopefully, "Perhaps you can write about it." But I told Steve that, try as I might, it completely repelled me with its wriggling fringe of legs.

Every June we have a number of bug invasions which are rarely of any serious proportions. One year, though, we experienced the second most prolific of the seventeen-year locust broods, number fourteen to be exact. Only brood number ten produces more locusts. This brood was impressive enough, however, as the woods rang with the songs of the male cicadas whenever the thermometer was above sixty degrees. It was like a continual ringing in my ears, and after several hot days in a row, I found myself nervously dreading the monotonous sound. Then the boys began perversely collecting the hard, brown, rejected skins in pint jars and showing them to me with enthusiasm. One day Steve came in with a white one that had just left the nymphal shell stage.

Day after day the buzzing grew louder as more kept emerging from their shells, and we saw them everywhere. But even with them dried, filled out, and winged I really did not like their looks. They were too big—large orange eyes on a black head, long orange legs for tearing plant leaves apart, and inch-long translucent wings which were edged in gold and black. Those wings were particularly intimidating, whirring with such vigor that they always startled me. Close up the seventeen-year locusts look like the horror movies about monster insects gone wild. Throughout this profusion of locusts, I found we had two allies: both our puppy Bobbin and all the brown thrashers enjoyed crunching them up.

Despite my aversion for the locusts, I have actually begun to appreciate certain insects with the help of Steve and his fascinating knowledge of them. Whenever I find an odd bug, in particular one of the many beautiful beetles, I collect it live for him. One early morning, as Mark and I opened the gate to the guest house lawn, Mark spotted an eyed elater click beetle crawling slowly along the top board. It had a salt-and-pepper-colored back, but most startling of all were the two large eye-like spots on its pronotum. Knowing Steve would appreciate such a specimen, I sent Mark up to the house for a collecting jar. Steve came tumbling down after him, very excited about such an unusual discovery. He put it in a jar and watched it for a while. Then he released it. His appreciation of insects prevented him from killing specimens for a permanent collection. He feels honorbound to let such creatures live. Even with some of the insects that invade the house—the wasps and bees in particular—he carefully picks each one up and takes it outdoors.

Some of the invaders, like the houseflies, I ruthlessly

exterminate. Especially in the month of June, the flies swarm in masses about the kitchen door, and "seven-at-one-blow" is no exaggeration once I sharpen my fly-swatting skills. Coupled with the flies, the kitchen is suddenly overrun with large black ants. I used to panic and buy ant traps, but then I learned to put away in tins all the brown sugar, dried fruits, honey, and molasses. After two weeks the ants decide that my cupboards are unsweetened, and they disappear for another year. One June, though, I really organized myself and put away all the sweets before the ants were expected. I also planted peppermint around the side of the house. That year I didn't see one ant in the kitchen, and yet they marched back and forth along my clothesline as they always had. Later I read in an old herbal book that mint is an excellent ant repellant.

As for the flies, they are always with us. Luckily for us, so are the flycatchers. One day I watched a great crested flycatcher fly down to the road, spread its wings in the dust, and touch the dirt with its belly. Then it thoroughly examined some dried grass flung on the road by the lawnmowers. Finally it flew off, and I was not certain whether it had been searching for food, taking a dust bath in the sun, or a little of both.

My porch watching time was dominated one June by another flycatcher—a wood pewee. No matter when I sat on the porch, the pewee always perched on the same dead locust branch down close to the lawn. It would take a brief flutter off the branch, launch out in a quick, short flight, and return to the branch for a few moments. This performance would be repeated over and over for hours. Presumably the air around the locust branch was filled with flying insects which kept the pewee well fed. I assumed it was a male because he never fed anyone but himself, and I never heard him make a sound either. He was probably a bachelor.

None of the red-eyed vireos in our woods want to be bachelors—they fill the June air with their courting songs. Each year it seems I become aware of new bird songs, and once I identify them, I hear them everywhere. So it was the first June I heard the red-eyed vireos. Every time I sat on the porch I listened to the unending, robinlike songs of the birds I couldn't see among the feathery locust leaves. Finally, after diligent watching, I spotted the rather plainly garbed songster, green in the midst of green leaves, hopping erratically around, snatching insects, and singing as he worked. Because he goes on all day with his song, he has been nicknamed the preacher in memory of all the ministers who delivered lengthy sermons in the old days. During June these woodland dwellers are everywhere, singing their unending patient songs.

One bright June morning a bird we hadn't seen since our Maine days landed awkwardly out in the field. Steve came yelling, "A gull, a gull, out by the barn." By the time I ran out in stocking feet on the dew-wet grass, the gull was soaring gracefully over the field—an incongruous but beautiful sight on a mountain farm, and I watched its flashing white wings as it flew up across the ridge.

By June most of the migrants have arrived, but usually there are a couple of latecomers. When the yellow warblers return, they make themselves seen and heard for several days, filling lilac bushes and apple trees with spots of flitting golden color. About the time they appear we begin hearing soft "coos" as well. If we are lucky, we will see the secretive bird hidden among the walnut leaves very high up in the tree. It has a white breast and brown back, but the distinguishing mark is the down-curving beak. If it is yellow, it is a yellow-billed cuckoo; if it is black, it is a black-billed cuckoo. We have both around here, and we count ourselves privileged whenever we get a long look at either, because they are more often heard than seen. According to Bent, their favorite food is caterpillars, the hairier the better, and they are liable to flock into any area that has a caterpillar infestation.

June is the month when we are likely to see lost baby birds. One evening we were charmed by an exquisite nestling perched confidently in the bridal wreath bush. Its behavior seemed extraordinary, because it sat quite calmly, looking us all over with nary a peep. Furthermore, there were no harried parents screeching around. It was beautiful, too, with a bright yellow belly, gray wings and head, and white wing bars. "Must be a flycatcher," I figured. It sat still for half an hour while Bruce took pictures. Then it began to chirp a lovely little song. "Can't be a flycatcher,"

I said. "That song is too pretty." At that moment a pair of Baltimore orioles appeared overhead, calling loudly. Our little foundling was a young oriole. We left it immediately to its parents' care.

On another occasion, as I sat on the porch, a pair of Baltimore orioles suddenly erupted into a fury, chasing, diving, and scolding a scampering red squirrel.

The Baltimore Oriole nestling poses for the camera.

They chased it up and down the walnut trees right next to the porch, unconcerned by my nearness. I assumed they were defending their eggs or nestlings from red squirrel predation, but I could not spot the nest in the tree. I never find oriole nests until after the leaves fall, so well do they hide them. But obviously the red squirrel had discovered one. To my surprise a catbird joined in the scolding, and off and on throughout the afternoon the orioles and catbird harassed the squirrel.

The catbirds are everywhere in June, giving their catlike calls, imitating other birds, and sometimes even mimicking peculiar noises. The first summer Bruce's parents spent in the guest house, a catbird learned to imitate the sound of a police whistle being blown. My mother-in-law had been using a whistle to call her husband at mealtimes, and one of the catbirds learned to reproduce it at odd times of the day. Frequently we wondered why the lunch whistle was being blown at 10 A.M. or the dinner whistle at 3 P.M., only to discover that we had been fooled by the catbird's uncanny imitation.

In addition to all the bird activity, the wildflower pageant moves from the woods to the fields and waste places in June. Dame's rocket grows thickly in pale purple masses, and I fill the house with them. They have a sweet scent and make magnificent long-lasting bouquets. Often mistaken for phlox, the flowers have only four petals rather than the five petals of true phlox. But by any name they are beautiful flowers, and I mix them with sprays of mock orange for striking displays.

I have a special dark brown vase made by American Indians which I call my daisy vase because it is the ideal size and color to display the field daisies of early summer that Mark faithfully picks for me. Daisy season always lasts long into July, and when it is ended the black-eyed Susans take their place in the Indian vase.

June also means roses—wild roses of pink and red

hues in the field and grape arbor, cultivated roses at the side of the house, and three enormous tea rose bushes that grow beside some cellar holes near the end of our road. Whenever I go down our mountain road to town I take my pruning shears and gather a bundle of the prickly stemmed flowers for my vases. One bush is white, another is pink, and the third is deep red, all domestic plants gone wild in a beautiful way. I never pick the true wild roses because they drop their petals almost immediately. I am content to appreciate the clumps of fragrant beauty in their natural setting.

Every year we manage to add a few more wildflowers to our list. One June, as Bruce was driving slowly down the road, he noticed a red flower over by the stream. He and Steve jumped out to look and were delighted to discover the red form of the Canada lily. Only one other plant was growing there, and unfortunately it had been broken off, so this one flower held the hope of future generations beside the stream. Almost reverently, Bruce took a photo, and we hoped that somehow that one plant would grow to be many in the years to come.

So each year we look forward to another June, because it begins the summer with the good and the bad—bugs and storms, fair weather and foul, heat, humidity, and dampness. But June also is filled with bird songs and box turtles, flowers and fresh lettuce, barefeet and school's out. The grass still grows too fast and the garden too slowly, but in June we can see the beginning of a hoped-for harvest, and that is the month's greatest promise.

July is a profligate month. Hundreds of deep orange day lilies spill down the banks below the house and cluster about the bases of the locust trees. They carpet the aisles between the grape trellises, making a magnificent green and orange display on the slope. Before they open I gather many of the flower buds, which I boil with salt, pepper, and butter. Sometimes for variety I sauté them in butter and flavor them with soy sauce. They make an excellent free vegetable that we can enjoy before the garden really begins to produce. I pick sparingly, careful to leave enough buds for blooming, and once they begin to open I stop picking altogether. I almost feel guilty about eating all those buds, having denied the blossoms their one short day of glory.

I do wish, though, I could deny the field bindweed the right to flourish and bloom. Overnight this choking vine springs up and wraps itself around corn plants, squash stems, and tomato seedlings—in fact, around every vegetable that tries to grow in the garden. Evening after evening I untwist it from around the delicate asparagus stalks and watch in despair as it takes over the pea fence. Finally the white and pale orchid blossoms of the bindweed, which look very much like morning glories, appear all over the garden, and again I am defeated by this persistent plant. I only wish the plant biologists could harness the secret of their rapid growth and use it to benefit the struggling vegetables.

However, I derive only joy from the fragrant purple blossoms of milkweed that grow along the driveway. Whenever we go outside, we wander over to see what insects have been attracted to their sweet scent. Bright orange and black monarch butterflies cling to the blossoms, extracting the nectar with their proboscises and gently pumping their wings as they work. Other blossoms are attractive to the magnificent yellow and black tiger swallowtails. Numerous brightly colored beetles explore the flowers, and the air is filled with the low droning buzz of dozens of honeybees swarming among the seductive blossoms.

One warm sunny day in mid-July I found myself standing with Steve in the midst of the milkweed patch. He was eager to give me a guided tour and introduce me to the countless shapes of fluttering life that swirled about me. Many of the straight stalks which supported the drooping flower clusters were taller than I. Each individual floret in the blossom was five-petaled and a pale, dusty, pink color, but its attractiveness to insects was probably due to its cloying-sweet odor.

As I stood surrounded by towering plants and buzzing insects, the fluttering butterflies at first all looked similar—orange and black colored mostly—and all were erratic flyers. But patiently Steve sorted them out for me. A great spangled fritillary flew in front of me, a medium-sized orange butterfly with varied black markings. "And I have found five different species of skippers in the milkweed patch," Steve reported. "Notice they are fast flyers with skipping motions." Indeed, they seemed small and nervous in comparison with the large, graceful, tiger swallowtails and monarchs. He quickly pointed out to me three of the five species—large orange ones called tawny skippers, dark brown ones with white markings on the underside, and orange and brown ones with silver spots on the underwings. After all this I was impressed with the amazing variation in one family of butterflies.

Occasionally a new butterfly arrived on the colorful scene. What looked like a white moth fluttering along became a spring azure when it landed on a flower. "But I thought spring azures were blue," I protested when Steve identified it. He explained that in early spring they are usually a deep blue, but the ones hatched later in the summer are lighter in color—in fact they are frequently more white than blue.

We found one hair-streak butterfly—often called the banded hair-streak, Steve said—a small bluish-gray butterfly with a minute orange-blue marking at the base of each wing. Then he shouted, "A yellow-collared scape moth!" and pointed excitedly.

"Looks more like a flying beetle," I commented. Certainly it was the least moth-looking of creatures with its dark-colored body and narrow wings. Steve explained that it was a day-flying species entirely.

Once we put a name to all the butterflies, we settled down to examining the beetles as they crawled all over the flowers and stiff leaves of the milkweed.

They, too, had predominantly orange and black color-ation. The long-horned beetles were the most notice-able, especially the pair that mated the whole time we were in the patch. They were a deep reddish-orange with seventeen black spots on their bodies. The sol-dier beetles, too, were mating and were a paler orange with only three black markings. The net-wing beetle with its black and orange wings flew by. Steve eagerly pointed out its fringed antenna, a refinement I never would have noticed.

Then he called, "Here is a beetle I haven't been able to identify, but isn't it a beauty?" And so it was. Its rounded body was colored and shaped like a lady bug, only larger. The back was bright orange with four spots at the edges and an inkblot marking in the middle. The head was a beautiful iridescent blue-green color. Whenever I really look closely at insects, I am amazed at the beauty of their diverse forms. Perhaps they, more than any other living thing, symbolize the miracle of earth life. Later Steve struggled to name the unknown. "Tortoise beetle?" he asked uncertainly, but I simply did not care. Our inability to name the insect added to its mystery and did not subtract from its beauty.

Still there were more wonders to admire—the long, thin, graceful waist of the thread-waisted wasp; the tiny flower bugs with minute etchings on their backs; the earwigs, long and narrow with pincers on their tails; the bee-like syrphid flies; the energetic honey-bees themselves; and, finally, a familiar sight, a daddy longlegs crawling over the leaves. But this daddy long-legs was different from the brown ones I often meet surrounding the black raspberries. It had an iridescent orange edging that enclosed a black back and legs that were light brown with a narrow band of black. It was a striking creature.

"And there are many other insects you can see here," Steve added as I left the hot sun, but I had been awed and impressed enough for one day. I needed time to absorb the wonders I had observed.

During July the flowers of the fields are endless, but in the woods only a few white blossoms stand out amidst all the cool green leaves. Indian pipes, those strange translucent flowers, glow ghostly white on the forest floor. With no real stems and leaves, they derive their nourishment from the green plants around them. Indian pipes are also called ice-plant, ghost-flower, and corpse-plant, all referring to their deathly pallor. In honor of their uniqueness we respectfully step around them where they grow in the middle of the trail.

Much harder to see are the tiny, white, bell-like flowers that nod secretly beneath the paired waxy green leaves of the wintergreen. Carefully I pick several fresh wintergreen leaves to make some tea, because when they are finely minced, steeped in boiled water, and spiced with a little honey, they make a delicate drink. Later, when those bell-flowers are replaced by red berries, they will provide a tasty snack as I hike along in midwinter.

The edges of the road are lovely with the clusters of white snakeroot, and now and then we see the stately white candles of black cohosh or bugbane. The name is rather disappointing for such a spectacular flower. Sometimes I wish I didn't have a passionate desire to identify all that I see. It is nicer, occasionally, to just admire the beauty and uniqueness of each wildflower.

But my penchant is vindicated whenever I see Queen Anne's lace, for how else could the beauty of that flower be described? The name certainly gives it the dignity it deserves. The naturalist Hal Borland in his book *Hill Country Harvest* tells how he counted the individual florets in a head of Queen Anne's lace. To his astonishment he found 2,450 florets in just one flower, which meant that one head could produce at least 2,000 seeds. All that delicate laciness is practical as well as beautiful and, as usual, nature has been generous in its attempt to ensure the continuance of the species.

Each July we make new wildflower discoveries. The year Bruce finally mowed the first field he found one small bush of brilliant butterfly weed hidden up in the far corner. Carefully he cut around it, leaving this beautiful deep orange member of the milkweed family to feed all the butterflies around. When he reported his find to us, we all went up to see and exclaim. Of course, Bruce had to take a photo of the flowers attracting butterflies.

Growing at the edges of the grape arbor are the bouncing Bets or soapworts. Their pale pinkish-white color makes a subdued background for the just-opened calendulas in my vases. The name soapwort describes its stolid feature—the bruised leaves make a soaplike lather when swished about in water. As for its other names—hedge pink, bruisewort, old maid's pink, and Fuller's herb—each suggests other characteristics.

My wildflower observation is sandwiched between harvesting the garden abundance and picking the wild berries, both of which occupy most of July. First come the tender sweet peas, with mountains of pods to shell in order to have a quart for dinner and a quart or two for the freezer. Luckily nothing tastes quite so marvelous as just-picked, shelled, and lightly simmered fresh peas. The frozen peas in the market do not resemble the ambrosial taste of garden peas, and certainly canned peas are a desecration. Growing, picking, and shelling fresh peas is no job for the efficient, time-saving, modern cook. First of all, it takes a lot of room to grow a reasonable amount, even if you do stick to the marvelously prolific Lincoln peas. Second, you should erect a very sturdy, four-foot high, chicken wire fence unless you plan to grow the nonclimbing Little Marvel variety. Third, when they finally fill out their pods, a process that seems to take forever, several hours a day should be devoted to picking, shelling, and freezing them. Finally, when the harvest is ended, you find that really there are less than ten quarts in the freezer and slightly over that served at the dinner table. But if you are a real pea devotee, as I am, you turn about and plant the fall crop.

The other thing you do, back in mid-April when you plant shell peas, is put in a much smaller amount of edible-podded or snow peas. This action is liable to drive you mad, because once they are ready to pick, there is no stopping their growth. In one day they go from edible to nonedible size, and no matter how I try, I generally miss about one quarter of the crop. So during the first several weeks of July, we alternate each evening between peas and snow peas, with an occasional helping of Swiss chard for variety.

About the time I call it quits with the peas, the green and wax bush beans have blossomed and begun to sport tiny beans. In less than a day, it seems, the bushes are loaded, and I spend long hours in the hot sun crawling down the rows, picking four or five quarts daily. But after pea shelling, bean preparation seems quick and easy—all I have to do is snap off each end and cut them in half. However, near the end of the month, just as I become terribly tired of the crawling routine, the beans finally slow down. Then, one bright day, I look up to see the pole beans absolutely covered with three-inch long beans. They make the bush beans seem puny by comparison! The Kentucky wonder pole beans always live up to their name, despite the Japanese beetles that crawl on their leaves. In a very short time I have nearly forty quarts of beans of all kinds in the freezer.

There are other vegetables that make their debut in July—broccoli, kale and, most notably, patty pan and zucchini squash. We do not like frozen summer squash very much, although when I'm forced to I freeze up some zucchini for winter stews. But mostly we eat it fresh, and I become a walking encyclopedia of zucchini recipes. Luckily, we all like both of these summer squashes, and there is no protest as I alternate one squash with the other each evening.

As if all the vegetables were not enough to keep me busy, the first of the wild berries, the luscious black raspberries, ripen in early July. They always choose the hottest days of the year to bear, and despite trying to pick only during the cool morning and evening hours, I usually end up broiled. But once the berries are picked, I put them into the freezer without any work at all, not even washing.

Once the berries are ready, I make a vow: all fruit, desserts, vegetables, and salads come free for my labor. It means that little housework is done while all my efforts are devoted to preserving and meal preparation. Of course, despite the work there are added benefits— sunshine, good health, and most of the day outdoors. Our meals are all feasts such as homemade ice cream covered with fresh black raspberries, fancy vegetable recipes, wonderful salads with six kinds of lettuce, and soups that use the surplus of vegetables. Summer is a gourmet's delight.

Once in a while, though, I rebel. I awake to a positively beautiful misty sunrise, and I struggle with myself. Should I hoe the garden or indulge in a walk? I justify the walk by carrying along a berry pail, just in case the blueberries are ready. I don't really think they are, but it makes a good excuse for walking in the cool woods. Indian pipes are emerging all along the trail. I see a wood thrush poised quietly on a tree branch, and I pause to watch it. But when I move on, it flies off. Then, along the side of the trail, the leaf mold is suddenly moving and humping like a live creature. I squat and watch as a small, black, furry animal surfaces for a second, then burrows down through the mold again. It must be a short-tail shrew, the largest of the shrew family, because it does not have the flipperlike front paws of a mole.

As I continue on, Laurel Ridge Trail is green and quiet, but emerging into the light of the powerline right-of-way, I don't even notice the view. Blueberries everywhere, of goodly size, are clinging ripely to innumerable small bushes. I simply can't believe the bounty—never have I seen so many. I kneel and begin picking, an almost religious rite in the early morning sunshine. A cock crows in the valley below, and I look down into the swirling mists. Only here on my exalted mountaintop does the sun shine brightly in a blue sky. They in the valley have wakened to shrouds of clinging fog, while I rejoice in the clarity of the mountain morning. I keep wanting to gather the warmth to me as a memory for next winter when I have to huddle against the cold. The only way, though, I can really preserve a summer memory is by freezing the berries and serving them on a cold winter's day.

The time goes quickly when I pick, and I am interrupted frequently by strange insects that crawl over the
bushes. At one point I see a small white walkingstick
looking freshly new as he delicately plods along. A little
later I notice a familiar leaf-hopper, only this one is reddish-brown rather than the plain brown species I usually
find on the black raspberry bushes. A powerline pole is a
drumming place for the pileated woodpecker or a calling
post for a young broad-winged hawk. Butterflies dance
and sway over the patch. It is so hard to tear myself away
from such beauty and abundance. But the pail is full, so
I go proudly home to bake a pie and a batch of blueberry
muffins and to rouse the boys with the announcement,
"Blueberries are ripening on the powerline."

Occasionally I do rest on the front porch and enjoy
the swaying of the locust tree branches and the frequent
arguments of the red squirrels. One July we had a particularly grand relationship with the birds. I had a feeling that if I had left the doors open, they would have
nested in the house. The window above the porch door
is recessed, but the recession had an old screen tacked
over it. However, a cheerful little pair of house wrens,
perhaps the same couple that had raised an earlier brood
on the veranda roof, discovered a hole in the screening.
It was such a nice little niche in which to build a nest.
And so they did. For days they stuffed sticks into a corner, interrupting themselves to carol on a locust limb
nearby. When Mamma began brooding, Papa serenaded, but when the eggs hatched, they both worked

frantically to feed their young. The babies seemed every bit as high-strung and energetic as their parents. As they grew older, the sound became more cacophonous. My quiet porch refuge had become a noisy nursery. Just as I began to accept the noise, I noticed a sudden peace. Another family had launched itself into the world while I had been busy in the kitchen.

Usually July is a hot dry month, and by the third week or so, we are looking for rain to keep the garden growing. When it comes, with intermittent storms, swirling clouds, and fog, I still have to go out in my rubber boots and slicker to do the chores. One foggy, rainy morning I counted thirty-four barn swallows lined up on the electric lines outside the barn, con-stantly reshuffling their positions, swooping through the air in and out of the mist, twittering, and calling to one another. What were they doing here? I had never seen so many on the mountain before, and I decided that the weather had somehow turned them around from wherever they were headed. As I stood admiring their grace, I was glad I had had a reason that brought me outside.

More common than a steady rainstorm, though, are those days when the July heat dissolves into a thunder-storm. One summer the month concluded with real fire-works. The day dawned fair and slightly humid, but as the morning progressed, it grew hotter and more breath-less. In the afternoon the faint breeze died away, and the leaves hung motionless and still on the trees. When I went out to take the clothes down, I noticed a few dark clouds gathering in the west. Panting in hot agitation, our dog Fritz edged over next to me and begged to go inside. The boys became quarrelsome and restless.

Then we heard the first distant rumbles of thunder. Fritz slinked whining to the door, and the boys dashed about gathering in their toys. I raced to the garden in bare feet to pick the vegetables for the evening meal. Then I stood on the back porch, waiting and listening. I heard a towhee calling in the grape arbor. An indigo bunting landed in the small cherry tree and gave several loud warning cries. Suddenly he was off and away in a great rush, just as the tops of the largest trees began to shake with invisible winds. "Listen, I can hear the rain coming," Steve cried. A wall of water rushed toward the house, and in an instant the ground, steps, and one racing cat were drenched.

At first the only sound was the pouring rain, which came as a needed blessing, perking up the drooping vegetables and the newly transplanted nasturtium plants. The boys frolicked in the rain, screaming their joy and dodging under cardboard shelters when an especially heavy deluge hit them. Clad only in shorts, their bare feet skimmed over the soaked lawn as they felt the delicious coolness of a summer rain. Hair soaked and shorts dripping, they were a picture of joyous free boyhood. No worry about colds or chills— this rain was merely cooling off the hot humid day we had just endured.

But the rain was only a prelude to more spectacular events. Fritz cowered in the cellar, waiting fearfully for the lightning and thunder, and the drenched cat retreated to the stone springhouse. The sky darkened until it cast a yellowish black glow over everything. The boys were subdued by the eerie color, and they came, awestruck, to stand on the porch and watch. The rain almost paused as we stood waiting. "Why is it so dark?" Mark asked, wonderingly. "It isn't night time yet."

But his question was answered by a flash of lightning and a deafening clap of thunder from a nearby ridge. Lightning stabbed down again and again, and I instinctively cringed from the sight. The boys watched with excitement as the lightning repeatedly struck the mountaintop. I was glad that the ridges on each side protected us from the full fury of the storm. Sometimes the strikes were so close that the roar of thunder followed the lightning with barely a pause. But gradually the grand pageant boomed and flickered its way down along Sapsucker Ridge, leaving only torrential rains and gusting winds in its wake.

Soon the sky lightened and the rain pattered more softly and then stopped. A single bird called, then another. The last rays of the setting sun brightened the sky as the wood thrushes began their evening serenades in the dripping woods. And Fritz came bursting out of the cellar, eager to tackle his evening meal. The thunderstorm was over and so was another July on the mountain.

August is the ripening month. All at once the garden is producing more food than any reasonable family can consume, and I hurry to preserve the bounty. Most of my time is spent picking, freezing, and canning. Tomatoes ripen rapidly on the vine, zucchini squashes have long passed the bounds of belief, pole beans grow faster than I can pick, and we eat about twenty ears of corn every evening.

The first year we grew potatoes though, the plants had been disappointing and had been attacked by everything imaginable. I had dusted them with lime repeatedly and had finally been forced to use rotenone. Still they had struggled along and had browned before they had blossomed, or so I thought. Remembering the vision of blossoming potato fields in Maine, I kept watching. Nothing! We mulched with hay, we searched for potato bugs, and we discussed the problem with everyone. The soil was too sweet, but we had hoped the hay would change that. Nevertheless, in mid-August the plants all upped and died.

"Let's dig for potatoes," Steve proposed enthusiastically.

"But the plants never blossomed," I protested.

"You never know," he answered as he began using his hands, mole-like, to dig down. A few seconds excavation and he pulled up a fair-sized potato. "You see," he crowed. "Come on, guys," he called to his brothers, "let's dig potatoes." I had never seen them so energetic about harvesting a crop. The other vegetables and fruits that grew above ground had never interested them very much. But digging for potatoes evidently seemed like digging for buried treasure. They labored for a couple hours, calling me whenever they unearthed a particularly large specimen, and finally we were able to weigh in thirty pounds of potatoes. It was not a large amount, but it was more than I had expected. Had they blossomed someday when I hadn't noticed?

I am used to flowers blooming spectacularly and with no nonsense, making an overwhelming show of themselves, especially in August. Large and small marigolds glow brown, yellow, and orange throughout the garden where I have planted them as bug repellants. They also flourish in unfenced flower beds because even the rabbits dislike their taste. They are easy, prolific, beautiful, and useful—I delight in growing them.

But above even the French marigolds in my estimation are the calendulas, or pot marigolds. Unlike their relations, a single frost does not kill them, and they have the longest growing season of any flower I know. The name calendula is Latin meaning "of the Kalends" or "the first of every month," because they can be found in bloom almost every month of the year. In Europe this may be so, but here in Pennsylvania the calendula season stretches from July until November, although they reach their height in August. Each year in early May I plant the black, crescent moon-shaped seeds in two rows. Thirty seeds or so of calendulas is all I need, because every seed germinates. The only care

I give them is keeping the bed weeded until the first flowers appear and, after that, snipping off all the dead blooms. Despite the solid lines of black aphids along their stems, they grow in a profusion of yellow and orange splendor at the side of our farmhouse. Until November, when the last bright blossoms are finally gone, I always keep an old brown wine bottle on a windowsill with five fresh calendulas in it.

The gladioluses I grow are just as easy, although their growing season only stretches from mid-July until late August. But during that time I feel as rich as Croesus when I fill my vases with their dramatic blossoms. So far I have only bought the cheap assortments of unnamed bulbs offered by various seed catalogs, but I have not been disappointed. Those simple collections have yielded some spectacular blossoms, and each year my bulb collection increases. In May I dig holes about four inches deep with my bulb planter, put the bulbs in, and cover them with dirt. That's it—in a few weeks the green spears appear, and from then on it is merely a matter of waiting and a little weeding. After the first frost, when all the flowers are spent, I dig up the bulbs, which have usually doubled in number, and dry them for the winter. What could be easier or more rewarding? Perhaps I shouldn't give the secret away, but growing gladioluses is a cheap and easy way to get a real thrill, if you happen to like showy flowers.

Even the wildflowers grow tall and lush. The heavy purple heads of joe-pye weeds tower seven feet above the unshorn grasses in the meadows. I love to cut the huge flowers and place them in large, narrow-necked bottles on the window sills. I wonder if Joe Pye, an Indian medicine man, would have approved of my use of his namesake flower, for he earned his fame in rural New England by curing typhus fever and other diseases with concoctions made from that weed.

Mingling with the joe-pye weeds throughout the meadows are spectacular splashes of rich yellow gold-enrod. I walk to the compost heap along a narrow path edged with them. Bees hover in clouds around each blossom, and I am careful not to jar the flowers. Monarch butterflies flutter around me as I walk up the path, and hundreds of tiny green aphids cling to the stems of the goldenrod. Yellow and black goldfinches flit about among the blossoms, filling the air with their tinkling songs. The abundance of life along this path makes each trip to the compost heap a memorable experience.

I have to compete with the wildlife for the rich harvest of elderberries which grow in masses behind the barn. We snap off the clusters and put them in a pot to simmer. The strange wild odor of cooking elderberries fills the kitchen. I strain the juice through cheesecloth and take time to admire the clear purplish-red color of the extracted liquid. I put some of the juice in the freezer, carefully labeled, and later I combine it with grape juice for a gourmet jelly. But in some years friends give us crabapples which I simmer, strain, and add to the elderberry juice, making the best jelly of all.

Wild black cherries are abundant, too, and Bruce perches precariously on a ladder trying to pick the trees clean. Fall webworms engulf some of the choicest branches, but still he fills a pail with the cherries. Again I extract the juice and combine it with wild apple juice for more batches of jelly.

August, with its beautiful flowers and bountiful harvests, has one drawback to my way of thinking: we almost always have at least one devastating heat wave and a good many days of high humidity. Nothing will dry, the books begin to mold, everything I touch is sticky, and the whole place seems dirty, even though it isn't. I react negatively to the hot humid weather, and I mutter over and over, "I could never live in the tropics." One year we had a particularly long heat wave. At the very height of it I awoke one day in the half-light of early dawn with just a sheet over me. No cooling breeze had come during the night, and it was 76 degrees. My body protested what my mind registered—this day would be hotter than all the rest. Yet there was work to be done. Pulling on my old gym shorts and tank top, I went down to prepare breakfast. Instead of hot cereal, which we eat most mornings, I poured out large bowls of cold granola. Then I packed a hot lunch for Bruce, who works and eats in air-conditioned comfort. Ah, how I envied him on such a day.

The air was heavy and still as the sun rose hotly in a metallic blue sky. No haze clouds shielded us from the sun's rays, which beat down on my head as I waved goodbye to Bruce. Before I retreated into the house, I noticed fluttering movements around a walnut tree. I walked over and discovered a horde of monarch butterflies flying about the upper branches in ecstatic mating flights. Heat is a welcome stimulant to insects—the more there is, the better they feel.

The tiny black gnats were active also, swirling about my face as I tried to hang up the clothes, and for once I was glad to be done with the job and back in the house. The shades were all pulled down against the sun's rays, and the darkness gave us an illusion of coolness. Not the reality, though, for as I struggled through the housework, my forehead grew wet, my face red, and my breathing labored.

The boys all lagged around the house, with no energy even for bickering. Finally they settled on the porch rockers in glassy-eyed comfort, lulled by the presence of a large box of comic books. Beyond that their minds ceased to function. The cats lay sprawled in varying positions near the boys and only squeaked occasionally for a little cold milk.

I could not rest yet, and I welcomed the breeze that blew through the kitchen. Even a hot wind was better than no air movement at all. I baked cookies, prepared cool salads, and handed out innumerable glasses of water and lemonade. In self-pity I brewed a pot of tea and sent David down to the back of the springhouse to pluck some mint leaves for flavoring. Certainly I could not labor down and up the slope in the pressing heat. With one eye on the clock, I drank my tea sloshing with ice and methodically prepared lunch. Immediately after the boys ate, I washed the dishes, mixed the gelatin for supper, read a story to Mark, and tucked him in for a nap.

Then I was free! I snatched a folding porch chair, a book, and my lunch and hurried down into the basement. In no time at all I was comfortably cool—I even thought of perking a cup of hot coffee for myself. The afternoon passed quickly as I read and wrote in comfort. I stretched out the time in my underground sanctuary by ironing and by cleaning the basement. But inevitably I had to go up again. Reluctantly I ascended the stairs and caught my breath as I opened the door. Surely I could not endure such heat. My thinking, which had been lucid in the basement, was instantly dulled; my body, which had felt energetic, grew lethargic, and I moved in a haze of heat and humidity, preparing supper and waiting for sunset.

At last the interminable day was over. The blaring light was gone, and the night settled darkly around me. A slight breeze stirred. Every time it began I hoped it was bringing cooler weather. Katydids screeched frenetically in the heated darkness and fireflies flashed their mating signals, but I sat dulled and defeated by the heat. When would it be over? I was too tired to care, and I drifted off to a restless sleep. Several times I awoke to rushing winds, but they still brought warm humid air. I knew that I would have still another day to suffer in the heat wave.

Eventually the heat wave faded into just an uncomfortable memory. Sometime in late August the nights suddenly grow chill and the days clear and crisp. The birds of winter come back from wherever it is they raise their families. In spring, when all the southern migrants appear, the winter bird population disappears, leaving center stage to flickers, wrens, indigo buntings, and Baltimore orioles. It is always their quarrels, their families, their nests, and their fledglings that we see. So when the winter birds return, I realize that summer is almost gone. First the chickadees appear and then the cardinals, closely followed by the titmice and the incredibly noisy nuthatches. The flickers are flocking, and the downy and pileated woodpeckers busily investigate the trees. As I harvest the corn, I pause, listening to the nuthatches, and realize that the warmth and light are waning.

Another sound in mid-August also tolls a warning. "Six weeks until frost," call the katydids as they fill the warm summer nights with their cacophonous pleas for mates. When each katydid finds a mate the noise is diminished by one, but for many weeks there is no real discernible difference in the hubbub.

While the katydids are a pleasant addition to late summer, the unsightly webs of the fall webworms are not. They hang prominently at the ends of branches, filled with squirming caterpillars, dead, chewed leaves, and droppings. They particularly like our black walnut trees and the wild black cherry trees that grow in the woods. When traveling to the city in August, I look at our mountainside clothed in white webs and shudder at the stupendous numbers of larvae that are feeding on the trees. After six weeks the larvae fall to the ground and bury in the soil to pupate, but the webs remain hanging in the trees, only gradually falling to the ground during heavy windstorms. Even in winter, while walking through the woods, I am liable to be bombarded by a falling nest. But despite their great numbers, they rarely defoliate a tree completely, although once they actually did us a favor and killed a small walnut sapling that was coming up in the grape tangle. However, it is the suburban visitors that they most disturb. Like the dandelions in the lawn or the autumn leaves that we never rake, the fall webworm is a deadly enemy and should be eradicated. "Better burn them out," they advise solemnly. Despairingly I wave my arms at the thousands of webs in trees much higher than any pole can reach. I do get tired of picking the caterpillars off my neck whenever I sit out on the porch, but we continue to live with them just as we live with dandelions and autumn leaves.

Eventually, though, all the caterpillars are safely pupating in the ground, and as we look around we notice that they and all the other insect pests have not totally vanquished us. The corn has grown despite an occasional worm, the tomatoes are abundant despite the slugs, and the squash has survived the squash bugs. Even the apples on the old apple tree have yielded enough juice to make some jelly.

The ripening apples, though, attract other harvesters besides ourselves. One morning in August I was abruptly awakened in the gray dawn by the snorting and stamping of a feisty young buck who considered the apple tree his personal domain. Sleepily I peered out through the mist, but I saw no creature. He went on and on with his thrashing until I was thoroughly awake and resigned to a very early Saturday morning breakfast. No one else had heard the noise, and I ate alone in the gray peace—after the buck had ended his protest.

As August ends the dawn is later, a reminder that summer is slipping away. The balm of Gilead trees in the yard rush the season. Their fading leaves rattle in the wind and litter the yard, giving a dried-leaf odor to the outdoors. The only harvest the trees provide is a waxy substance extracted from their buds in early spring which mountain people still use to make salves. Pioneers prized the tree for its rapid growth and planted it in farm dooryards. As I sweep the curled dead leaves from the porch, I sigh. Summer is coming to a close, the boys will hasten back to school, and nature will prepare for its fall climax. There is much more harvesting to be done, but I can feel the hush of the quiet time beginning to descend on me once again as August gives way to peaceful September.

Chapter 9
The Lesser Creatures

A S A CHILD I had a morbid fear of snakes. But over the years I have consciously trained myself to observe them dispassionately. Our years in Maine helped me, because I knew that there were no poisonous snakes in that state. Still, I could never control the lurch in my stomach whenever I stumbled over a large milk snake. They are beautifully colored creatures with rows of reddish-brown blotches bordered in black that contrast with cream-colored bodies. I lavishly admired the younger milk snakes, which show the strongest contrasts in color with their bright coppery red blotches, and I was charmed by the small grass-colored green snakes. Of course, the garter snakes were everywhere. To us snakes were a harmless part of a benign environment.

When we moved to Pennsylvania all the old poisonous snake fears returned. People who had lived on the mountain, and even those who hadn't, rushed to tell us of their snake experiences. "Dad killed a nest of rattlers in the stone wall a couple of years ago," one young lady reported.

"Don't tell me you let your kids play in the corn crib?" another asked in a horrified voice. "It's just crawling with copperheads."

Grown men announced that they wouldn't live up here for anything—"too many poisonous snakes." After a few weeks of this, I was definitely nervous. I rushed out to buy the boys high-top leather boots and issued instructions that they must wear them whenever they went outdoors. "No bare feet," I declared, "and stick to the trails if you go hiking." I could hardly wait for the cold weather when, presumably, the hordes of poisonous snakes would be hibernating.

The following spring the boys shed their boots and their shoes and socks, but I remained nervous at their daring. And in midsummer my caution seemed justified.

"Mom," Steve shouted, "there's a strange snake out by the back steps. It's curled up and hissing. I think it's a copperhead."

"Stay away," I screamed, as I crept slowly out to the back porch. The snake certainly did look ferocious—ready to strike at any minute—and yet something in the back of my mind said "just a milk snake."

"No, no," Steve insisted as he pulled out our guidebook on reptiles. I had never seen a poisonous snake close-up, and I had no idea how big the pits were that distinguish pit vipers. Nor did I know exactly how flat their heads should be in comparison with the thicker heads of the nonpoisonous snakes. Painstakingly, I read and reread the descriptions of both snakes and compared the colored drawings, while Steve jumped around saying, "I'm sure it's a copperhead, Mommy."

Finally I called Bruce at work, twenty-eight miles away. "What shall I do?" I wailed.

"Call our neighbor and ask her to come over," he suggested.

Hesitantly I called Margaret. "I've only seen one copperhead in my life up here," she said, "but I'll be right over." A few minutes later she marched up the road carrying a garden hoe.

"Don't want to waste a shot on a snake," she explained.

All the while the snake remained coiled and hissing. "Could be one," she commented, "better kill it to be sure." While she stood calmly talking, she suddenly chopped the snake across its middle and slowly mashed its head with the back of the hoe. "Now this is the way you kill a snake," she instructed as I watched, frightened and revolted.

"Forget it, Margaret," I answered. "I could never do that."

"Nothing to it," she replied. Thanking her when the deed was done, we left the snake where it had fallen. A couple of hours later Bruce came home and scooped the remains onto a newspaper. Then he got out the reptile book, checked the snake's belly, and announced that we had, indeed, killed a harmless milk snake. Steven was particularly heartbroken because had he not persisted in his belief that the snake was a copperhead, I would have been certain that our brave reptile was only a milk snake. Painstakingly, Bruce showed me the divided scales just behind the anal opening, which were different from the single row of scales under the tail of a copperhead.

"And did you see any pits on the side of its head?" he asked. Shakily I pointed to the passage in the book that warned against approaching live snakes close enough to see their pits.

"What about the head shape and color?" he asked.

"Well, it looked flatter than usual and reddish, although I told Steve I was sure that V marking on its head made it a milk snake." Finally, after reading the book further, we took a little comfort in the statement that many harmless snakes are killed because they resemble copperheads.

After that I adopted an almost blasé attitude toward snakes. Once I learned that children do not drop dead on the spot when they are bitten, I stopped fighting "bare feet fever." I still tried to make the boys wear shoes when they went blueberrying, but usually they would sneak off shoeless anyway. One bright August morning a few years later, I sent them up to the powerline right-of-way where the blueberries were plentiful with an assigned quota for the day: Steve had to pick one quart, and David and Mark were each to pick a pint. Steve quickly filled his bucket and returned, but his little brothers mostly stalled and ate—their blue mouths a dead giveaway. In exasperation I sent them back up in the afternoon. For a while I heard their caroling voices on the mountaintop—more playing than picking I surmised with a sigh. Then suddenly they burst into the yard, empty pails clanking.

"Where are your berries?" I demanded angrily.

"Mommy, we saw a poisonous snake up there," David yelled excitedly.

I hardly reacted. Just a story to avoid picking. But David grabbed up the reptile field guide, looked up the picture of a copperhead, and said, "Yep, that's what we saw." Still I was not wholly convinced, but I did listen intently to their story.

Mark was the hero of the tale. As David started to step over a brush pile, Mark suddenly spoke up.

"Look out for the poisonous snake, David."

"Of course, I thought he was kidding," David related. "But I did look down. And he was right. A foot in front of me a large snake was coiled up, and I could see his fangs. I've never been so scared before.

My teeth clacked together, and we turned around and ran home."

By this time, Steve was glaring jealously, annoyed that he had not seen the snake, and he begged me to let him go back and look. My doubts had evaporated, and after congratulating David and Mark on their escape, I forbade Steve to go back to the berry patch. As far as I was concerned, blueberry picking had ended for the year.

But when Bruce came home he was annoyed that I hadn't gone up the mountain and checked on their tale.

"Now we'll all live in fear because of two little kids' story."

Grabbing the rifle, he and the boys went up to look for the snake, although four hours had elapsed since the incident.

A half hour later they all returned. Steve was triumphantly carrying a snakeskin with a row of single undivided plates under the tail, a primary identifying characteristic of a poisonous snake. Once again four-year-old Mark had saved the day. David had led them to the wrong brush pile, where they searched for evidence of the snake. But Mark had protested. "No, it was over beside this brush pile, David," he insisted, even though, according to Bruce, all the brush piles looked identical. Nevertheless, everyone respected Mark's opinion enough to search his brush pile as well. It was then that Mark spotted the snakeskin in the brush, and that was all the verification any of them needed. Evidently the copperhead had just shed its skin and was still resting there when David came along. I was deeply thankful for Mark's alertness, grateful that neither had been struck, and reminded that our mountain is not wholly safe, at least not in the summertime.

In fact, it took considerable courage for me to enter the blackberry patch the next morning even though it is not on the powerline right-of-way. Of course, one copperhead in nearly four years of continuous wandering was not unreasonable to expect. The mountain is not crawling with poisonous snakes, as the people in the valley had indicated, but obviously there are some around. Mostly, though, our snake experiences here have been interesting and pleasant. Not long ago Mark came running toward me with a small garter snake in his hand. For the first time in my life I had an urge to hold the creature myself—however, I resisted the impulse. Someday that final barrier will be crossed when my intellectual acceptance of snakes will be joined with an emotional acceptance as well.

Despite all their affection and easy handling of the garter snakes, the boys have been far more leery of the big black rat snakes that we frequently see around the farm. One hot summer day they discovered an enormous one twining through a large lilac bush. Excitedly Steve called Bruce to help them capture it, because they wanted to study and measure the creature. After a good deal of poking and prodding with a large stick, Bruce succeeded in maneuvering it into a deep box. Rattling its tail furiously, the snake reared up and started to slither out of the box. As Steve saw his prize quarry about to escape, he quickly pushed it back down and was sharply bitten. Despite blood spurting from the wound, he declared that "it doesn't hurt a bit." Nevertheless, he was more careful after that. The snake measured five feet long, an enormous specimen, and I tried to calculate how many rats and mice were necessary to keep it filled. I welcomed its vermin-controlling presence, even though its size and ferocity repelled me. Shortly afterwards it escaped from the box while we were eating dinner, and I was glad.

Black snakes do have the unnerving habit of climbing bushes and trees, evoking all those jungle visions of ferocious snakes dropping down on top of the unwary. One evening I stood in the driveway talking to a visitor when there was a sudden thud directly behind me. A large black snake had been curled up on the branch of a wild cherry tree when the limb suddenly shattered. It lay there confused and stunned for a couple minutes before slowly slithering off into the woods. Our female visitor stood horrified while Bruce and the boys quickly calculated its size and I continued conversing, unmoved and apparently calm. She was completely convinced that the mountain was, indeed, "crawling with snakes."

"Oh, but it's just a black snake," I said, "and they eat rats and mice."

She shivered. "It's big and ugly, and I would kill it."

But not all black snakes are pugnacious or threatening, as the boys discovered one September afternoon when Mark found one stretched along the big grate in the driveway. It was very sluggish from having just eaten something which bulged out its middle. The boys and I went down to see it because Mark reported that it was gigantic. As I watched warily the three boys sat down quietly beside the snake, and Steve, confident and affectionate as always, began talking to it.

"Hi, fella! Aren't you a handsome snake?" Perhaps the snake really did sense his kindly intentions, because in just a few minutes Steve had tamed it and was carrying all five feet of it gently coiled around his arm.

"He really is beautiful," David declared as he stroked its body, "and look at those little bits of white on his black skin."

Finally, after Bruce had a chance to take several photos of the snake twined around the boys' necks, they released it beside the veranda where it instantly slithered down a chipmunk hole.

I was glad to watch the boys develop a sensible, affectionate attitude toward snakes. Many people fear and hate them, and they will kill them at every opportunity. In fact, some herpetologists are beginning to worry about the marked decline in the numbers of snakes found in our country. One spring morning Mark was happily playing with garter snakes by the well when a large delivery truck drove up. A big burly man got out to unload roofing paper for the barn. He glanced up at the well.

"Hey! What's your kid playing with?" he asked.

"Oh, just a nest of garter snakes," I answered. A look of loathing crossed his face.

"Snakes!" he exploded.

"But they're harmless," I protested.

"I hate all them things. Kill every one I see. No snake is harmless. They're sneaky things. Never know when they'll turn on you."

I didn't answer. I merely compared his enormous size to that of the tiny garter snakes and wondered how such a man could be frightened by a harmless snake.

"I'd never live up here," were his parting words as he rumbled back down the mountain.

While my acceptance of snakes is still not total, I have no reservations at all about the numerous kinds of amphibians we have on the mountain. I am getting particularly fond of the large variety of salamanders found in Pennsylvania. Being anxious to see how many we could find on our mountain, I set off down the road with Steve one bleak, damp, and overcast day to hunt under rotted logs and large rocks where salamanders spend their daylight hours. Only during rainstorms and at night do they roam the forest floor.

Since I am not too strong, I let Steve turn over most of the heavy rocks. At first we found only red ant nests, large black ground beetles, earthworms bulging with eggs, and various kinds of centipedes. Then we made our first strike. With a lightning swift lunge, Steve grabbed a small, dark, and slippery salamander. I frantically leafed through Roger Conant's *A Field Guide to Reptiles and Amphibians* and finally decided that we had found a Wehrle's salamander, named for R. W. Wehrle of Indiana, Pennsylvania, who discovered this gray-bellied species. These salamanders live under stones in the upland forests of the Appalachian Mountains, and they eat earthworms, beetles, and ants. Under another rock we discovered red ants attempting to eat a Wehrle's salamander. Its tail had been severed from its body and was off wriggling by itself while its body was covered with ants. "He'll grow a new tail," Steve declared confidently, as he gently brushed the red ants from the salamander. Then he placed it under another rock. "Just made it in time to rescue that fellow," he said.

Steve went leaping down to investigate under the rocks in the still pools of the stream. There he found several dark salamanders with white lines behind their eyes. We identified them as northern dusky salamanders, a lungless species that breathes through its skin and mouth lining. A very common salamander, it lives in streams, springs, or moist spots in the woods.

Steve also brought a medium-sized crayfish from the stream to show me. As I worried about him getting pinched by the formidable looking claws, he purposely allowed one pincher to grip his forefinger.

"Doesn't hurt," he insisted, but when he tried to release his finger the crayfish held on tenaciously. Steve finally wrenched his finger out, and I wondered if it had been as painless as he had maintained. He made no comment after the incident, and I hadn't the heart to question his bravado.

Feeling the need to show his great nine-year-old strength, he began to heft up much larger rocks. Under a particularly huge flat one we discovered two large black salamanders completely speckled with white spots. As he picked one up, Steve's hand became covered with a sticky skin-gland secretion that clung like glue. This was the slimy or "sticky" salamander that lives in moist wooded ravines and hillsides.

I noticed Steve's infinite care toward each salamander he handled, and I remembered a hard lesson he had learned in Maine. As a small eager boy of four, he had found an exquisite woodland salamander and happily toted it home, despite my warnings. He was entranced by its shape and movement, and he recoiled in horror and tears when the delicate creature died before his eyes.

"You took him away from his proper environment," I explained. "He could not live anywhere but in the moist woods soil under a damp rock where you found him."

"I'll never, ever do that again," he had replied tearfully. Ever since then he has always made himself familiar with the needs of the creatures he catches and studies, and he quickly releases them when he has finished his work. As we studied the salamanders during our walk, Steve constantly stroked their backs with a gentle wet forefinger to keep them moist and unharmed.

Then it started to rain, which brought out of its hole one of the most charming of all the salamanders. Walking deliberately and boldly along, looking like a miniature dinosaur, was a red eft. It was a lovely orange-red color with bright red spots. Efts are not as slippery as most salamanders because their skins are rougher and not at all slimy, and I enjoyed having this slow-moving creature walk over my hand and up my arm. It really seemed to have a definite personality. In one to three years it would return to the water from whence its egg had originally hatched and become an aquatic, olive-colored, red-spotted newt. But in the midst of the downpour it delightfully and brightly concluded our salamander hunt for the day.

Despite our mountain stream environment where salamanders flourish, the boys have missed having a pond here. Just below the kitchen window of our home in Maine we had had a small pond that teemed with wildlife of all kinds. Muskrats built their homes on its banks, wood ducks and black ducks stopped off on their migrations, and barn swallows swooped down for occasional drinks. In the spring the boys waded at its edge, collecting water bugs and frogs, and summertime found us watching the great blue herons as they hunted for frogs and fish. So one summer after we moved here the boys began haunting the mud holes and watery ditches, the springhouse, and the old well, looking for the familiar creatures of a pond environment.

Once in a while they were rewarded. A bullfrog lived along the ditch next to our driveway, and it startled us with a loud plop whenever we came near. Steve spent hours stalking it, but the bullfrog always jumped the instant before he struck. In despair one day Steve retreated underneath the cedar-shaked roof of the old well. Because the well is silted up, there are only a few inches of water in it, but it is cool and dark, with large rocks lining the sides. From out of the well that afternoon a cry of surprise came echoing up to the house. "Mom, there's a spring salamander in the well! I can see his head peering out of the rocks!" We all went running to see, but we were rewarded with only a look at the dank still water. No creature lurked there. "Just wait—I'll catch him. Then you'll see," Steve declared.

And so began the long attempt to hook the spring salamander with a fishing line. Patiently Steve dug worms, baited the hook, and lay quietly waiting. Each time he dropped the line in the water the spring salamander had itself a feast but avoided the hook. As the week progressed, more and more small heads peered out from behind the rocks, and more and more worms were devoured. Soon five spring salamanders were joined by two mudpuppies in the daily feeding of worms. Steve was frequently joined by a curious grandfather and two inquisitive brothers, while Bruce and I waited eagerly in the background for a look. As we waited and watched, we were liberally educated by Steve in the ways of spring salamanders and mudpuppies.

We learned that they are agile salamanders that usually live in cool springs and mountain areas. They are also found beneath logs, stones, or leaves in moist forest environments. Mudpuppies, or waterdogs as they are called in the south, were so named because it was believed that they make a barking sound (which they do not). They do have three sets of bushy red gills which they retract when they are taken out of water and a long flattened tail which they use as a fin. They, too, like the shelter of underwater rocks, and they grow quite large—a full foot when mature.

Explaining everything he knew about the creatures did not help Steve catch them. They were simply too quick for him. In disgust one day Steve flung down the rod. But all his feeding of the salamanders had made them less wary of his presence, and they no longer stayed hidden behind the rocks when he was around. That afternoon he made a quick grab and caught a slimy seven-inch long spring salamander which he carefully put in a bucket. We heard his jubilation all over the mountain, and we went down to look. The spring salamander stalked about the bucket with great dignity. Everyone admired the specimen as Steve measured and examined it. Then he returned it to the well. The next morning Steve caught a mudpuppy the same way, and he showed us its red gills and finlike tail. Then it, too, went back into the well.

Every spring and summer now the boys go frequently to look in the well and watch the spring salamanders and mudpuppies. And they don't seem to miss the Maine pond quite so much anymore.

Another thing about Maine that we don't miss are the black flies and mosquitoes. Our Pennsylvania mountain is almost a bug-free paradise. We can plant our garden without getting a single bite, and we can sit outside on the porch at night without hearing the ominous hum of mosquitoes. By bug-free, of course, I mean the biting insects that make life miserable for people. Certainly we do not lack other forms of insect life. By summer, as I go about my work, I have an idea of what it must be like to live in a jungle: surging, constant, humid heat; thick green foliage in the woods and fields; and, most of all, a great profusion of insects that fly, jump, crawl, and wriggle everywhere. Aphids are strung out in black-beaded rows along the stems of nasturtiums and calendulas, small green worms hump along the ripe broccoli heads, and the iridescent dogbane beetles are clustered all over the spreading dogbane bushes. August is definitely the best month for budding entomologists, and the boys drag in all kinds of specimens for me to admire.

One time Steve came in proudly bearing a black, two-inch-long, tilehorned prionus beetle, with its large pincers clacking ominously. Almost everyone backed off in the company of such a fearsome creature, but Steve knew just how to hold it to avoid those pincers. Since the beetle was a female, Steve placed her in a jar as he wished to keep her until she laid her eggs. To my great delight, she dined on Japanese beetles for a week, but then she refused to eat anything at all. Steve assured us that this was normal; female beetles never eat just before they lay their eggs. In due time she laid a cluster of tiny yellow eggs. Then, with her life's work completed, she promptly died. We all mourned her passing, because the boys had enjoyed holding and watching her. No tilehorned prionus beetle had ever received more affection—and after all, she liked to eat Japanese beetles, didn't she?

Any creature that feeds on those imported pests is welcome to live here. Nothing repels me more than the sight of Japanese beetles piled on top of each other—bundled masses of shiny green—on every plant in the garden. Blackberries, pole beans, zinnias, and marigolds—few crops escape their rampage. The boys stuff jars full with them, and still there are countless numbers everywhere. Because of the damage they do to my favorite plants, I cringe from their hard bodies and avoid touching them.

Yet when Steve brings in a praying mantis to show me, I handle it easily, allowing it to plod all over my arm. Some of its peculiar habits seem strange to me, such as the female's custom of frequently eating the male during or just after mating. But I also know that praying mantises are fierce warriors which consume huge numbers of garden pests. In addition, their unusual appearance, manner of walking, and "praying" habit make them seem almost like pets. The naturalist Edwin Way Teale in his book *Near Horizons* tells of his pet praying mantis named Dinah. She lived on a plant in his study and roamed freely all over the room. She ate voraciously any insects offered her, even those that had been killed in a cyanide bottle. But near the end of her life cycle she simply stopped eating, rested quietly, and slept her way into death. Teale claims that she had been a very companionable and interesting pet and that she seemed to have a lively curiosity. Judging by Teale's experience, my fondness for praying mantises is not so strange after all.

Another creepy, crawly creature that I like is the ordinary spider. Although many people sweep them out with a vengeance, I always apologize each time I destroy a web, especially if it has a few houseflies trapped in it. Spiders are really our allies against the insect invaders, and many of them are beautiful, too. Often as I work in the garden the bright yellow or red crab spiders scurry off, a striking contrast to the brown earth. And when I pick blackberries in early summer mornings I am fascinated by the intricate beauty of the webs of the common garden spiders. I step carefully around them to avoid disturbing the black and yellow occupants as they wait for prey.

The insects and spiders are preyed upon by many of the birds that live on the mountain. Of all the bug catchers, the eastern phoebes are the most delightful to observe. They have always allowed us to watch them raise their families in the variety of odd, unusual localities they have chosen for their nests. According to Arthur Cleveland Bent's *Life Histories of North American Flycatchers, Larks, Swallows and Their Allies*, phoebes have nested "on a strip of wallpaper that sagged from the ceiling . . . on an abandoned farmhouse to which the only entrance was a two-by-four-inch opening in a broken windowpane . . . in an air shaft of a coal mine . . . and on a portable cider mill." Bent says the birds frequently nest "on the porch of an abandoned farmhouse, over the door, perhaps, on the narrow wooden ledge." He adds that "even in inhabited houses . . . the presence of people passing in and out all day has not driven them away."

One summer the phoebes chose the portico above the guest house door to build their nest. Our various city friends were delighted to step outside the door and look up at several little heads looking down at them, while the parents waited patiently on the fence for the guests to move off so they could continue feeding their nestlings. Occasionally one of the boys would pull a stepladder over to the nest, climb up, and peer in at them, but they never touched the young phoebes. One day the nest was jammed full, and the next day it was empty, although we never saw any flying lessons. Later in the summer they raised a second brood in the same nest.

The next spring in early April the male phoebe appeared. Monotonously singing his froggy song, he perched on the fence, his tail flicking, waiting for a likely female to appear. In due time a female arrived, and for a few weeks they happily chased around in the drizzly rain, the male singing and calling to the female. Soon Steve reported that they were busy constructing a nest just underneath the eaves of the stone springhouse. That year I was determined to watch their progress more closely. Because of the placement of the nest we could not see directly into it, even with a stepladder. But by May we knew the female was incubating eggs. One day Steve verified that there were several eggs in the nest by gently thrusting his hand into it when the phoebe was off catching bugs. On May 20 the eggs hatched, and we picked up the remains of the pure white eggshells on the ground beneath the nest.

When I complained to Bruce that I could not see into the nest, he found a large pocket mirror for me. Eagerly I ran to the nest and saw the reflection of several naked, large-eyed, long-beaked babies. They were in such a tumbled mass that I could not accurately count them. Each day I went to look just once in order not to disturb them. After three days I saw the beginnings of black down on their wings, and two days later they were completely down-covered and cheeping loudly. By the end of the first week I no longer needed the mirror—five lusty nestlings were stretched out above the nest. That whole week had been rainy and cold, and yet they had survived and thrived. Both parents worked endlessly, catching bugs to feed them in a constant relay.

The second week the weather warmed, and the days were beautiful. Gradually the little phoebes grew feathers and bulged from the nest. Then, on June 6, I went down at 10 A.M. to check. As I approached the nest, they suddenly flew off in all directions, low to the ground, and I had to duck down quickly. Five new phoebes had launched themselves out into a bright new world.

Another bird we grew quite fond of was hen pheasant. One late January morning I discovered her in the brush near the garden. I was walking back from the compost heap through the dried crackly weeds when I heard a slight movement. A large mottled-brown hen pheasant stood in the brush about seven feet away. Neither of us moved. Finally, I spoke softly to her. She continued to stand still, looking at me. Then she slowly stalked around the small green fence that encloses the Plummer family gravesite and several enormous lilac bushes. I circled the fence, too, and came within a few feet of her. Her hen-like body, long trailing tail, and enormous white eye rings fascinated me and so did her calmness. It was I who finally wandered off—she remained immovable.

As the days passed it became obvious that she was settling down into the grape tangle. Steve often came upon her as he wandered through, and once the puppy Bobbin tried to flush her. "She just ignored her," Steve reported. Her coloration was excellent camouflage. I would ask Steve to point her out to me, and unless she moved it was quite difficult to see her. She usually foraged at the edge of the tangle near the back porch

*Hen pheasant stalks around the small, green fence
that encloses the Plummer family gravesite
and several enormous lilac bushes.*

in late afternoon, and we could watch her from the
kitchen window. We did wonder, though, why she was
alone. Normally hen pheasants flock together for the
winter in the weedy edges of valley grain fields. Whatever was she doing off by herself on our wild mountain?
We couldn't answer that question, but we could enjoy
watching her gracious presence as she strolled slowly
through the grape tangle or picked and scratched the
ground near a fallen pole.

She stayed around into mid-April, eventually coming
up to the back porch for birdseed. Then she disappeared,
and we assumed that she had left us and gone searching
for a mate. One day in mid-May, as we were getting ready
for dinner, Bruce glanced out the back kitchen window.

"Here comes the hen pheasant," he exclaimed. She literally rushed across the lawn and up the porch steps, her head bobbing about, as she looked for birdseed. When she didn't see any, she headed for the lawn to eat dandelion seeds. She frequently looked up at us hopefully as if she were pleading for food. Bruce ran down to the barn to get some chicken scratch. While I continued looking, she climbed back up to the porch and began tapping loudly at the dog's dish and eating some of the scraps. She obviously was starved.

When Bruce returned he carefully opened the door. The hen pheasant started away down the steps and across the lawn. Splat! The chicken scratch hit the porch floor. The sound stopped her in her tracks. She spun around and dashed back up the steps. Her beak stabbing down at rapid-fire rate, she quickly consumed the feed and then hurried off toward the grape tangle. Her haste and extreme hunger made me guess she might be nesting somewhere nearby. She came once more a few days later, and that was the last we saw of her. But she and all the other so-called lesser creatures have added amusement to our lives here on the mountain, and we are just as pleased when we find a new salamander, bird, insect, or snake as when we see a new mammal. To us even the life cycle of the lowliest insect is a fascinating tale.

Chapter 10
Autumn Peace

SEPTEMBER COMES QUIETLY in with the waning goldenrod, the fading purple asters, and the drooping joe-pye weed. I welcome the brisk beginning of autumn that September gives us. It is a month of change—from blistering heat wave to almost frosty nights—and tucked in between the many glorious days are the turbulent equinoctial storms. September is also the month when birds and insects begin migrating south.

The first wave of warblers sweep through in mid-September. We are enjoying breakfast when we suddenly notice that the old apple tree is filled with a lively, fluttering mass of birds. Grabbing binoculars and bird books, we all go out to sit on the back porch and watch. Not only the apple tree but also the grape trellises, the sumac bushes, and the oak trees along the woods are covered with feeding warblers. They are so preoccupied that they don't mind our presence or our excited discussion of them.

Many warblers change their bright spring colors to more uniform olive and yellow shades in the fall, making them very difficult to identify at this time of year. Called the "butterflies" of the bird world, they never alight long enough for us to focus our binoculars. Steve and I keep up a continuous argument about whether we are seeing Cape May warblers or yellow warblers, black-throated blue warblers, or blackburnian warblers. But at last I am triumphant as I call out "black-and-white warbler." There is no argument on that score, because they are black and white all year long, which distinguishes them from all their olive and yellow relatives. We watch for over half an hour, dizzy from following their rapid movements. Then they are gone, as suddenly as they had come.

I walk through the woods watching the migrating birds each morning before the sun tops the ridge. One day, just beyond the garden, the small patch of trees was already sunlit and filled with warblers. A single bird stood out from the rest with its pure white breast and bluish-gray back. A black-throated blue warbler was heading south, with all the golden throngs, leaving the country for the warm shores of Cuba, Haiti, and Jamaica. What exotic traveled lives the warblers lead!

Sometimes I wish I could follow them on their pursuit of constant warmth. Yet I feel compelled to endure the cold along with the hardier birds.

Monarch butterflies, too, migrate through this area most of the month. Some years are better than others. One September they must have had an exceptionally good summer. They fluttered across the country roads, and I noticed countless broken bodies on the pavement. Our van contributed to the toll because of its broad flat front. I flinched whenever I heard the loud splat as still another monarch died on its long trip south.

Many monarch butterflies migrate from as far north as Hudson's Bay, traveling an average of 12 to 15 miles an hour. They fly by day and rest in trees by night. Several branches of two particular black walnut trees in our yard were covered with resting monarchs for many nights. Early each morning they would flutter off, only to be replaced by more travelers that evening. When they finally reach their southern destinations, they will settle in crowds on particular trees used by them year after year. There they rest in semihibernation until spring when they head north again, the females laying eggs on the milkweed as they go. All the adult monarchs die on the northward journey, so none ever make the southern migration twice—yet the new generations always travel south to the same chosen trees in Florida, California, and Mexico.

*A migrating monarch butterfly
stops in to investigate a flowering
Jerusalem artichoke plant.*

Woolly bear caterpillars seem to be just as purposeful in their movements, be it across highways or through our backyard to the outside cellar stairs. Some years they have broad brown bands in the center with black tips at each end; other years the brown bands are narrow and the black bands thick. Supposedly the size of the bands foretells the severity of the coming winter. However, experts in such things vary in their interpretations. Some say that broad brown bands mean a harsh winter, and others say just the opposite. I find it all very confusing, and I wonder each September what kind of winter the caterpillars are foretelling. Whatever it is, they will be unaware, since they all curl up in tight dormant balls until spring.

In spring they will resume their feeding on the leaves of common plantain until they finally pupate. As the plantain begins to bloom they emerge as pinkish-yellow Isia Isabella moths. The moths feed on the plantain blossoms until they lay their eggs on its leaves. After they lay their eggs, the moths die. The new crop of woolly bears hatches from the eggs and feeds on the plantain leaves until autumn. By September they are so soft and cuddly that all our boys have them curling in their hands, crawling over their legs, or treasured in their pockets.

September also gives us many beautiful clear evenings to watch the waxing of the harvest moon, that last full moon before the autumnal equinox. At this time of year the orbit of the moon at sunset lies almost flat on the eastern horizon. Because of this, the full moon appears to rise at sunset for three days in a row. The evenings are lightened and lengthened by the bright moonlight, allowing farmers in northern lands around the world to gather in the harvest long after sunset.

By day's end, though, I am so tired from harvesting the garden crops that I am content just to sit and admire the moon's light as it bathes the fields and woods in white splendor. Despite the scientific explorations we have directed toward the moon, I still find it mysterious and romantic. Human landings have not altered its beauty one whit for me.

While the moon is lovely to gaze at from our fruitful earth, I certainly would not wish to live on such a barren dead land. I wonder, sometimes, as I observe our galloping consumption of earthly treasures, whether we won't turn this miraculous world of ours into a similarly barren place. Every time I hear that we must lower our hard-won pollution standards, that we must build more atomic power plants, and that we must carelessly strip more coal from the earth, I wonder: Why must we keep increasing our consumption of electricity? Why can't we learn to curb our desire for worldly goods? Why are we so eager to live in a synthetic environment, with all the plastic luxuries and comforts that human beings can invent?

I shudder when I think of the earth becoming completely human-dominated. I know that my very spirit would shrivel and die if I could never see waste fields glowing with goldenrod and aster or watch wild turkeys running clumsily through the woods. To be enclosed, instead, in concrete and asphalt, breathing polluted air, and experiencing the natural world only through television and movies would be devastating to my soul. Already many people live that way in American cities and towns. Have they nothing more than material possessions in their lives, no other thoughts than their own pleasures, no appreciation for the wonders of the natural world?

Certainly such people are not able to walk down a country road in September and see the turtleheads in blossom. They could not stand quietly and watch a fat carpenter bee pull down the pink lower lip of a large white blossom and crawl inside, its back legs dangling out, to gather pollen. As it moves about inside, it wiggles the blossom, making it look like a turtle's head which is stretching itself about. Slowly, slowly it backs out and tries another blossom for size. Such a scene is worth far more to me than any televised nature spectacular.

Rather than depending on electronic marvels that waste so much of this world's riches, why shouldn't we try to enjoy life firsthand? In September I find all my senses intrigued by the common spicebushes that grow along the stream below the corral. Their leaves are yellowing, and their green fruits are turning red. I pick a red fruit, shiny smooth to the touch, and break it open. The most delightful spicy odor emanates from it, and I take several home to dry and grind. They make an excellent substitute for allspice in baking.

How much longer will I be privileged to discover and enjoy such things? Through my lifetime, perhaps. But my children—what about them and their children? What kind of heritage will we leave them—a life of moon gazing, turtlehead watching, and spicebush sniffing, or one of concrete, pollution, and television. During the beautiful, opening days of autumn I sometimes brood about such things.

I am thankful for our own small corner of Eden and the bounties we reap, especially in September. We finish off the first planting of sweet corn, and I carefully harvest the ears that have grown too tough for eating. Those enormous kernels make marvelous corn relish for the canning shelves. Then we wait anxiously as the second planting of corn ripens. No matter how much we plant, there is never enough, because our uses for corn are unending. Fresh corn chowder is a daily lunch treat, and each evening we have at least three ears apiece. I follow the old rules for fresh corn on the cob: I put water in a kettle on the stove to boil, go out to pick and husk twenty ears right in the field, and run back to the kitchen where the boiling water is ready. The haste is vital, since the delicate sugars in the kernels start changing to starch almost immediately. I dump the corn in, set the timer for three minutes, and call the family. As soon as they are seated, the corn is served. I used to waste time by spreading on butter and liberally salting each ear, but Bruce persuaded me to eat my corn plain. Not only is this better for my waistline, but it also allows me to eat more of this most delectable of garden vegetables. As a child I had always liked corn, but I knew it was a rather starchy vegetable. However, when it is picked, husked, and cooked immediately, the sweetness is unforgettable. I am able to retain this taste in the freezer by cutting the kernels off the cobs right after they have been boiled for three minutes and freezing them in pint boxes. At times during the middle of the winter I bring out a package, heat the corn slowly, and serve it for dinner. Except for the absence of cobs, the corn tastes much as it did in September.

The tomatoes ripen about the time the corn does, and sliced tomatoes always seem to go with corn on the cob. I usually grow several different kinds of tomatoes, including the bright orange ones that are exceptionally high in vitamin C. And I learned that if I grow pear and cherry tomatoes, the boys will eat them right from the garden. Slicing tomatoes for dinner is as quick and easy as boiling corn. But I need all the time I save in dinner preparation to can the excess tomatoes.

September is also bean month. The bush and pole beans have usually quit producing, but I notice that I have missed picking several bushels of the long tough pods. So Mark and I pull up all the plants and strip off the pods, which we carry up to the attic. We leave them spread out to dry on newspapers so that sometime in midwinter we can shell out our supply of dry beans for soups and stews.

We also grow green soybeans. By early September the small fuzzy pods are finally filled out, and Bruce helps me with the tedious picking job. It takes a lot of pods to make a meal, but we feel the unique taste is worth it and, of course, soybeans are very rich in high quality protein. The first year we grew them I laboriously twisted the tough pods to shell them out, much as I do limas. During the winter I read about an easier way and determined to try it out even though it sounded improbable. I washed all the pods and put them into a large pot of boiling water for five minutes. Then I rinsed them in cold water and proceeded to "shell" the beans by squeezing the pods between my thumb and forefinger. The soybeans shot out like bullets into the cooking pot, and when they were all shelled, I heated them again for several more minutes before serving them. They are absolutely delicious—better than lima beans and as tender as peas, with a sweet nutty taste. And they freeze beautifully, too.

During September we harvest at a frenetic pace with one eye on the thermometer. Usually in Pennsylvania the first frost does not come until October, although the nights are nippy. And by October we are willing to relinquish the garden work. But in September we are just beginning to reap the lima beans and green peppers, and we hate to give in. After several years of late frosts, though, we began to relax. Then one year, on September 23, it suddenly turned cold. As night approached I went out to dig up a marjoram plant, and I clipped off all the blossoming marigolds. When Bruce got home from work, I persuaded him to help me cover most of the tomato and pepper plants with black plastic. But he insisted that it would not freeze, so we decided not to bother covering the rest of the garden.

The next morning it was 26 degrees. I struggled with the icy hose in an attempt to wash the frost off the uncovered vegetables before the sun came up, but it was useless. There was at least a quarter of an inch of frost on every small leaf. After nearly freezing my fingers I gave myself up to the beauty of each white-etched plant. Even the weeds were lovely. I walked along in the cold light-filled dawn, watching the sunshine creep across the white field and melt the frost with its heat. Woodpeckers and nuthatches called, but the birds of summer were silent. Once I entered the woods there was no sign of frost. The leaves of the trees had formed a thick canopy that had kept out the frost crystals. Only the powerline right-of-way cut a white swathe through the woods. But as I walked on in the silence, I knew that soon the time of peace would be here. September was almost over—I welcomed the coming of fall.

Sometimes October creeps darkly in, with no sign of the bright blue weather we all expect. For weeks we are enclosed in deep clouds that swirl over the mountaintop. Occasionally we hear a robin's song or the brilliant call of a cardinal, but mostly the outdoors are silent and dingy.

During other Octobers, however, we are rewarded by the most glorious days of the year. Weeks of Indian summer drift hazily by: doors and windows are flung open, shorts are retrieved from bottom dresser drawers, and bare feet are again in fashion. The garden grows on and on, producing scores of squashes, bushels of tomatoes, baskets of green peppers, and pounds of pole beans.

Nature recognizes the falseness of the season, however, because the birds continue migrating south despite the warm weather. The most spectacular migrants during the month are the great flocks of Canada geese which follow our mountain south each October. Usually they fly in high wavering formations, but one rainy evening, as we sat at the dinner table, we suddenly heard the cries of the geese coming much closer than usual. We rushed outside in time to see them skimming just above the treetops. The low cloud cover had forced them down so near to the mountaintop that we had a marvelous close-up view of them as they flew over.

Sometimes the geese stream over for several days and nights, keeping us awake with their incessant barking cries. But one glorious October I heard them only once. During an early morning fog, as I quietly walked the Short-Circuit Trail, the muffled silence was suddenly broken by the far-off calling of the geese. I paused to listen, stirred as always by the wild sound, and I strained to see them through the white mist. Later in the month a friend called to find out whether we had heard any geese. "Do you think anything has happened to them?" she asked anxiously. I tried to reassure her with my report of one distant flock, and we both hoped that the geese had only changed their migration route this one autumn.

The smaller birds, however, never seem to vary their routes. The warbler migration reaches its height in early October. We can sit for hours on our warm, sunny back porch watching them fly about the yard and the grape tangle. The most common are the myrtle warblers—small, streaked black and white with vivid yellow rumps. Intent upon foraging, they pay no attention to us as they flit around the black walnut trees and chase each other in the lilac bushes. Our first year on the mountain we were puzzled by the tiny olive green birds that often accompanied the myrtle warblers. Smaller than warblers, but with the same nervous haste, they often stopped to flutter on the wing just as hummingbirds do, and yet they were not hummingbirds. After long and patient watching, we suddenly noticed one excited fellow bend his head, displaying a striking scarlet patch. "Ruby-crowned kinglet!" I exclaimed immediately, and I began leafing through the bird guide. As I read the description—tiny size, hummingbird-like actions, and white eye ring—all the criteria matched up. Each year since then we have watched the ruby-crowned kinglets and myrtle warblers playing and feeding for almost a week before they eventually drift off for the Carolinas and other points south.

Each autumn many migrating birds are attracted to the old apple tree which stands among the grape tangles. Sometimes we can count over a dozen kinds of birds at once in the tree. One beautiful day the tree was filled with myrtle warblers, black-throated green warblers, black-and-white warblers, and the brilliant yellow-breasted magnolia warblers. Most of the birds seemed more interested in chasing than feeding, but one magnolia warbler sat on a lower branch where a stray grape vine hung, laden with clusters of Concord grapes. Eagerly the bird pecked away at the fruit, making an unforgettable picture in the late afternoon sunshine. However, the magnolia warblers never stay very long, because they have to migrate clear down to Central America for the winter.

During October many of the juvenile birds are quite evident. Usually they are less cautious than their elders, and often their coloring is quite different. The immature robins with their spotted breasts, the young white-throated sparrows that lack the white throats, and the juvenile red-headed woodpeckers with their striking brown heads are all noticeable among the adult birds. Once we were puzzled by a large, black and white woodpecker with slightly yellow underparts that landed grandly on the dead limb of the old apple tree. We were unable to identify him as he moved up and down the branch, investigating the bark but never pecking at anything. But our mysterious visitor turned out to be an immature yellow-bellied sapsucker, probably hatched on our own Sapsucker Ridge. He stayed around the old apple tree for a few days, keeping company with the warblers and kinglets. Then he was gone again, off to the southern states and traveling alone as yellow-bellied sapsuckers usually do.

Some birds end their migrations right on our mountain. The white-throated sparrows return early in the month from their Canadian nesting grounds to spend the winter foraging here in the grape tangles and weedy undergrowth. They are particularly fond of our grapes, although they consume only the pulp, discarding the skins and seeds as they eat. Almost half their diet during October is comprised of ragweed seeds, according to studies done for the U.S. Department of Agriculture, and they certainly can harvest all they want from the abundance in the brushy edges of our garden. Their food is supplemented by the scattering of seeds beneath our feeders and, in constant company with the dark-eyed juncos, they spend hours each day scratching busily around the yard. We are pleased to hear once again their familiar cheery song about "poor Sam Peabody, Peabody, Peabody," even though in autumn the call sounds somewhat rusty and flat at the end.

Shortly after the arrival of the white-throated sparrows, the tree sparrows come winging in from their Arctic nesting grounds. Their chestnut-capped heads look very much like the rufous crowns of the chipping sparrows, and hence they are nicknamed "winter chippies." However, the one prominent dark spot on their breasts distinguishes the tree sparrow from other sparrows. So do their beautiful, tinkling calls, sounding almost like church bells, that fill our winters with musical sound. They scratch in the ground beneath the feeder in company with the white-throated sparrows, but frequently they can be found perched up on the feeder as well.

The golden-crowned kinglets also spend the winter on the mountain, but they prefer the patch of woods just above the Short-Circuit Trail for their foraging. They have found two of the very few white pine trees that grow on our property, and at the tops of those trees they search for the bark beetles, scale insects, and eggs of moths and plant lice that they particularly relish. Watching them work at such a height is a neck-cramping exercise for an earth-bound mortal. They move constantly and quickly, but I always hope to see the yellow streak on the head of the male or the reddish-orange streak of the female. As with ruby-crowned kinglets, the streaks don't always show— they must be triggered by excitement or, in spring, the mating urge.

The month progresses, and the flurry of migration slows. Some of the summer birds still remain: the doughty phoebes flick their tails as they perch silently in the trees, the robins call in the woods, and the goldfinches bounce over the fields wearing their winter coats of olive green. On one memorable early morning walk, a brown thrasher startled me with a loudly aspirated hiss that sounded like the alarm call of a deer. When the hissing continued, I looked all about for a deer, but I soon realized that the startling noises were coming from a thrasher perched in a maple tree just above my head. As I watched him, I could see the slight movement in his throat as he hissed over and over. Evidently I had thoroughly surprised him in the damp foggy dawn.

Nothing, though, can alarm the migrating bluebirds when they stop to rest in the black walnut trees around our yard. Sitting peacefully on the branches, they exhibit none of the frenzied, hurried appearances of the kinglets and warblers. As we stand with binoculars raised, admiring their incomparable blue color, there are no frantic alarm calls or sudden startling noises. They sit until they are rested, usually no more than half an hour, and then they are gone until the next spring. Because they are so quiet and stay for such a short time, we sometimes miss their fall migrations. Usually, though, Steve's sharp eyes notice them, and he comes to call me from the kitchen where I am chained, for most of the month, by the harvesting.

Often I must will myself to the task of canning while nature continues on without me, and sometimes the choice is difficult to make. What am I missing outside as I can the countless jars of fruits and vegetables? It is almost a pity that this most glorious of months also must be the most bountiful.

Yet I feel an obligation to reap all the planted and wild crops without wasting even a small amount during our short harvest season. The pumpkins are baked, pureed, and frozen; the grapes are made into juice, jams, jellies, and pies; and the last glut of tomatoes is turned into chili sauce, relish, and chow-chow. Green peppers are frozen, baked, sautéed, and stuffed. And before the first frost I pot up some of the herbs—sage, thyme, marjoram, and chives—and put them on the windowsills. There they make beautiful houseplants that are useful for flavoring soups and stews. The basil, dill, and parsley are frozen, and I dry the surplus of thyme, marjoram, sage, and mint by hanging them upside down from the kitchen beams. The boys help me pick four kinds of winter squashes, which we load into their wagon and haul to the house. Carefully placing them in baskets, the boys carry them to the attic and spread them out on newspapers for storing.

On a gusty cold day Bruce brings out the high ladder and props it precariously among the brittle limbs of the enormous old pear tree out behind the guest house. I never watch as he slings a burlap sack around his shoulder and climbs up to begin the hazardous picking. It takes several hours just to pick the reachable branches. Then the baskets and baskets of pears are taken down to the basement to ripen. Sometime in mid-October they are ready. I can for days, with juice running down my arms as I peel bushels of unsprayed specimens. When I cannot face another quart jar, I turn to making orange and lemon pear honey to spread on our home-baked bread. Finally I sigh, finished, and the now-rotting remnants of the bumper pear harvest are tossed on the compost heap.

Another October task is the harvesting of black walnuts. One glorious year there were no walnuts, and I was grateful. But that was a rare and unexpected blessing. Our first year on the mountain we innocently and eagerly gathered several baskets. On a cold windy day we spent hours carefully cracking the green outer husks off the hard-shelled nuts and getting walnut stained shoes and hands in the process. But we persevered and at last carried the nuts down to the basement to dry. Then our lazy streak and the red squirrels settled in. Just once, on a cold wintery day, Bruce smashed open a large number with a hammer while I spent several long boring hours picking out the meat, getting only enough to flavor one nut bread. Except for that day, the rest were left to the squirrels, who ransacked our basement in the wee early hours and carried their treasures to their nests in the walls of the house.

The next autumn, when we had an even larger crop, I felt energetic once again on a cold windy day. Marshaling the boys, we carried the baskets of unhulled walnuts down to the paved part of the driveway outside the guest house. We dumped all the nuts on the hard macadam and, trying to find a less exhausting way to crack off the hulls, I carefully drove the jeep back and forth over them. But there were still pieces clinging to the nuts which we had to pull off, and we worked the entire morning on it. This time Bruce did not help, declaring it a waste of time. He suggested that we should not dry the nuts in the basement and give the squirrels free meals all winter. So we trundled them to the barn in Mark's little red wagon and left two husked bushels. Three days later I went out to see if they had dried at all. Over half the nuts were gone. Apparently the red squirrels had themselves a fine time. In dismay I hauled the remaining nuts up to the garage, my last refuge on the farm. The squirrels only pilfered an occasional nut there, but the dank, damp weather of a rainy autumn defeated me. Miserably I watched as the nuts molded and rotted into a fuzzy white heap. All our work had gone for nothing—we ate not a single nut. That is why on years when the crop fails I am secretly grateful. The squirrels, though, have to spend many hours out in the woods hunting for acorns to tide them through a thin winter.

Then there was the year when we finally found a use for the bitter little apples growing on the old trees scattered around the farm. Scrounging around in a cluttered corner of the basement, Bruce discovered an old wine press, a relic belonging to former owners. "Why not use the wine press to make cider?" he suggested.

"Ridiculous," I scoffed, but nevertheless I pulled out some old government pamphlets on cider-making. We gathered a basket of the runty apples and grated them into an enormous old crockery bowl. Then we carefully lined the press with cheesecloth and dumped in the apples. Slowly Bruce turned the handle while I hopefully held a pitcher beneath the opening. To our amazed delight, cider poured from the spout. Those worthless apples produced the sweetest cider we had ever tasted. It took a lot of grating to produce much cider, but each evening we pressed enough for two full glasses, congratulating ourselves on our originality. Even when we discovered that the "wine press" was actually a lard press, we didn't feel too deflated.

Sometime in October much of the bounty is killed by the first frost. If we are lucky it comes later in the month, but occasionally we have a frost by the first or second week. Whenever it comes, we both welcome and dread it. Usually the wind begins to blow, the thermometer drops to around 40 degrees, and the skies are piled high with deep purple wind clouds. Then, overnight, the wind stills and we awake to intense silence. A white crunchy layer of frost covers the lawn and fields. Most of the garden sags and dies under the coating, while only the parsley, Swiss chard, and carrots survive. Along the house the calendulas still sparkle amidst the fallen marigolds and zinnias. Some people try to save their gardens by hosing down the plants before sunrise, but I am content in October to let the natural harvest cycle end with the first frost. I am once again free to roam the fields and woods in the stillness of dawn, admiring each white-encrusted leaf and branch.

Snow is a rare phenomenon in October, but one year, after an early hard frost, it remained cold and windy for more than a week. On October 18 the gray damp morning was especially cold and penetrating. As Mark and I went off to shop that day, I paused to look up at the sky. "If it weren't October, I would say that it's going to snow," I said to him. In less than an hour, when I glanced out of a store window, I noticed fat flakes beginning to sift down. "Certainly won't last," I replied to Mark's excited chatter, but it continued snowing steadily the whole day. As I drove back up our road the hemlocks hung heavy with the wet snow and all the colored leaves were etched with white. The full seed heads of goldenrod and joe-pye weed were large, fluffy powder puffs, and every tall dry blade of grass had an outline of snow accentuating it.

To our amazement, it snowed on through the night. We awoke to a silvery gray and white day with the snow so heavy and wet that it weighed down and blurred the outline of every tree branch and obscured the color of every leaf. A cardinal appeared near the feeder and perched on a snow-covered bush, the only bright spot among the pale colors. The dark-eyed juncos, or "snowbirds" as they are so aptly nicknamed, gathered in the grape tangle, marshaling forces with two tree sparrows, one white-crowned sparrow, and a song sparrow. They were all timid about coming up to the feeder for the first time that year. Eventually they approached, though they fled if anyone came too near the windows.

By afternoon the sky had taken on some blue amidst large clouds. A slight breeze blew, dislodging snow from branches and leaves. Eagerly I went out to enjoy the beauty of snow in October, tramping through patches of colored trees and white snow along the Short-Circuit Trail. Suddenly a large doe darted across the path in front of me, and I had a brief second to admire her brown eyes and soft gray coat before she slid off among the snowy laurel bushes. But very quickly the glory was melted by the sun, and we were moving back into the unadorned but colorful beauty of autumn.

In October we tread on paths of gold. The yellow leaves lighten the woods, even on gloomy days, and I rarely stay indoors. I am out with the fog of early morning, waiting for the sunrise which highlights the waves of autumn color. The color change begins in late September in the lowest story of the forest when the black gum trees turn a deep red. Soon the birches, hickories, black walnuts, and tulip trees begin to turn their various shades of yellow. Soft shades of red are displayed by the red maples and, toward the end of October, the different species of oaks fill the woods with yellows and browns.

Perhaps the edges of the fields are the most spectacular. There the deep red of the staghorn sumacs contrasts with the yellow of the wild grape vines which festoon many of the large trees. Closer to the house, one of the tall red maples growing in the lawn always turns to flaming crimson, and the mums, calendulas, and marigolds provide deep, rich, contrasting colors in the flower beds.

But all too soon the display is gone. A few days of blustery wind near the end of October, and most of the trees are bare. With the leaves down the few animals and birds still left are easier to see, and deer-watching becomes a favorite pastime. Much as I delight in October, I enjoy following the season through to the inevitable gray November.

November is a very uncertain month, with freezing wind and snow flurries one day and benign Indian summer another. The month rarely passes without at least one good snowstorm, sometimes as deep as six inches. It isn't winter, it isn't summer, it isn't even always fall—it is merely cantankerous, unreliable, and extraordinarily variable.

Throughout the month the grape tangle is filled with wintering birds that come to the feeder. Shy, elusive Carolina wrens, with their reddish-brown coats and perky tails, dart through the underbrush, busily feeding on the insects they find in the fallen timbers. Occasionally, if we are very still, they come to take some seeds from the ground beneath the feeder, but generally they prefer an insect diet. During severe winters with heavy snows, we worry about these nonmigratory birds. Originally they were a southern bird, but gradually they extended their range northward along with the cardinals and tufted titmice. Ornithologists have noted that the number of Carolina wrens in the north fluctuates according to the severity of the winter. However, their survival is more certain if they live in sheltered localities, such as our grape tangles, which offer them ample protection and plenty of food. We often hear them singing and calling during the coldest days of winter.

The cardinals and tufted titmice have also been around all year, but it is only when the feeder is full that we see them. The titmice are bold and scold angrily at me if I sit near the feeder in the sunshine. After a while, though, they ignore me and come flipping in for their favorite sunflower seeds. The cardinals are never bold. One movement at the window and they are gone. Usually the female is the first to come, and only after she has been feeding for a while does the brilliant male join her.

On bright warm November days the back porch is an ideal place to sit and enjoy the sunshine. Sometimes Mark quietly joins me on the step as I drink my morning coffee. At first the birds stay in the grape tangle, calling nervously, but after a short while a bold white-breasted nuthatch darts into the feeder for a seed. Then the black-capped chickadees suddenly whiz over our heads, calling as they feed. Mark sits transfixed at their nearness; they are so close that their wings whistle as they flit by. In the meantime the juncos and tree sparrows advance slowly from grape tangle to grassy slope. If we remain still, they are soon feeding confidently just beyond the doorstep. But the least movement sends them fleeing back into the grape tangles.

Usually in November, during a cold spell, I will suddenly hear a new call. Cautiously I steal to the window. A couple of female evening grosbeaks sit in the middle of the feeder, cracking sunflower seeds with amazing speed. For a time the other birds are cowed by the presence of these large birds, but finally a chickadee zooms in and out quickly. The nuthatches, though, try to go about the business more politely. One lands precariously at the very edge of the feeder, opens and closes its wings, and slowly sways back and forth. For its politeness, it gets pecked and driven off. Evening grosbeaks are a quarrelsome lot, constantly jumping and thrusting at each other, and rarely can even four coexist on the feeder at the same time. The rest of them feed on the ground, waiting for an empty space on the feeder. Once the females discover us, it is only a few days before the male evening grosbeaks join them. Then I sigh and go out to buy more sunflower seeds, but their beauty and antics are worth the price.

Feeder watching is one of the many indoor activities I engage in during the cold days of November. Much as I love the brisk weather, I also enjoy rediscovering the comforts of a warm home. Automatically I pick up my knitting needles to begin the winter's supply of mittens and caps. I am an indifferent and unskilled knitter, and months pass each year during which I never touch my needles. But somehow, with winter approaching, I love to handle the brightly colored wools and create gay and warm accessories. Some years I elaborate and knit a sweater if one son particularly needs it, and occasionally I do a tie for Bruce's Christmas stocking.

About the same time I discover that my wardrobe possesses only worn-out slacks, threadbare aprons, and nothing with any style. I spend days at the sewing machine whipping up some new clothes and repairing the old ones. Handling the bright fabrics is cheery work when November is at its gloomiest.

Usually we get our first gusty cold days in November when the wind slams over the mountainside. All the cracks in the old house whistle, and the furnace cannot keep us toasty-warm. On those days I make soup, bake bread, and serve up casseroles for dinner. And I save the applesauce canning for those days, too. The steaming pots and jars warm the kitchen wonderfully.

Then suddenly the winds are quiet. We awaken to our first snowfall: usually just an inch or so, but enough to evoke the magic of an untouched world. Eagerly the boys trot out the sleds and polish the runners, and we all take our first run down the long sloping lawn. The nights are enchanted, glowing with moonlight and reflected snow. Screech owls hoot eerily about the mountaintop, and on a clear night we hear the baying of coon hounds. One night I awoke abruptly to the far-off singing-howling noise of the dogs. I opened the bedroom window wider to listen, gazing at the multitude of stars. The muffled distant sounds went on and on. Then there was a pause, two shots were fired, and silence came at last.

I wonder, though, why people need to hunt raccoons. And I remembered a sad sight one Thanksgiving. It was a particularly fine day, with an inch of snow on the ground. The view from the top of the first field was ethereal—the sun was shining on the isolated mountains, reddening them, while the valleys lay in deeply purpled cloud shadows. I entered the woods with Fritz leaping on ahead. Suddenly my joy was blunted by the sight of a dying raccoon on the path. It was the first raccoon I had seen on our mountain, although I often had discovered them down beside the river at night. It lay near a log, on its side, kicking its upper hind leg convulsively and licking the snow. Its eyes were open and alert, but I could see the suffering in them, too. Anxiously I turned home, calling Fritz before he could spot the sick animal.

As quickly as possible I summoned Bruce and the boys, and leaving Fritz in the basement we hurried back up to see if anything could be done for the raccoon. By then it had stopped licking snow and its eyes were almost closed. Steve stroked it, and we all spoke gently to the animal. It didn't struggle to escape us, and it almost seemed to sense our pity and our inability to help. There was no blood or any sign of attack nearby, and we watched it sigh its last breath, the victim of some illness. I have never forgotten those fine, intelligent eyes. Later I learned from the game warden that raccoons had been dying of disease. "But why do people hunt them?" I asked.

"Because they get $6 for every pelt," he replied. I had forgotten that animal's fur is more valuable than its life.

While I do hear some coon hunters, November on the mountain is mainly the month for wild turkey hunting. The local hunters all want the "real thing" to grace their holiday table. Our road is known as a good place to spot turkeys, and for weeks we are beseiged with hunters parking illegally on our roadside. Wherever Bruce goes he is questioned by eager men: "Seen any turkeys up your way?"

Once he had a marvelous tale to tell them. "I drove through a huge flock the other day, more than I could count before they flew off."

"Have your gun with ya?" one hunter asked.

"No, I didn't."

"Wish't ya had, I bet."

"Well, not exactly," Bruce replied. "I really wished I had my camera."

Seeing a large flock of wild turkeys is a rare occurrence, even in these days when turkeys have reappeared in all their old haunts and are gradually spreading into areas where they never lived before. Back in the 1880s wild turkeys were rare—they had been ruthlessly hunted and had been pushed off their traditional grounds by spreading settlements. The Pennsylvania Game Commission, formed in 1896, set out to prevent market hunting and to control the annual turkey kill. It purchased game lands as refuges for turkeys in the south-central mountains of the state, where they still survived. In 1930 it began a game farm, hoping to artificially propagate turkeys from half-wild breeders, but the experiment didn't work. The resultant turkeys were simply too tame and were unable to resist predation. Other states, meanwhile, were live-trapping totally wild turkeys and transporting them to depleted areas. This approach was and is so successful that turkeys are now found beyond the limits of their ancestral range.

Mating season for the turkeys begins in the spring. We can hear them gobbling on Sapsucker Ridge, although so far we have not been able to witness their courtship displays. After mating, the hens go off alone to lay their eggs in the forest. Once the poults are born, the mothers move them into clearings where they can find grass, insects, and water. In the late summer several broods combine to form a larger flock, which forages together for acorns and other nuts throughout the autumn. No doubt the flock that Bruce saw was such a grouping. As winter approaches the flocks break up into smaller groups again. Many toms remain in solitude, roosting alone in treetops, and several times I have startled a single roosting turkey at dusk. Once the snow falls I find the large turkey tracks in the woods and on the path between the first field and the far field. That area certainly has all the criteria the turkeys need—plenty of woods filled with oak trees, water seepage areas, clearings near the dense woods, and, except for us, total isolation.

Usually they are wary enough to be gone before we come near, but one blustery March day we went tramping through the woods with some friends.

"Turkeys!" Steve shouted.

We looked up in time to see several go flying out over the mountainside. One look for all of us was worth more than a thousand rifle shots, although I understand that wild turkeys make superb eating.

We are content to settle for a freshly killed domestic turkey on Thanksgiving Day, and usually a bevy of friends and relatives gather around the table. The entire holiday centers around food, certainly a skilled cook's shining hour of the year. In our home I always dig out the traditional recipes, and so do the guests who bring their own favorite dishes to add to the bounty. The feast begins with our home-canned grape juice. Then the turkey is brought on, stuffed with homemade cornbread and sausage. We always have a sweet potato casserole and a large cranberry salad, pumpkin muffins with elderberry jelly, and green beans with mushrooms. I proudly trot out the side dishes of chutney, corn relish, spiced apples, and canned applesauce. After polishing off the main courses, we turn to the desserts: my sister's special mince pie, my mother's fresh pumpkin pie, and my apple nut crumb pie. After the dishes are done, most of us go walking, sometimes in six inches of snow. In the evening we gather around the old organ to sing the Thanksgiving hymns. Invariably, though, someone will thumb on through the hymnal to the Christmas carols, and as one holiday ends another begins.

Deer hunting season begins the Monday after Thanksgiving, and it lasts for two weeks and two days with only Sundays off. Normally we stay out of the woods except on Sundays, although when I get stir crazy, I go walking anyway, making plenty of noise. Both we and our neighbors require hunters to park at the bottom of our road and hike up, so we are not overrun by them. Most of the ones that do walk up are polite and considerate, staying well up on the ridges, and only an occasional shot reminds us of the season.

One year, though, we did have an incident, or rather a series of them. A few days before hunting season was due to begin I set out for the Laurel Ridge Trail intending to explore down the left turn beyond our property line. The trees are much younger there and the land more open, and I hoped to see some deer. The sky was white—it was a penetratingly damp day— but it was a weekend, and I was free to wander for a few precious hours. As I neared the top of the ridge I heard a low roaring sound. "That certainly doesn't sound like any animal or bird I've ever heard before," I mused to myself and paused to listen more closely. Then I realized that what I was hearing was a motor. I went dashing on up but was too late to get even a glimpse of the noisemaker. However, traces of snow along the trail made tracking fairly easy. The vehicle had gone right, but I turned left, curious to discover how it had gotten up the mountain. I walked for at least a half mile before the trail petered out onto a wide open knoll. To my right a very steep, narrow, and leaf-clogged jeep trail wound precipitously down the mountain. The imprint of the tires was very plain to spot in the deep wet leaves.

I started back, eager now to see the culprit and find out just how far he had traveled on our trails. As I walked along I listened to incessant gunshots resounding up from Sinking Valley. Hunters were practicing for the "big day." Nearing the edge of our property line, I suddenly heard a motor coming toward me. Quickly I ducked into the woods, hidden from the occupants but able to see them as they cruised by. Two men sat tensed up in an ancient hand-painted green jeep, their eyes roving the woods, obviously watching for deer. As the jeep disappeared over a rise I continued on my way. Branches crushed, bushes bruised, and moss marred—all the growth showed signs of their passing. In several steep places they had skidded up the trail, doing great damage to the trailing arbutus and laurel bushes. Angrily I followed the tracks all the way to the far field where the trail ended, and they had been forced to turn back. Of course our trails had been originally built for access in case of fire, but I had never expected them to be used as public roads. We had reserved the trails for foot travelers, and I was upset as I contemplated the destruction of our peaceful refuge.

The next afternoon the jeep returned. This time it roared boldly up our main road, turned sharply left at the guest house corner, and clawed its way up the steep trail. I threw down my knitting, snatched up my hat and coat, and went running down to the road. Fritz bounded along as I started a mad dash up the trail after the vehicle. But of course by then the culprit was out of sight, and I was left with only my anger and a feeling of impotence. When I reached home the phone was ringing. Our neighbor had seen the jeep as it had driven past her place, but she had not recognized it. She agreed to give me a quick warning call the next time it came up.

The following day buck season officially opened. That afternoon the phone rang. Our neighbor, breathless with anger, warned, "They're on their way, and I know who they are now. They stopped to talk to me, and I told them to stay off the mountain with their jeep. But they said they are coming over to set you straight on a few things."

"I guess I'll gird my loins and go out to do battle," I replied. Quickly I pulled on my jacket, called to Fritz, and started outside. This time the jeep drove on up our driveway. A young man emerged cautiously, because Fritz was barking furiously, and I did not restrain him. Another fellow remained in the jeep, gazing indifferently ahead.

"We want to hunt on your property in our jeep," the young man began confidently.

I smiled but answered firmly, "I'm sorry, but we don't allow motorized vehicles on our trails. They erode the paths. We only permit people to walk on them."

He looked at me with disbelief and began to bluster. "Why my uncle used to work here, and he drove a jeep all over the place."

Again I smiled and said, "I hope we won't have to post our land and put chains across our road and trails, but we will if we can't keep cars away. It's too bad because this is prime hunting land." Apparently convinced by my threat of posting, he hastened back into his jeep and retreated down the road.

Two days later I was hanging out the clothes when Fritz suddenly erupted into a frenzy of barking. Walking down our driveway with their guns were an old man, a middle-aged man with a huge belly, and a small boy. I didn't restrain Fritz because I was annoyed at their nearness to the house. As they walked past I asked them politely to confine their hunting to the ridges. "Don't worry, lady," the middle-aged man replied, "we're heading up there now." Then the old man pointed at Fritz and piped up angrily, "You better keep that bugger tied. He's been chasing deer over the fields. I'll shoot him if I see him doing that."

"Did you see him chasing them?" I asked.

"Oh, no! But we saw the tracks."

I managed to hold my temper—after all, they were the ones with the guns. "Those tracks probably belong to a stray that was hanging around here this morning, or perhaps to the pack of wild dogs I've seen on the mountain." The old man continued to stare hostilely at me, muttering something as they walked off.

The more I thought of that encounter, the angrier I became. There they were, hunting on our land, telling me what to do, and threatening to shoot our dog on our property. Unfortunately, these are the same types of people that protest the loudest as more and more landowners post their property. They take it as their inalienable right to tramp over other people's fields and woods, to shoot at any moving object, and to drop their beer cans and candy wrappers wherever they go.

The Pennsylvania Game Commission works hard to promote good relations with the owners of prime deer country. Every November I can depend on a visit from our local game warden. The first year I was a bit overwhelmed by the individual attention. He drove up and asked if I had had any trouble with hunters.

"Just you take their numbers and call me. Don't tangle with them," he warned. "Most of the bad ones we know about," and he whipped out his list of people forbidden to hunt in the county. "They spoil it for all the rest, you know."

On and on we talked about the outdoors, swapping animal tales and bird stories. Eagerly I listened as he told me how he startled a big bear once.

"It was getting near dark, and I saw this big black hump near a tree. Quietly I circled around till I got in front of it, about thirty feet away. Then I hollered

'Boo!' and that bear reared up, about 300 pounds, biggest black bear I ever saw, turned, and went scooting up the mountain. You know, the older I get, the more I love the outdoors and nature," he added. Then he launched into tales about the Pennsylvania Game Commission, telling me how "we bought some more land over to Bald Eagle Mountain the other day. Almost own the whole mountain now." Because of the commission's aggressive and far-sighted policies, many Pennsylvania mountains belong to the people. And those that they don't own, they strive to keep open by fostering good relations with landowners.

So November and autumn go out in a volley of shots, and wintery December is saluted with more. Sharing our land for a little over two weeks each year is not too great a hardship, though I am glad when deer hunting season is finally over so I can return to my daily walks in peace.

Chapter 11

What Do You Do with Your Time?

OFTEN WHEN COUPLES visit us, as the man gazes about envying Bruce's existence, the woman will say to me, "It's very pretty up here, but I don't think I would like being so isolated. How can you stand being unable to get out in the winter—doesn't it drive you crazy? What do you do with your time?"

I mumble something polite about not minding it, about enjoying the peace and quiet and isolation. Afterwards I always reflect on their lives, which require the excitement of going places in their cars, the sustenance of commercially produced foods, and the thrill of televised entertainment. Then I reflect on our lives, which are filled with a variety of self-directed activities. All the things we do, in fact, keep to the rhythms of the seasons, with many of the same tasks performed at the same times each year. My life here is never boring, not even during the long, cold winter months when I am imprisoned by our icy road. In fact, it is then that I see things most clearly, because there are many winter days on the mountain in which I do very little but watch and walk and bask in the sun.

Once in late winter a day arrived without a definable pattern—it was not like February, as the calendar faithfully recorded, and it was certainly not like May, as the thermometer indicated. It had begun raining in the early morning, shrouding the mountain with mist and cloud. Yet there was a warm, soft feeling to the air. This was no cold winter rain but a balmy spring rain, gently falling on the thawing ground. Still I settled in for a rainy day. About 10 A.M. the rain began sheeting down, the downspouts gushed, and the wind flung the rain against the west-facing windows. An hour later the rain had slackened and, to my surprise, I noticed a ribbon of blue sky and puffy white clouds streaking toward the farm from the west. In a few minutes the sky had totally cleared. By then I had given up any idea of working indoors. The sun was shining, it was 70 degrees, and spring had come. I ran about flinging open doors and windows, letting in the soft, sweet air. I dragged my chaise lounge near the back porch and settled down to absorb the sunlight. The woods glittered with the reflected light of gleaming wet laurel leaves. Tree trunks and branches were shiny and scrubbed black from the rain. I squinted my eyes against all the incredible light from the open cleansed woods.

The clouds and wind, though, wrestled with the sunshine that whole day. Occasionally spatters of rain fell, but I remained immobile, watching the sudden proliferation of birds. In the balm of Gilead tree overhead the normally dominating, juvenile, red-headed woodpecker worked patiently and quietly. Then a quiet little brown creeper began skittering up the same tree. I wondered if the woodpecker would rout the smaller bird as he had other intruders. But when it came to the branch where the woodpecker was working, the brown creeper suddenly zoomed off to another tree and continued its unending quest for insects. I could not tell if it had changed trees because of red-headed woodpecker, because neither bird showed any outward signs of noticing the other.

I had been still for some time, and the chickadees and juncos came closer than usual. They, too, seemed stimulated by the unseasonable warmth. A few titmice began singing, while tree sparrows crowded the nearby bushes. Nuthatches "yank-yanked" up and down the tree trunks, and a busy downy woodpecker made a loud rattling noise as he banged industriously on a forsythia bush at the side of the house.

Then, suddenly, I heard a new note coming from the side yard. No winter bird sounded like that—such a familiar sound and yet so unfamiliar after several months of not hearing it. Slowly and cautiously I walked to the veranda, my eyes casting about for the origin of that loud call. There, high in a black walnut tree, perched a robin. I could scarcely believe its deep orange breast and black back, its matchless dignified poise, and its unseasonable appearance. I had not seen or heard a robin since early November—was this creature a maverick, a loner, and an adventurer, or had spring come prematurely?

Later, when I walked up to the muddy garden, the robin was running sedately over the thawing earth, looking plump and businesslike as robins always do. As I watched I heard another springlike call: the killdeer were screeching in the fields. I wandered along, hoping to see just one, to verify with my eyes what my ears were hearing. But always the sounds were far off, and I couldn't even catch a movement.

I walked on down the road and surprised a chipmink emerging groggily from its burrow. I stopped and watched as it sat eating nervously, keeping a wary eye on me. When I finally moved slowly on, it continued feeding in the warm sunlight, thinking no doubt that I had not seen its red-brown body against the brown earth. I counted it as a spring arrival also, because it had been sleeping since late autumn. Like me, it had been made restless by the balmy air and had come out to see if winter was actually over. For just that day winter had retreated, and I had been able to mark the advance of spring.

As winter days rapidly lengthen and the sun's rays warm the earth, I am able to sunbathe at the Sinking Valley overlook. Wearing a ski jacket and wool slacks to insulate myself from the cold ground, I lie down on a thick patch of moss, face the sun, and soak up the warmth for a half hour of lazy rapture.

Pennsylvania has at least a few good sunbathing days every month of the year. I never take my lawn chairs inside. Whenever the sky is clear and the thermometer is 40 degrees or more, I can face my chaise into the sun and enjoy a bit of summer. The therapeutic effect of such a simple act, especially in January or February, is amazing. Getting out of the stuffy house and lying in the winter sun is very satisfying.

I also get a lot of free entertainment. One warm January day I took the chaise out on the lawn, turning it to face the field and Sapsucker Ridge beyond. At first it was very quiet as I settled down with binoculars, pen, and paper. But as I sat still writing, I began to hear the wildlife resume normal activities. First the birds started calling and flitting nearby. They seemed to sense the lengthening of the days, and already they were tuning their pipes for the spring. The white-throated sparrow sounded rusty, but the organlike tones of the "tomtit" were beautifully polished and full.

Then I noticed a red squirrel dashing up and down a nearby walnut tree. With a careful eye on me, he raced to the hole at the base of the tree where he had cached his winter supply of black walnuts. Zooming back up to a safe branch, he gnawed away at a tough-shelled nut. Suddenly at the edge of the field two deer leaped gracefully through the grape vine tangle and then slowed to a leisurely walk.

Ears pricked up and white tails high, they watched my motionless figure. Finally they moved off, unhurried and unafraid. Later I saw four deer feeding in the corner of the pasture. In March the appearance of deer in that spot means the first blades of grass are showing, but when I went up to examine the area a little later in the day I found no signs of green.

Years ago, when we lived on a country road in Maine, deep snow covered the ground four months of the year. During that time the chaise was stored and there was no sunbathing. But in early March one small slope would melt before the rest of the land. On the first day with temperatures above freezing, I would troop up with the boys, then preschoolers, and bask in the sunlight. The only trouble was that I could be seen from the road, and I did get very peculiar stares from the local residents as they slowly drove past. They knew it was not spring yet, but apparently I, an outlander, did not.

Because of our present isolated location on top of the mountain, I can now sunbathe without a thought of spectators. One November, however, my recumbent figure at the powerline right-of-way startled an innocent hunter. Mark was sitting on the path building with stones, and Fritz, our dog, was off exploring. I was enjoying my favorite pastime when I heard a sudden noise. Lazily I opened my eyes. A very disconcerted man looked from Mark to me and said, "Lady, are you alright?"

"Of course," I replied, "I'm just sunbathing."

"Oh!" was all he said as he walked on quickly. After he disappeared along the ridge, I burst out laughing, realizing how ridiculous my reply must have sounded to him. He probably thought I was crazy, or at the very least, a little "woods queer." Too bad, I thought, that more people haven't discovered the fun of winter sunbathing. No need to go to Florida to get the benefit of the sun's rays. The same sun shines here, too. It is merely that the air is somewhat cooler!

Gradually, though, my time of peaceful walks and sunbaths ebbs away as spring slowly and hesitantly

The author and Mark sunbathe
at the top of the power line right-of-way.

makes its appearance. By then I am ready for a little action, and I pace impatiently through the many days of rain and fog. Often we live among the clouds, and instead of being elevated, we feel closed in. A rainy overcast day in the valley usually means thick mist and fog swirling around our home on the mountain. Waking up in the morning, we groan as we look out into a neutral world of gray and white.

After a while I almost become a victim of cabin fever. From inside the warm house the thought of going out into the gloom of yet another gray drizzly day dampens my already dismal spirits. Usually, though, I convince myself that I need the exercise, and donning slicker and boots, I go out for a look at the moist world. Once outside I am amazed at the fresh-smelling air and the stark beauty of a wet day.

One day I went walking just as the clouds lifted from around our home. It was still completely overcast, but at least the rain had stopped falling for a time. Everything was wet and sloshy on top of a frozen layer of earth and leaves, and occasionally I broke through the ground where it had begun to thaw. I moved along in utter silence, enveloped in the moist, heavy air, and paused at the Sinking Valley overlook. Most of the farmhouses below were clear of fog. A heavy cloud blanket covered the valley from our ridge to the nearby mountains.

When I was home again, the wind rose and a storm cloud came whirling toward the house. Suddenly it was very dark. The rain slashed with great force against the windows, and I could hear the roaring tumult of rushing water as it spilled out of the drainpipes and thundered through the ditches. Just as suddenly the cloud was gone, the rain eased and darkness lifted. The first time we were cloud-covered, Mark and I were very awed and a little frightened. Now I just say to him, "Here comes a cloud over us," and we wait and watch. But no matter how often it happens, it is still a unique and quieting experience to be cloud-smothered.

About mid-March we begin to think about daffodils and forsythia, especially when still another snow squall blows up. And sometimes we even think about heading south for a premature spring. One year we actually succumbed to temptation, took the boys out of school, locked up the place, and went to see our nation's capital.

Many years before we had left Washington, D.C., "forever." Wiping the soot ungratefully from our feet, we had headed for a new rural life in central Maine. Our three years in the capital had been long enough—too long, in fact. We were finished with cities and crowds; we were tired of living in fear.

When we had lived in Washington we enjoyed seeking out all the green places—the parks, the botanical gardens, the National Arboretum, and the many natural areas Louis Halle wrote about in his classic book *Spring in Washington*. In 1945 Halle had set out on his bicycle to record the coming of spring to the capital, and we found, when we lived there twenty years later, that many of the places he had visited were still intact. The same beauties could still be appreciated; the same species of birds still sang.

On the first day of our visit the city welcomed us with hazy warmth, the bright yellow of forsythia, and the deep rose of flowering magnolia trees. With daffodils blooming at every doorstep and the thermometer at 75 degrees, it looked as if spring had indeed come to Washington. We set out for the National Zoo, located in the heart of Rock Creek Park, a beautiful woodland refuge that winds through the city. During Lincoln's second inaugural in 1865, John Burroughs observed that "Rock Creek has an abundance of all the elements that make up not only pleasing, but wild and rugged scenery. There is, perhaps, not another city in the Union that has on its very threshold so much natural beauty and grandeur." All the birds that Burroughs wrote about in his book *Wake-Robin* can still be seen in the park. As we drove slowly along the winding road we spotted numerous wild mallards swimming in the creek, their green heads shining in the sun.

The following day we awoke to plunging temperatures and howling winds. All the flowering plants looked cold, and we huddled along in our coats from one museum to another. Ascending the long flight of stairs to the Capitol Building was a real struggle, so we conducted the rest of our historical tour in the car. The Tidal Basin at the Jefferson Memorial was a churning mass of crashing waves. A few cherry trees were prematurely blooming; a few herring gulls risked the waves. But the ducks, grebes, and loons that we used to see there were probably in some protected cove along the Potomac River.

Our last sentimental stop was Roaches Run, a water-fowl sanctuary on the Virginia side of the river, tucked away between the National Airport, the Washington Memorial Parkway, and some railroad tracks. The sanctuary was always noisy with the jets, cars, and trains, but the ducks never seemed to mind. It was there that we had seen our first wild pintails, American mergansers, and the comical coot. To our dismay, that week the wind and waves kept the waterfowl away, but we were pleased to see that the sanctuary still existed as it had when we lived there. Then we went on to the airport to watch the manmade "birds" swoop in and out, undeterred by the elements. "So that's a city," Mark commented. "Let's go home!" And we did.

Eventually, though, our Pennsylvania spring does come, with warmth and sunshine. During May I move the rockers out to the porch and begin one of my favorite activities—porch-watching. The porch, nestled in the tree tops, makes a wonderful bird blind. Stretched out on the chaise lounge, binoculars near at hand, I settle down expectantly.

From the huge lilac bush at the left of the porch comes the mewing of a catbird. Periodically it is interrupted by the excited nervous twittering of the house wrens. Occasionally, too, a brilliant goldfinch or a masked yellowthroat will join the chorus. One afternoon the lilac bush filled up with male and female goldfinches which were twittering so loudly that they actually made my ears ring with their noise.

Once I have determined the contents of the lilac bush, my eyes scan the sweeping lawn far below me. If it is dandelion time, I can be assured of a visual treat. Not at all concerned with territorial rights, four indigo buntings, two chipping sparrows, and numerous goldfinches eat the dandelion seeds. They land on the tall stems and ride them to the ground, then they feed easily from the fallen heads. One beautiful day in mid-May two migrating white-crowned sparrows joined the banquet, resting on their long journey to northern Canada.

The four large locust trees that encircle the porch usually shelter several species of birds which are easily seen because the porch is so high above the ground. The foliage of the locusts is thin in comparison with the maples and oaks, and several branches of one tree almost touch the porch. If I sit very still, I am apt to be rewarded by the sight of several different birds perching nearby. One day a yellowthroat landed, followed closely by a scarlet tanager and a goldfinch. Frequently downy woodpeckers and white-breasted nuthatches probe for insects along the locust trunks, while blue jays, robins, wood thrushes, and song sparrows use the branches as brief caroling posts. Occasionally the common songsters are upstaged by a brilliant newcomer. Once I heard a more beautiful song than all the rest:

something like a Baltimore oriole, only more complete. Excitedly I scanned the trees with my binoculars and finally located the mysterious singer. First I saw his back, primarily black but highlighted with white and beige. Then he turned and displayed a deep rose breast below his neck, accented by his white belly. I was being serenaded by a rose-breasted grosbeak. He sang for ten minutes before flying off toward the garden.

Sometimes I turn my attention to the fence and the watery ditch beside the road. Almost always a phoebe is perched on the fence, flicking its tail. Generally it is the female phoebe taking a break from brooding her eggs. The indigo buntings and goldfinches also use the fence as a resting place. Often they dip down to the ditch for a drink and a refreshing bath. Sometimes the chipping sparrows and Baltimore orioles use the ditch also. One year a pair of red-winged blackbirds decided to nest on the mountain, and every afternoon I would hear a few loud "Okalees" as the male would swoop down and give himself a vigorous bath.

Finally I scan the balm of Gilead tree outside the guest house for a glimpse of the flickers and Baltimore orioles that nest there. Then I range along the line of red maples beside the driveway. Suddenly I see a flash of red and black as the scarlet tanager flits among the branches of a maple tree. I debate with myself—is the scarlet tanager the loveliest of all the birds? What about the indigo buntings, the goldfinches, and the Baltimore orioles? All are so brightly beautiful that I cannot decide.

When at last I become satiated with color and movement, I settle back and close my eyes. Even then I cannot rest. I am busy putting a name to all the bird calls. That loud, penetrating noise is a great-crested flycatcher. The warbling is a robin's song. "Drink your tea," the towhees call incessantly from the grape tangle. Then suddenly the sound of a giant bumblebee comes terribly close. My eyes pop open in time to see a ruby-throated hummingbird zip off. If I want a nap, the porch is no place to take one. Not for a bird watcher, that is.

By the middle of May, though, porch-watching is a rare treat. Mostly I am caught up in planting the garden and freezing the early crops: rhubarb and dandelion greens. From then until November, food raising and preserving occupies the major portion of my time. While Bruce gets started on the rototilling and planting, the lawn mowing, and the big outdoor projects of the year, I do all the garden planning, hand weeding, harvesting, and preserving. Each spring we both feel as if there is never time enough to do all that needs to be done.

During May, however, the wanderlust comes heavily to all of us, and sometimes we break away from our work to take walks, either alone or as a family. Once in a great while Bruce and I go off by ourselves to explore the mountain. One particularly beautiful cool Memorial Day, we asked Bruce's mother to babysit so we could go for a walk. Setting off at 10 A.M., we told her we would be back by lunchtime. But once we were on our way, we were unable to turn around. The day lured us on and on—along the mountain ridge, past the far field, and through the trees that boldly marked our property line. We clambered over a rock-strewn hill and entered the environs of a hunting lodge. A turkey gobbled loudly not far away. In a few minutes, as we neared a tiny sun-lit meadow, the turkey gobbled again. Quickly we sat down, straining our eyes for a look at the gobbler. As we waited quietly, the turkey gobbled once more. This time the sound came from the opposite side of the meadow. Finally Bruce inched up to the meadow's edge, screened by some bushes, while I stayed seated. We hoped that the gobbler would strut across that meadow, but although we waited for over a half hour, we didn't see or hear him again. Reluctantly we walked on along a wide grassy jeep trail with large fields on either side and a beautiful view of other mountains. As if to mock us, the turkey gobbled several times. He had obviously moved off when he realized we were watching for him.

The hunting lodge property was very different from ours—almost like a mountain park, with cornfields plowed and randomly seeded for the deer. In the woods there was very little underbrush, no blueberries or blackberries, and not even any laurel bushes to screen the deers' passing. Many large apple trees were scattered about for fine deer food, and we noticed a huge flowering dogwood blooming in a sunny spot beside the rusting hulk of an old stripped car.

Eventually we left the property and continued on along the crest of the mountain—a very narrow ridge that plunged down steeply on both sides. Along one side the trees were plastered with "no trespassing" signs. About all we could see beyond the signs was the steep drop-off, and we wondered exactly what the jealous landowner was protecting. We were hiking on a well-kept foot trail that led to an enormous rock slide. As I clung to a picturesque rock, Bruce snapped my profile against the background of a magnificent sweeping view of the valley and Allegheny Mountains beyond. The footpath threaded on through the tumbled rocks for several hundred yards before it dipped back into the woods for a short span. Then we went onto the first road that crosses the mountain, nearly four miles from our home. Cars whizzed along as we hiked down the road, and we got many peculiar stares. "Why walk when you can ride?" the stares seemed to mean.

At the bottom of the mountain we walked through a neat, well-kept little village, each backyard filled with irises, peonies, and a prospering vegetable garden. But despite the "drive carefully, we love our children" signs and the low speed limit, cars streaked past at 60 miles per hour, destroying the peace of the quiet village.

Somehow we missed the dirt road that leads back up the mountain to the hunting lodge. Instead we hiked along a small country road through Sinking Valley, which paralleled a stream and the mountain. Only an occasional slow car drifted past. Once we passed a large farm family with seven children of various ages playing baseball.

"Hey! You got a girlfriend," one bold little fellow called out.

"Does he mean you?" I asked Bruce.

"There's nobody else but us around," Bruce said, grinning. Well at that point, my almost thirty-four-year-old body straightened up.

"We must really look young," I bragged happily.

"Or maybe he figures that only young lovers would be off walking by themselves," Bruce replied.

By then some rarely used muscles were beginning to ache, and I searched eagerly for our powerline right-of-way as a route back up the mountain. Despite my "youthful appearance," my sagging bones needed a rest. We sat down beside the stream in a delicious bed of highly aromatic mint and, after sampling some mint leaves, we finished the water in our canteens. I was becoming anxious to get home, because it was well after two in the afternoon and we had had no lunch.

But the powerline right-of-way was still a distance away, and we trudged through fields, pleased to get a long look at a killdeer. Once I saw a female red-winged blackbird fly up, and I found her exquisite nest woven inside a protecting circle of tall weeds. It contained two light beige eggs with delicate brown tracings on them which were reminiscent of Chinese calligraphy.

Our cool day had grown hot as we finally reached the base of the powerline. The climb up was fierce, steep, and breathless for me as I clung to Bruce's hand and stumbled through the seemingly endless brush. Lungs bursting and heart pounding, I gratefully reached the top and the welcome soft coolness of our shaded, moss-covered trail. How quiet our mountain seemed after the hustle of the valley.

Such interludes are very welcome during the bustle of spring. Some years are more hectic than others, though, especially the year we received a phone call from Bruce's parents in early April. They had just sold their large country home in New Jersey and wanted to make their summer home in our guest house. They planned to move in on June 1.

"Just get somebody to wallpaper the place, and we'll put in a modern kitchen when we get there," they requested cheerily. I groaned to Bruce.

"They don't know how hard it is to get anyone to do anything around here." But I went ahead, trying to choose appropriate wallpaper and to browbeat a local service person into doing the job. It wasn't easy, especially when Mom gave me samples of all the curtains she had for the various rooms. Pop's was particularly difficult—large, flowered, blue and purple curtains—and I finally settled on an uneven blue-striped pattern. Getting the serviceperson to come was even harder, but at last he began work on Memorial Day.

In the meantime Bruce was quietly going crazy. His parents had hired an enormous moving van to lug the entire contents of their huge house and a furnished

garage apartment into our barn until they could purchase a winter home in Georgia. There was only one
problem: the barn roof had begun leaking badly. We
could not afford to hire someone to put on a new roof,
so Bruce squared his shoulders, got hold of some books
on barn roofing, and ordered supplies. We also could
not afford to buy a forty-foot ladder. After thinking
about it, Bruce chained two heavy wooden ladders
together, and I helped him hoist them up against the
roof. It was ticklish heavy work. The jeep was parked
next to the ladders as a further brace, and Bruce clambered up with his bucket of asphalt, nails, and roofing
paper. I watched below with sinking heart. That roof
was devilishly high. The first part was comparatively
easy, though, with just a gentle slope, and Bruce went
cheerily to work. Usually he would manage to get only
a small portion finished before it would begin raining or become so hot that he would have to retreat.
But when the weather was not right, which was almost
every weekend, Bruce occupied himself by drawing up
plans for a modern kitchen in the guest house which he
and Pop would install themselves. And then, of course,
there was the inevitable garden work and lawn cutting.
Life had become very complicated indeed.

Eventually, though, the first part of the roof was finished, and I looked up doubtfully at the second part,
which was too steep to even stand on. "Now what?"
I wondered. But Bruce began hammering and sawing
and quickly built himself a bench. Then he threw long

heavy ropes over the barn roof to anchor to the jeep on the other side. By moving the car from one side to the other, he could adjust the location of his support scaffold. As a further safety measure, he looped a nylon rope from the cupola to his waist. Then he was set to go again. But it was nearing June, the guest house was only partially papered, the barn roof still leaked at the ridge, and the guest house kitchen still had its old coal stove with a gaping hole in the ceiling above it.

A few days later Bruce's parents drove up. "You'll have to stay with us awhile," I said.

"Oh well," they answered, and carried in their suitcases. "The moving van is coming in two days," they added. "Is the barn roof finished?"

"Are you kidding?" Bruce asked. So they sighed gently and went out to buy plastic sheeting to cover their possessions.

The giant moving van arrived in town early on Sunday morning, but with all its roaring, straining effort it could only make it about 700 feet up our steep, narrow, twisting, and very muddy dirt road. After agonizing its way back down, scraping against the mountain on one side and hanging over the ravine on the other, the van charged up again for a second try, only to slip to a halt a few hundred feet further up. By late afternoon it rested, sighing in defeat, at the bottom of the mountain. So Bruce and the three moving men went off to the city for a smaller rental truck, which they used to transfer the furniture from the van up the mile and a half road to the barn. The black wild night was punctuated with thunderstorms as they brought load after load up in the twenty-two-foot rental truck, and the moving men, who had never been far from Trenton before, were terrified of everything, especially the wildlife they imagined to be lurking everywhere. But finally at dawn the saga ended as they closed the big barn doors on the last load.

Next Pop and Bruce turned to remodeling the guest house kitchen. They removed an old window and installed a new one designed to fit above the new sink. They replastered much of the walls and ceiling and installed new built-in cabinets, including a wall oven and countertop range unit, doing all the wiring and plumbing themselves. When the wall and ceiling paper was finally hung and a new vinyl flooring was laid, Mom was happy to go to work in her new kitchen with its panoramic view of the woods, field, and stream spread out below. And Bruce was free to return to the dangerous tyranny of the barn roof.

By that time it was mid-July, and I was deeply involved in freezing peas and harvesting black raspberries. In fact, for more than two weeks each July I exist in a haze of black raspberries. Early each morning I don long pants and rubber boots, snatch up my large berrying pail, and hasten out into the cool quiet day to pick the berries. The boys are still asleep, Bruce is off to work, and I have a peaceful time to pick and watch the day advance.

Very quickly the dew soaks me to my hips, and my dungarees cling to me. My bare arms and hands are a welter of ugly red scratches. An occasional buzzing mosquito finds me a juicy target. But I feel joyous as I plop quart after quart of the enormous black caps into my pail. Now and then birds protest my invasion of their larder. The crows are especially loud in their abuse, and the towhees move reluctantly away as I approach them.

But they are not the only creatures that enjoy the feast.

One morning, as I followed a deer trail along the edge of a patch near the woods and watched a cottontail rabbit startle off through the brush, I instinctively sensed that I was very close to another living creature. Right above me a long, shiny, black snake lay twined among the prickly branches, waiting quietly for an unwary bird to alight. We paused and watched each other, he unblinking and I with a racing heart. I stood motionless as slowly, slowly he undulated himself backward and away. Soon he was gone, and I was alone again.

Other creatures find the berry patch just as attractive as the snakes do. Large American toads often wait there to eat the many kinds of bugs that live among the berries. I frequently see swarms of black ants on the sweet black raspberries or mottled-brown froghoppers jumping along the raspberry leaves. Most common, though, are the prowling daddy longlegs, or harvestmen. They sit on berries, surrounding them with all their thin black legs, and I have to brush them away as I pick. They glide quickly off, wanting to cause no trouble, for there are always more raspberries to sit on.

Another morning, as I pushed my body through a particularly heavy tangle, seeing only the large black fruit just a bit beyond my grasp, I felt a small movement at my toe. A large, shiny, wet, box turtle lay at my feet, its head and neck outstretched, eating the berries. I was careful not to disturb him in his chosen patch, because he, too, is entitled to the fruit that neither of us had any part in growing. Box turtles make themselves gluttons over the berries, just as we do. Sometimes they eat so many that they do not have room under their shells for their back feet and tails.

We all eat our way happily through black raspberry season. We have them with cereal in the morning and with honey and milk at lunch. In the evening I experiment with more complex recipes—cold fruit soup, pie, custard, and cobbler. And then, so we will not forget their goodness over the long winter months, I freeze several dozen pints. When I take those boxes out later I will remember the sounds, the smells, the sights, and the beauty I saw in the berry patch on warm July mornings. Perhaps this memory will be the most precious harvest I have reaped.

No sooner does black raspberry season end then I am into blackberries and blueberries. Every day I harvest in the cool morning hours and after sunset—

there is no time for walks, because so much needs to be done.

Finally, when Bruce begins cutting lawns in his sleep and I start picking blackberries in my dreams, we decide that it is time to take a vacation. One August we found ourselves headed north on a bright blue Saturday morning, off to visit old friends who owned an island in the Georgian Bay, an eastern extension of Lake Huron.

We met our friends in Parry Sound, Ontario, a bustling little tourist town halfway up the eastern shore of the Georgian Bay. Parking our car in town, we transferred our gear to their large, inboard-outboard cruiser. Once we were out of the harbor it seemed strange to see water that stretched over the horizon but was fresh and pure enough to drink, to see large oceangoing vessels and no ocean and, strangest of all, to see birds of the lakeshore and those of the ocean intermingling. Seagulls soared overhead, common terns dove down into the water, and black ducks quacked away at our approach. All around us were the innumerable large and small green knobs of land that help make up the 30,000 islands of the Georgian Bay. The day was beautiful and clear, but there was a brisk wind, enough to make novice boat travelers a bit nervous as we smacked into the small waves at 35 miles per hour.

Fourteen miles south of Parry Sound we docked on a three-acre island called Budopecong, an Indian name meaning "place where the alders grow." After a tour of the island and a swim in the clear cool water of the bay, we set off in a canoe to look for beaver dams. As evening approached we slowly and silently paddled along the wooded shores of several islands. Soon we landed on a small rocky ledge and set off to explore a boggy area. Mosquitoes hummed about us as we pushed our way through the brush. Just as we neared some open water, we suddenly heard a loud slap—the beaver warning signal. Emerging on the shore of the pond, we saw not only a beaver dam but the beaver as well, swimming toward his lodge with a stick in his mouth. Standing motionless, we watched him through binoculars. Only when he neared his home did he dive underwater into the tunnel that led up to his lodge. No doubt the stick he was carrying would be added to his winter food supply. Reluctantly we withdrew to the canoe as the mosquitoes became too much for us.

During the three days we were on the island we were kept busy observing and identifying the varied bird life of the Georgian Bay. On one boat trip a huge silent bird of prey flapped overhead. When I saw the white head and prominent black mask, I knew we had seen the now rare osprey, or fish hawk. Once a very common bird, its numbers have decreased because of pesticides. Tiny fish that eat the poisoned insects are eaten by larger fish. The osprey eat those fish, thereby getting the poison into their own bodies. This seems to inhibit fertility, and it causes the eggs that are laid to have soft shells. We felt privileged to see this rare bird in a relatively wild setting.

We frequently saw common loons around the islands, and their weird yodeling calls in the early hours of the dawn—one of the most thrilling sounds of the north—woke us out of our sound sleep each morning. But even the common loon is becoming threatened by the activities of humans. Their nests, which are built in mounds of debris at the edges of quiet coves, are being swamped and destroyed by the wakes of powerful motorboats.

On the last day of our visit we went on an expedition out to Pomeroy Island, located at the edge of the open Georgian Bay. The Precambrian shield, an extremely old and very hard granite that forms much of Ontario, is easy to examine and study on the wind and wave swept ledges of this ten-acre island. The boys climbed, shrilled, and swooped over the beautifully striped rocks, but they paused with us to study the patches of yellow lichen and the tiny pools of red algae. Round-leaved sundew, a tiny insect-eating plant, and the blue flowers of brook lobelia provided additional contrast to the weathered rocks. White and red cedars thrived in the crevices and small patches of acid soil, but the blueberry bushes, which grew everywhere, were withered and yellow from a month-long drought.

As we sat on the ledges having a picnic, we heard the low rumblings of distant thunder. We fled for the boat and raced back to Budopecong, arriving just as the sheets of rain brought the drought to an end. The

days of unending sunshine were over—and so, regret-
fully, was our vacation interlude.

Such interludes, though, are rare with us, especially
during the busy summer and autumn months. Besides,
as many of our visitors point out, we already live in a
vacationer's paradise. The trouble is that our home and
land needs constant upkeep and improvement, and our
minds brim over with all we can and must do here.

The boys, though, see our place in a different light.
One dark windy night Bruce came home from work
and announced that the road was washing away badly
from the rain and melting snow. A stream running
off the mountain had been unable to flow through a
badly plugged culvert, and it was roaring across the
road instead. After a quick dinner, he and Steve set
off in the jeep to dig out the rocks and debris and
open the entrance to the culvert. Two hours later,
weary and soaked to the skin, they returned. Later
Bruce told me about it.

"It took a lot longer than I expected, and I began
grumbling about it to Steve. But he said quickly, 'Oh,
Dad, it's still worth it to live up here.' "

All the boys think the mountain is an exciting place
to live. Not once have any of them complained about a
lack of playmates. And surprisingly, neither Steve nor
David have had any social problems in school. In fact,
Steve has always been gregarious, and David has been
able to handle anyone, even bullies, with a few well-
chosen words. But they are happiest when they get off

the school bus on Fridays and know that they have the whole glorious weekend ahead of them. Occasionally friends of the boys will walk up for a weekend visit, but mostly they are each other's best friends.

Our fourth winter on the mountain, when Steve was almost 11 and Mark had just turned 5, a very close relationship sprang up between the two. Both boys have similar exuberant personalities, but Mark was willing to let his big brother lead. Previously Steve had taken several long solitary hikes down into the valley. David had never been interested in really long walks; he preferred to stay on our own trails and poke around quietly. Then one day Steve said, "Do you want to come with me, Mark?" Mark's face was jubilant. Tucking apples in their pockets, they headed down the road. Five hours later they returned full of tales. They had walked down our mountain, crossed the highway, and wound their way up the next mountain to the radio tower. Then they had circled back down, wandered over the valley roads, and come back up our road, a total of nearly seven miles according to the geological survey maps. I looked at Mark's short sturdy legs and wondered at his strength.

But several weeks later they took off again, and despite my entreaties, they still took just two apples. "We won't be gone that long," Steve assured me as they set off across the first field at ten in the morning. It was January, but as the day progressed the cloudy sky cleared and the thermometer hit 65 degrees. David and I walked and sunbathed, and eventually we had a late lunch without the two hikers. As the hours passed, I tried not to worry. Steve was trustworthy, he knew the mountain, and there would be no snakes abroad despite the warm weather. But as the clock hands crept past 4:30 and the daylight began to wane, I grew more upset. Surely they couldn't have been walking so long. Finally I went out to take down the clothes, wondering desperately where we should begin searching. And then I heard Steve's voice coming from down the road. "Come on, Mark—we're almost home."

"Where have you been?" I called down joyfully.

"Oh, Mom, we saw a huge flock of turkeys," Steve answered happily. Later we traced their hike on our maps. They had followed the mountain ridge down past the hunting lodge to the first road that crosses over the mountain—the same route Bruce and I had taken on Memorial Day. Then they had hiked down to the village to play with friends Steve had made on a previous walk. After a time they had started back along the valley, but instead of coming back up the powerline right-of-way, as Bruce and I had done, they had followed on out around the end of the mountain and come up our road—a total of eleven miles, Bruce discovered on the map.

"Aren't you tired, Mark?" I asked.

"Oh, no," he answered. "Come on, Steve, let's play Parcheesi."

David is quiet and introspective, and he enjoys the title of curator that his brothers conferred on him because of his interest and work in the corn crib museum. Every guest we have is led down along the brick and gravel walk which David laid up to the metal edifice. As soon as anyone enters they notice the gently swaying multicolored clumps of sea whip that hang picturesquely from the rafters. And they also exclaim over the shell collection neatly spread out on three old tabletops. The Maine, New Jersey, Florida, Georgia, and Hawaii coasts are all represented because our visitors usually remember the boys and their museum wherever they travel.

Anything and everything may be found there at one time or another: David's string sculptures, a huge hunk of anthracite coal, and an Australian aboriginal boomerang. Steve keeps his coin collection in the museum, including a particularly interesting 1864 two-cent piece that he discovered on our driveway. Many of the display shelves are old bureaus that we found in the barn. When we removed their drawers they made perfect display cabinets. One venerable old specimen contains the highlight of the museum—four shelves of animal skulls. It is particularly amusing to watch visitors as Mark enthusiastically points out the small skull of a woodchuck and the enormous one of a horse.

"But how do you know that it is a woodchuck skull?" they inevitably ask.

"Oh," Mark answers cheerfully, "we saw Fritzie kill it, then we waited till it rotted and dried, and we brought it here."

Other bureaus and tables are filled with rocks and fossils, birds' nests, pine cones, a bleached turtle shell, and uninhabited hornets' nests—everything, in fact, to delight a boy's heart. And it is kept cleaner and neater than their bedrooms. On rainy days David troops down to rearrange and sweep up, sometimes joined by his brothers. But he feels, being curator, that he has the final say in running the museum. Occasionally this leads to bickering, though usually his brothers respect his judgment. In the spring he plants flowers in front of the museum. One year a friend gave us a hundred moonflower plants, which I helped David set out in a large oval. Then we filled the center with transplanted marigolds. The boys waited eagerly until August, when the marigolds started blooming. But they were even more excited the first evening that the large white moonflowers opened. Every night they proudly counted the blooms of this night-flowering plant, and they were especially pleased when the moonflowers kept their blossoms throughout the gloomy days. Fostering many of their interests, the corn crib museum remains one of the focal points of the boys' existence on the mountain.

We have tried to give them a sense of adventure and independence by allowing them to do such things as taking long hikes on their own at fairly early ages, a privilege that apparently very few children have today. Steve caused a minor sensation the first time he appeared in a village five miles away. The parents of the boy he was talking to asked him where he came from, and when he gestured at the mountain, they were dumbfounded. In fact, they were so curious that they drove him home just to see where he lived.

We are continually amazed at the lack of confidence modern parents have in their children, and we are astonished by the fears most townpeople have toward country living. When we first moved to the country in Maine, we were barraged by a battery of "what if" questions from well-meaning friends and relatives. "What if one of the boys gets sick and Bruce is at work?" (In Maine we only had the one car.) "What if you have an accident out there all by yourself?" "What if you are snowed in and the electricity goes off?" And so forth. A number of these "what if" propositions did occur, but we always managed to cope successfully.

Here my isolation is much greater, particularly in the wintertime. And Bruce is much farther away when he is at work—almost unreachable during crises. Luckily I have had only one time of sheer panic since we have lived on the mountain.

It was a matchless first day of spring. Geese barked overhead as they headed north, crows constantly cawed across the fields, and one bluebird heralded the new day. I bustled about happily, hanging up clothes with Mark's help and then going inside to bake custard. Mark came in to watch, but he quickly went back outside. A little later I went out to drink my coffee in the sunshine. That was when I noticed the silence. The birds sang and the squirrels scolded, but I heard no cheery talking sounds of a four-year-old boy and his puppies. "Probably just went up to the powerline right-of-way with the pups," I thought, because Mark had recently begun taking short hikes by himself. Nevertheless, I could always tell what trail he was on by his singing voice. I listened extra hard; still there were no sounds. One of the pups came sniffing up, but Bobbin and Frisky were gone. They were with him, no doubt. I tried to relax and wait, but as time passed and I heard nothing from Laurel Ridge, I grew uneasy. Suddenly all the possible dangers to a little boy off by himself became magnified to great proportions in my mind. Grabbing my binoculars, I walked about the immediate vicinity of the buildings, calling and searching. My calls echoed hollowly off Sapsucker Ridge, and I felt truly alone for the first time since we had come here.

"Maybe he hurt himself in the barn," I worried, and I ran to see. Searching the barn from top to bottom and calling desperately brought no relief. He seemed to be nowhere at all. Desolation swept over me, and I searched the nearby fields with my binoculars. A large pile of dirt caught my eye. It had been left by the backhoe two years before when we had made a seven-foot deep test hole for a possible pond site. Eventually it had filled in with water, and the boys had been warned to stay away from the straight-sided hole. But as I looked, I panicked. I dashed down the road and across the stream. Then I stopped. I could not bear to climb the fence and actually peer down into the murky water. Besides, there was no sign of the pups.

As I walked sorrowfully back, I noticed Mark's tricycle parked between the springhouse and the old well. My heart lurched, and I dashed over, tore open the springhouse door, and looked into the muddy two-inch depth of water. Of course he couldn't be there, my mind reasoned, but my emotions were totally ruling me now. I thought I heard the faint sound of a child's voice up on Laurel Ridge, and I raced to the top as if possessed, my heart pounding. The crows were screeching about something. Could it be Mark and the pups?

The ridge was empty when I finally reached the top. I had to wait several minutes to quiet my breathing before I could call again. Nothing, not even an echo this time: just the desperate sound of a frightened woman. I ran along Laurel Ridge Trail, still hopeful that I might meet him, but when I reached the Dump Trail, I reluctantly headed home. Nameless fears tortured me—fruitlessly I swept the woods with my binoculars. He was so little to be alone.

Then I had a sudden surge of hope: he must be home by now, probably looking for me. But the house was dark and empty. He had been gone almost two hours. Reluctantly, unwillingly, I called our neighbor, trying desperately to keep my voice steady. As usual she was optimistic and comforting, and she promised to search around her place. Bleakly I went out to stand helplessly and look at the barren fields and woods. How tenuous were the strands that bound me joyfully to this place. If I lost Mark I knew I would hate the mountain—I could no longer live here.

And then Bobbin bounced into view. "Where were you?" I asked joyfully, as Frisky came tearing up behind. Finally Mark burst into sight—pink-cheeked, vibrant, and beautiful. But he stopped uncertainly when I cried, "Where have you been?" He heard the panic in my voice, and he stood dumbly, refusing to answer. Patiently I curbed my anxiety to give him confidence.

"To the far field," he muttered uncertainly.

"But you never went there before. Why didn't you tell me?"

"I guess I won't go walking again," he said resentfully. I knelt down gratefully and hugged his sturdy body. And after a while, he told me about his hike.

"I wanted to see the view from the top of the first field," he said. "And then I went on to the far field. I climbed the hill there, too," he added proudly. I praised his efforts, and I emphasized that after this he must tell me before he went off. Finally I noticed how very beautiful the day was.

Chapter 12
A New Life

FOR YEARS PROMINENT environmentalists have warned of impending energy shortages. In recent years the increase in the price of imported oil has plunged the United States into a dramatic fuel shortage. Like so many other Americans, we began to carefully examine our own energy uses. Both houses were heated with oil and equipped with a surplus of electrical appliances. Furthermore, Bruce had a long way to commute to work each day. So one by one we began hacking away at the problems. Bruce placed a classified advertisement in the local paper and was able to start a car pool. As a result, when gasoline doubled in price, our gas bills remained even lower than before. We turned our thermostats down to 60 degrees and saved money to buy storm windows and insulation for the house. In addition, we made plans to incorporate wood-heating stoves and fireplaces into our home as we fixed up the downstairs rooms.

As for electricity, we made a list of absolute priorities: which electrical appliances were most important and which were not. Obviously the water pump and hot water heater were essential, although we saved on both as much as we could. And I am fond of my refrigerator, freezer, electric stove, and washer. But I decided I could do without my clothes dryer and my dishwasher. A couple of lines in the basement during the winter solved the clothes-drying problems, and I never have minded washing dishes. We did not own many of the smaller electric gadgets, but I conscientiously wrestled over the use of the blender, the portable mixer, and the waffle iron. Whenever possible, I used arm power rather than electric power, and gradually our kilowatt-hours usage went down. Someday, perhaps, we will be able to invest in solar and wind power, but until then we are trying hard not to waste anything.

At about the same time that people were becoming energy conscious, the environmentalists predicted that overpopulation and fertilizer shortages would lead to massive famines. Many humanitarians started pleading with us to help, and a book entitled *Diet for a Small Planet* by Frances Moore Lappé offered some interesting new ideas. She maintained that we could no longer consume meat in large quantities, because it was a wasteful way of getting protein. All that grain used to feed animals could be used instead to feed people, in combination with eggs, cheese, rice, milk, beans, and nuts. In other words, she espoused a highly sophisticated vegetarian diet. Various humanitarian groups exhorted us to have meatless days or even days of fasting so the starving peoples could have the food we didn't eat on those days. Coupled with this, of course, were the skyrocketing food prices. We began to rethink our eating habits and, indeed, our whole philosophy of peaceful coexistence with all creatures. Previously our family had been content to let butchers do our killing for us, although we had always eaten what is called "low on the cow," for example, liver, hamburger, and chuck roasts. We had never been able to afford expensive cuts of meat, and our meals had always tended toward casseroles, fish, and chicken, with occasional treats of pork chops and ham roasts. I was already an expert on home-baked beans, cheese soufflés, and soup. No bones were ever wasted in our kitchen. They only reached the dogs after the soup was made.

Still we were consuming meat. During the meat boycott, I whimsically joined in, using it as an excuse to test out vegetarian recipes on the family. And after a week of such fare we all had very mixed feelings. Some of the dishes, usually those that contained large quantities of eggs, cheese, and milk, were delicious to our palates. But others, particularly the ground nut loaves, were unacceptable. Clearly we wanted some meat in our diets: we were absolutely starved for a juicy hamburger or a fat sausage.

Then we looked at our lovely land and realized that our lives as romantic naturalists would have to be tempered. If we used our land well, farmed it organically, raised our own animal feed, and slaughtered what food animals we needed, would we be taking food from hungry mouths overseas? We thought not.

With an eventual goal of self-sufficiency in our own food supply, we began changing our mountaintop retreat back into a farm. And our lives took on even more interest than they had before. We still had time to observe the wildlife, but now we had the opportunity to study domestic animals as well. And some of their antics proved as interesting as the doings of our wild friends.

We were quickly launched into livestock ventures when I called an acquaintance who raised chickens. Once I mentioned that I, too, was interested in raising chickens, my acquaintance became a friend. At dinnertime on the first day of spring she called me on the telephone.

"I have a banty rooster and two hens tied up in a feed sack for you. I have to go out of town, so I'll just leave them at the Gulf station with some young fellows," my friend said.

"But what'll I do?" I asked.

"Just get some old pans and fill them with laying mash and water and scatter some scratch on the ground. That's all they'll need," she answered firmly.

There was another problem. The old chicken coop needed cleaning, repairing, disinfecting, and white-washing before it could be used. So the boys and I optimistically filled two horse troughs in the barn with clean hay and settled down to wait for Bruce. He was due home any minute, and I had no intention of meeting him on our one-lane road in the jeep.

An hour later we were still waiting. Bruce had never been so late before. My taut nerves began crumbling—at the very least, I expected a car accident. But luckily the explanation was far simpler. One of the new members of Bruce's carpool had misunderstood the meeting place, and the others had spent an hour searching for him. When Bruce drove up at 7 P.M., we immediately piled into the bus and headed downtown. As we pulled into the gas station, six teenage boys stood staring at us. What they saw were three grubby, excited little boys; one nervous, long-haired, dungaree-clad woman; and an immaculate, white-shirted man with a suit and tie. It took considerable effort on my part to get out of the car and ask a faltering question.

"Do you have my chickens?"

They pointed silently to a wriggling, cackling bag in the corner.

One boy burst out rudely, "Take them, lady, and get them out of here." I couldn't understand their obvious hostility and disgust with me and the chickens.

Eagerly we drove back up the mountain, and Bruce lugged the bag into the barn. Carefully cutting the twine, he upended the bag into the horse trough. Out jumped a striking reddish-brown and black rooster with a bright red comb. Another shake and the lovely brown and white hens emerged. The darker and prettier of the hens stayed in the trough while the rooster and the lighter colored hen fled to the other end of the barn, cackling excitedly. Eventually they all flew wildly up to the stone sill of a small window. That window became their roost and refuge from curious little boys.

For several days, through rain storms and cold weather, we kept them in the barn. Hunt as we could, we found no eggs. When the weather finally turned nice, we began letting them outside to range. This led to a protracted hunt each evening as we attempted to herd them back in for the night. The rooster, named Laffite by the boys, and the lighter hen, Gabrielle, were usually together. But Doris, the darker hen, was definitely a maverick. She was always off by herself in some out-of-the-way place. However, she was easier to catch, and she let the boys pick her up without too much protest. As a matter of fact, she took to perching on Steve's forefinger, looking like a caricature of a trained falcon. Every child that came to visit fell in love with her, and even though she never laid an egg in her life, she was the most pampered hen imaginable.

One afternoon the rooster wandered off and did not return by nightfall. After an unsuccessful search, we left the barn door open in case he came back. The following day was icy, damp, and miserable with heavy sleet.

Laffite still had not returned. Steve thought he heard him crowing once in the gray cold morning near the tool building, but Bruce and I spent an hour searching in the sleet and found nothing. I felt really heavy-hearted about Laffite's disappearance.

The next day was even worse—freezing rain which coated everything with a thick layer of ice. We had just about given up hope for our new banty rooster when suddenly, just outside the dining room window, there he was, in the midst of the sleet, foraging in the grape tangle. He looked almost ludicrous—a spot of gaudy color in a silver and black world. Bruce and Steve charged out into the dismal slippery day, running hard to head off the independent rooster. The rest of us cheered lustily from the back porch as time after time Laffite came almost within reach. At the crucial moment, Steve would lose his footing and upend himself on the ice. They chased that rooster from the grape tangle to the stream and into the woods. Suddenly, as Steve cut him off, Bruce lunged and grabbed the sodden creature, tucked him under his arm, and carried him back to the barn and his small harem. He was a pitiful, sorry sight, so wet and defeated, but he managed to make a small triumph out of his inglorious return, puffing his soaked feathers proudly as he strutted before the admiring hens. "I sure hope he doesn't get sick from the cold exposure," Bruce worried. We didn't yet know what hardy creatures banty roosters could be.

April came with its warm weather. Gradually the bantams settled into a routine. The window ledge remained their roost, while one horse trough, in which I placed a plastic egg, became a nesting box for Gabrielle. They would have their morning meal and then sally out to the barberry bushes where they foraged all day. By 6 o'clock Laffite was rounding up the hens and herding them back into the barn for supper and early retirement.

In the meantime Bruce and the boys tried to ready the chicken house, in between all the other pressing spring chores. The large tool building which had had a portion walled off for chickens many decades ago was divided into two separate enclosed areas, one considerably smaller than the other. There were several large removable windows which needed screens, numerous nesting boxes that had to be repaired, and ample roosts with dropping boards beneath. In the middle of the larger enclosure was an old trap door which led to the windowed dirt basement beneath. Lying in the dirt was an enormous and very heavy old plank which would have to be hoisted up to the trap door so the chickens could go down the ramp and take their dust baths in the dirt. Many of the windows below had been smashed, and both the basement and the chicken house were jammed with the cast-offs of an old farm. Much of it was large and bulky and had to be hauled to the dump in the jeep.

Once the junk was gone, Bruce mended the nesting boxes, took the tons of old hay and manure to the compost bins, put mesh over the windows, and finally whitewashed and disinfected the whole place. Then we covered the floors with three inches of fresh hay, stuffed new hay in the nesting boxes, hung up the mash feeders, and put down the waterers. The small enclosure was ready for the bantys. But instead of three bantys, we now had six to catch, because my friend had brought me three more hens. We shut up the barn, called for the boys to help, and spent an hour chasing and catching the frightened birds. Once we put them in their new home, though, they quickly adjusted. The roosts were occupied instantly, and the next day I collected three eggs from the nesting boxes. I opened the trap door, scattering some grain down the ramp, and within two days Laffite and his five hens were trooping up and down, scratching in the dirt and laying eggs in the boxes. At three each afternoon, when I opened the lower door, Laffite led them outside, where they wandered all over the yard searching for food. Promptly at 6:15 the rooster rounded up his flock and herded them back through the basement door, up the ramp, and into the chicken house. Patiently they waited for their feed, a change of water, and some greens before settling down on their roosts for the night. Occasionally Doris strayed, and we would inevitably discover her lurking under the barberry bushes. But by and large I grew very fond of my dependable hens and the proud, dominant rooster.

I could never quite escape the thrill I felt whenever I discovered a fresh, beautiful egg lying in a nesting box. It was miraculous to my town-bred eyes.

The bantys, though, were only the beginning of my ambitious plan to raise all of our eggs, to supply our garden with manure, and to fill our freezer with chickens. From a nearby hatchery I ordered 25 day-old pullets, and near the end of May, Pop, Mark, and I drove down to pick them up. The hatchery, reputed to be the oldest in the country, specializes in breeding various types of hens with Rhode Island red roosters. Following the advice of my friend Mary, I had requested their black beauty pullets, which were the result of crossing barred rock hens with the Rhode Island reds. The tiny chicks were coal black and peeping lustily when we lifted the lid of their ventilated carton. We brought them home and installed them in a large box in the dining room. For a brooder, Bruce took the shield off his trouble light, jammed the handle through an inverted aluminum pie plate, and tied the cord to the middle of a long board. In order to gain a high enough support for the board on each side of the big box, he pulled over two dining room chairs and piled on them a number of his fat old Smithsonian Annual Reports. To adjust the temperature at the bottom of the box, we simply had to add or subtract volumes.

Carefully following directions from the hatchery, I had lined the box with newspapers, filled a chick waterer, and put some starter mash in a little feeder. I lifted the first chick from the ventilated carton, dipped its beak in the warm water and then in the feed, and released it. Immediately it began scurrying busily around eating, drinking, and messing up the clean newspapers. The other twenty-four chicks followed suit. All the books had said that chicks would need several lessons in eating and drinking before they caught on. Ours did not—they ate and drank lustily from the beginning.

Of course, this installation in the dining room was only temporary, a month at the most, until the chicks were big enough to go into the henhouse. However, despite changing the newspapers several times a day, the dining room began to smell distinctly of chickens, and I began to exhort Bruce to do something. Luckily, we only eat in the dining room when we have guests, and for a couple of weeks none were expected. Then Bruce came home one day to say that he had invited his boss over to view the laurel and stay for dinner. She is a lovely person—in fact, she was raised on a farm—but still I didn't feel that I should subject her to a dinner accompanied by the peeping of twenty-five smelly chicks. I set the date of the dinner as the deadline—the chicks had to be out by then. While I cleaned the house and prepared the meal on the day she was expected, Bruce and Pop scrounged around the barn and shed for materials to construct a predator-proof pen for the chicks inside the henhouse. With two old wooden doors, some corrugated steel, and an old screen door, they fashioned a large enclosure that could be opened from the top to permit access to the chicks. They also drilled a hole through the screen door and threaded the electric cord for the pie pan brooder through it. We lined the pen with hay and newspapers, deposited the chicks, and left them playing "chase the chick with the piece of straw in her mouth," their favorite and only game. With barely an hour before our guest's arrival, I opened all the windows and drew a deep breath, the first I had drawn in the dining room since the chicks had arrived.

Now that our henhouse was filled with chickens, I felt satisfied; but I had reckoned without Mary. Several weeks later she called to ask if I would like some guinea fowl and a pair of six-week-old Mallard ducklings. I had never heard of guineas and had no idea what they looked like except, as Mary told me, "They're ugly with big lumps on their heads and awful noisy." When I told Steve of Mary's offer, he said that he wanted to raise them because their feathers were beautiful. Of course, none of us had to be persuaded about the ducklings. We did wonder, though, what they would do without a pond to swim in.

By then, since the black beauty hens were nearly as large as the bantys, we released them from the pen and partitioned it into two sections for the guineas and the ducklings. The three baby guineas inherited the chick waterer and the brooder, and they obligingly ate starter mash from a paper plate. The ducklings splashed merrily in a large enamel pan and siphoned up starter mash mixed with water. The boys were thrilled with the brown ducklings that huddled uncertainly in a corner of the pen, frightened by the abrupt change in their lives, and it took several weeks of patient coaxing before they finally lost their fear and settled down. The guineas, of course, remembered nothing and were quite pleased with the situation. They were beautiful little creatures, showing no signs of their impending lumps and raucous voices. They peeped just like every other baby bird.

We had a month of relative peace in the henhouse—the black beauty hens quickly learned to follow the bantys outside and spend their days foraging in the sunshine. The ducklings and guineas thrived and grew in the pen. And two banty hens stopped laying and became broody. Mary supplied us with thirteen fertile eggs for the one mother-to-be and eight eggs for the other. The thirteen-egg hen was due to hatch out on the fourth of August. But just before that date, tragedy struck. Mary had told me that the guineas and ducklings were old enough to go outside the pen, so I released them. The ducks promptly went outside, waddled under the barberry hedge, and settled in. The guineas flew up to the henhouse roost. That night I neglected to turn on the light in the henhouse, and the next morning only one guinea greeted me when I went in to feed the chickens. The boys found the mangled body of another stuffed in a hole in the floor. The third was badly injured down in the corner of the basement. We put it and the healthy guinea back into the pen, but the injured one died the following night. Obviously a rat had seized its opportunity in the dark, and only the fact that the second guinea had been too big to fit through the hole had saved the third guinea from capture and death. Bruce plugged the rat hole and set out rat traps and poison. After a few days we discovered the body of a rat killed by the poison just outside the henhouse. The remaining guinea, fondly named Gin-gin (with a hard G), roamed about calling cheerfully all day, but each night the boys engaged in a wild chase to capture him and put him back in the pen.

Promptly on schedule, mamma banty began hatching out her chicks. Along with the banty eggs, Mary had

The author lets the hens out of the shed for the day.

slipped in two colored eggs, the product of Aracuna hens that had been fertilized by banty roosters. We were especially anxious to see if they would hatch. They did, and so did nine banty chicks—only two of the thirteen eggs were infertile. Every time we went down to the chicken house there were more tiny golden heads peering out from underneath the mamma. She patiently let Steve pick her up to count and admire her offspring. After two days we cleaned out the eggshells, scooped up mamma and her chicks, and deposited them in the pen for safety during the night, divided from Gin-gin by the wooden barrier. Banty mothers do not pamper their diminutive chicks: she had them outside foraging within a week. They were a beautiful sight—downy yellow and incredibly small with black stripings on their backs. Two of them, bantacunas according to Steve, were slightly larger than the others, but mamma treated them all alike as she led them through the henhouse each morning, down the ramp, across the basement, up and out the door, and over the dew-covered grass.

The other mamma was not so smart. When her first egg hatched, she promptly deserted the nest and thus became the proud mother of one chick. But neither the chick nor its mamma were tolerated by mamma Number 1, so I was forced to displace Gin-gin in order to give a safe place to the new arrival. Gin-gin was as large as the bantys, so I felt he should finally be safe in the open henhouse at night. But a peculiar relationship developed—Gin-gin really didn't want to leave the pen, and he kept trying to get back in whenever the screen door was open. After he had a few tussles with mamma Number 2, she suddenly accepted him as part of the family. Gin-gin took his role quite seriously, helping to train, guard, and protect the small chick. For over a month the happy threesome were constantly together as they explored the lawn and barnyard.

In the meantime the eleven little chicks were growing rapidly. The sight of mamma Number 1 clucking along with her eleven peeping chicks strung out behind never ceased to amuse me. Then, when the chicks were almost a month old, the picture was spoiled. Coming back from the garden around noontime, I heard a fearsome squawking in the chicken yard. As I looked down from the lawn I saw mamma Number 1 chasing a large bird. The bird rose into a nearby maple tree, while mamma still squawked below. As it turned its head slightly I saw the curved beak of a hawk with something clutched in its talons. I went charging down as the Cooper's hawk, the most notorious of chicken killers, sailed away. I yelled for the boys, and they joined me in the chicken yard. It was strangely silent and deserted except for the distressed hen who kept searching about and calling. There was no sign or sound of the chicks, and for a minute I feared the hawk had killed them all. Steve stoutly maintained that the chicks were hidden, and we looked in all the likely places. Under the hedge the two mallard ducklings were huddled. Under the henhouse the black beauty hens, the bantys, and Gin-gin squeezed as far back as possible. Mamma Number 2 and her chick were in the henhouse itself. At that moment Pop drove up and parked his car beside the stone wall outside the guest house. Baby chicks exploded from the underbrush beside it. Fearfully we counted as they fled for mamma—only ten were left. The hawk had made a killing and would likely be back for more. As Pop oiled his gun, the old conflict between wildlife and domestic animals occupied my thoughts. No one else worried about it- the hawk had killed a chicken and would have to be killed in turn. With all the rabbits and mice around, its attack on the chickens seemed unforgiveable. Still, I hated the thought of killing any wild animal. Luckily it never returned.

The next chicken killer we had to face posed a much sadder dilemma. When our puppy Bobbin grew up, she seemed inordinately interested in the chickens. Twice we caught her stalking the banty hens, and the third time only Mom's intervention saved the life of one. We tried disciplining the pup, but whenever she could she was back after the chickens. One day I caught her skulking around beneath the henhouse, so I spanked her and sent her out. That evening when I went down to feed the black beauty hens, there were only twenty-four. Desperately I recounted, but one was gone. I discovered her uneaten body under the henhouse. A predator would have eaten its kill—it was obvious Bobbin was a chicken killer. Perhaps her wild mother had taught her that any small creature was fair game. Sadly we were forced to tie her permanently to her doghouse. "On any normal farm, that dog would be shot," Bruce growled as the boys begged for mercy for their little pet. They bought a chain and a leash, and Bobbin began a life of almost total imprisonment. Farm life certainly had its problems. Eventually the boys reached the decision to give her away to the humane society, and so she left us. It is hard, even now, to forget her winsome ways.

Luckily, though, all the boys were thoroughly distracted by the chickens and ducks, and there was even talk of getting geese and peacocks. Mary did present us with one more oddity. When the boys and I went to visit her, she pointed to a huge, male, Muscovy duck wandering around her yard. "If you fellows can catch him, you can have him," she challenged. That was all the encouragement they needed, though it took them half an hour and an incredible struggle to finally trap him. He was a magnificent specimen with his striking black and white coat and red head and beak. But he did act as if he were lord of everything—particularly the much smaller mallard ducklings. And there was nothing endearing about his hissing personality or his malevolent beady eyes. Mary had dubbed him "Big John," and Big John he remained. When he waddled majestically into view, chickens and ducklings scattered, but he did maintain a healthy mistrust of human beings, which enabled me to keep him away from the feed dish when the mallards were eating.

Summer passed, and autumn was upon us. The black beauty hens were fully grown, and the banty chicks were becoming discernible as roosters and hens. Mamma Number 1 went back to laying eggs, and Gin-gin took on the shepherding and training of the ten half-grown chicks. We were liable to hear his raucous call almost anywhere as he discovered a new source of food. The bantys would come running. Particular delicacies were the rotting grapes and spilled seed beneath the bird feeder.

To our delight we had one large white and red rooster. We were hopeful that he might service some of the black beauty hens since we had no black beauty roosters. When he was only half-grown he began practicing his crow—a squeaky uncertain noise, but gradually his expertise improved. He also began mating quite decisively with the old banty hens. They were not amused, but since Laffite didn't object, the chosen hen always lost the struggle.

Near the end of October, when we were finally certain that Gin-gin was a male, Mary gave us a slightly younger female. After protesting for several hours, she finally settled down and followed Gin-gin outside. By evening, though they seemed admirably suited, she would not follow him back into the henhouse, and she insisted on roosting in a tree for the night. Later that night I was awakened out of a sound sleep by a squawking noise. In a few seconds there was silence, followed by the call of a great-horned owl. The next morning the guinea was gone, and only one of the two female mallards appeared with Big John. We never found a trace of the other duck or the guinea. Mary gave us three more baby guineas to raise and train, and we figured that by spring we would finally have a mate for Gin-gin. In the meantime he began venting his mating frustrations on the black beauty hens.

After the death of the mallard, the remaining ducks also went into the chicken house at night. We didn't even have to train them—they were just there every evening at dusk.

Evidently they sensed danger outside, or at least that was the only explanation we could figure out, because they had never gone in before. Big John and the little mallard duck became constant companions after that night.

The black beauty hens started laying in mid-October. At first there were just a couple of pullet-sized eggs, but by the first week in November we were averaging eighteen per day. Many of the first layers had already progressed from pullet-size to enormous, brown, double-yolked eggs. It took me awhile to adjust my thinking from scarcity to bounty. Finally I had more eggs than I needed—nearly two dozen a day—and I was able to sell the surplus. Each cold, dreary November day I shivered my way down to feed the chickens and to collect the warm, just-laid eggs in my chilled hands. Noon was the highlight of Mark's day when he picked up the egg pail and went down to gather the morning-laid eggs.

"Ten more eggs, Mommy," he would announce proudly upon his return. In his eyes, and mine too, eggs were truly one of the great miracles of creation.

Our farming ventures hinged on keeping the first field open for future pastures and cultivated crops. Since we had moved in we had been trying to convince farmers from the valley to come up and cut the field. But even offers of free hay didn't tempt them. Our road and the difficulty of getting equipment up was just too much for them. As briars, brush, and locust trees began springing up throughout the field, Bruce grew increasingly upset. For the millionth time he would say plaintively, "We can't let that field go back to woods."

"But we can't afford a tractor, either," I would answer.

Into this miasma of despair stepped a young local sheep farmer. Would we rent our field to him? After it was cut once, he said, the sheep would do a good job of keeping the field down. And since the field was completely ringed with woods, which the sheep wouldn't go into, all we would need to do would be to fence them out of the garden and lawn area, and they would stay in the fields. It sounded like the ideal answer to our problem with the field. Best of all, the sheep would be his headache, not ours. Maybe we could painlessly learn something about sheep-raising from a real expert. The proposal was made in August, and the farmer promised to cut the field over that autumn in preparation for putting in the sheep the following spring. But despite several pleas, he could not find the time to cut the field before winter set in. We heard nothing from him all winter until one sunny day in late March when he drove into the barnyard.

"Well, guess the field will be ready in another month for the sheep," he drawled.

"You mean you still plan to use our field?" I queried.

"Oh, yeh!" he answered, "soon as I get back from sheep-shearing. Go all over the country," he added.

I greeted Bruce with the good news that evening, and we began to hope. We hoped all through April and into May as the grass grew higher and higher. Finally Bruce called him up.

"Have them there in a few days," the farmer answered, "soon's you get the sheep fencing up."

"I'll wait until the sheep are here. Then I'll put the fence up," Bruce answered, not really believing that they would ever come. We waited two more weeks on into June. Again Bruce called him.

"Truck's broke down," was the answer.

"Well, either pay the rent for June or the deal's off," Bruce said impatiently.

"Have 'em up Monday," the farmer promised.

On Monday afternoon a large, slatted, livestock truck drove up. The farmer pulled in front of the barn and opened the back of the truck; out leaped thirty-eight sheep. They certainly were frisky little creatures, I marveled, as all we could see was a maze of white backs awash in a sea of enveloping green. The boys were fascinated, but I cautioned them to let the sheep alone. After learning that the sheep were Suffolks, Hampshires, and Suffolk crosses, I retired to the front porch. The farmer drove off and the boys, along with their grandfather, went closer to look at them. Suddenly I heard a shout: "Head him off, Steve." I looked out to see one sheep racing the length of the field with Steve and Dave running desperately to catch up.

A few minutes later Steve yelled, "What'll I do, Grandpa, now that I've caught him?" This call came across from the edge of the woods beyond the powerline.

"Let him go; he'll come back," was the advice. Several minutes later Steve came down over the field and told how he had caught the sheep, wrestled it to the ground, and attempted to calm it. "But when I let go, it ran into the woods."

I went back to search with Steve, remembering the farmer's parting words, "The woods form a natural barrier. They'll never go into them." When I reached the spot where Steve had caught the sheep, I could clearly see the trampled path that led deep into the woods of Sapsucker Ridge, but there was no sign of the strayed sheep. By the time we got back to the house the farmer had returned with a large bucket of brown granules which he called "minerals." Sorrowfully I told the story of the lost sheep. To my surprise, he didn't even seem annoyed. He looked over his flock and said, "Oh yeh! I know which one's missing. She'll probably wander back tonight."

"But she's way up in the woods," I pointed out.

He took one look at the distance and the hot sun and said, "Don't worry about it," as he drove off in his truck.

For a while the rest of the sheep stayed in a huddled group off in the field, but near dusk they came running. Our unfenced yard was a real boon to them. They surged over the lawns, through the garden, and into the barnyard. Eagerly they chomped at the neat, trimmed edges of the lawn. Once they discovered the cultivated crops, they forgot all about the field. "Why traipse through the tall grass when there's all this lovely trimmed stuff?" they seemed to reason. The thirty-three ewes and lambs ran together while the four rams stayed off by themselves. The "bachelor boys," as my in-laws called them, were large, slow-moving, and placid; but they seemed menacing to me. The others ran when I came near. The rams stood their ground, making almost imperceptible rumblings in their throats. I remembered all the stories I had heard about butting rams, and I kept my distance.

Since the sheep were here now, Bruce went out to purchase fencing. To his dismay, he quickly discovered that there was none available. It would have to be ordered. In the meantime we would just have to put up with sheep grazing on the lawn. If only they had stayed just on the lawn! Two days after their arrival, as

I set off on my early morning walk, I glanced fondly at my flourishing strawberry patch, where I had fought sod and weeds for two years. But this spring the plants were loaded with blossoms, and now the unripe berries were abundant. To my surprise, several leaves had been nipped off. Innocently, I wondered whether the bunnies had been sampling them. The next morning I looked again at my patch, only this time I saw nothing but four rows of leafless stems. The berries and leaves were gone. Sprinkled liberally throughout the patch was sheep dung. I thought of my two years of hard labor and cried. It was hard to believe that I would never see the culmination of all that work and concern.

Once the strawberries were gone, the sheep moved into the corn. They dug up the marigolds, nipped off the portulaca, and ate the forsythia leaves. They never grazed in the fields. They were either resting in the barnyard or sampling all the cultivated goodies. We spent evenings until ten o'clock chasing them, and we were awakened each morning at five by their bleating just under our windows. Once my in-laws looked out on the tiny front porch of the guest house and found it packed solid with sheep. Another time they were all trapped in the small, fenced, guest house yard, unable to get out. Or we would hear a sudden bleating at the side of the house late at night and race out just in time to save the bridal wreath bush from total destruction.

They seemed to be incredibly stupid animals. Invariably one or two lambs would be separated from the flock and would run around desperately bleating "ma, ma, ma" as loudly as possible. One morning Pop and Mom looked out the window and saw a ram with three legs jammed down through the large grate across the road. It took patience and strength to pull him gently out.

By this time we were all nervous wrecks. The sheep had made no headway at all in the fields, and to top it off, we were told that the fencing we had ordered was unavailable. After a sleepless night and much figuring over the checkbook, Bruce announced, "Let's go tractor hunting today. I'll cut the fields myself." By the end of the day we had bought a second-hand tractor. Then Bruce called up the sheep farmer. "Either lend us some fencing or the sheep must go. They're ruining the place," he told him. The next morning the farmer brought up two rolls of sheep fencing and a bucket of fence staples. "I'll have a fence up in no time," Bruce announced confidently.

He and Pop labored all day, fencing off the yards and gardens from the sheep. They started in the woods above the garden, stretching the fencing taut with the help of the jeep. Previously they had pirated steel fence poles from the part of the pasture that had once been fenced with barbed wire. The stretching did not work well wherever the ground was uneven, and there were gaps beneath the fence in a number of strategic places. Even in using two entire rolls of fencing, we still had to depend on barbed wire to finish the job. The corral was missing a number of crucial boards and also had to be repaired, but by nightfall a fairly adequate fence was in place.

Or so we thought. At their accustomed dusk rampage, the lambs and ewes gathered above the barn and began running down the now-fenced road. They pushed and butted against the fence; the lambs tried to jam their heads underneath. Unfortunately, Bruce had been unable to make the fence very taut at that spot, and we sat up on the stone bench watching first one and then another slip quite easily beneath the barrier.

By this time Bruce's chin was set hard. He would defeat those sheep. He hauled heavy oak planks from the barn and stapled them to the fence bottom. The added weight eliminated the sag, and they were stopped for that night. Wearily we went inside at 10 P.M.

From my reading I learned that sheep establish definite patterns and are most active at dusk and dawn. These sheep were no exception. Promptly at 5 A.M. the first "ma-ma's" began as a lamb struggled under a fence and then couldn't get back to the flock. Bruce and his parents were up chasing and rescuing each morning. But every day the fence was meticulously inspected and shored up with various make-do methods. Six strands of barbed wire worked in one spot for awhile. So did black plastic stuffed in an impossible hole (my contribution, one desperate evening, when several lambs discovered the escape hatch). Gradually the lambs and ewes adjusted to the new situation. Our dusks and dawns were no longer a nightmare of chasing.

The rams were different—more persistent, but not nearly so damaging a problem. They liked the guest house lawn, our lawn, and the weedy flat area between the woods and the bottom of the grape arbor. They had not participated in the destruction of the garden. But they also did not give up as easily as the lambs and ewes. Most evenings they would suddenly appear on one of the lawns, peacefully grazing, and once again Bruce and his father would pace the fence line, trying to figure out how they were getting through. Each time they would find some small overlooked hole and plug it up. It was a slow, aggravating battle, but after a week we were mostly freed from the plague.

For the first time I actually looked at the sheep without loathing. A couple of the lambs began approaching me boldly. One lovely morning I stood and watched as Bobbin and two curious lambs nosed each other. Under the watchful eye of the ewe, Bobbin ran, rolled, and flicked her tail and then moved in to lick the faces of the lambs. It was a bucolic scene. Maybe, just maybe, I would get to like the sheep.

This peaceful state of affairs lasted less than two weeks. Then suddenly the whole flock appeared in the driveway. This time we could find no escape hatch. The following morning Margaret came up the road, driving a large flock of sheep ahead of her. She had discovered them over a mile down the road and running hard. They began following the fence into the woods and turning around it to come into the garden, no matter how far

Bruce extended it. Wearily we admitted defeat, and Bruce called up the farmer. He came and got his sheep, and we were left with $60 worth of sheep fencing and a shaggy field. The next day Bruce began cutting down the fields with a bush hog attached to the tractor. But for weeks afterward I dreamt of chasing sheep. Even now the mere sight of a flock of sheep turns me cold and reminds me that not all our ventures here have been successful.

Once the field was cut down we began to plan for more livestock. Eagerly we walked about looking for ideal places to raise pigs and graze goats. And we discussed the possibility of growing our own feed. Much as we rejected the idea of big-time farming with lots of expensive equipment, it was obvious that we would have to invest in some more implements for the tractor if we intended to raise all our own food. We had neither the time nor strength to do all the work by hand.

Looking over the supermarkets and fruit stands that summer and fall, I was appalled by the prices and scarcity of fresh produce. A small clump of Concord grapes sold for an enormous price, and there were no blackberries, raspberries, currants, or gooseberries at all. Strawberries were scarce and expensive, and blueberries were large, tasteless, and overpriced. We discovered that small fruit farming was practically an extinct art. Suddenly our broken-down grape trellises seemed sinfully wasteful. Surely it could still be a haven for wildlife and also produce large crops for sale to local markets if only Bruce would replace the rotten poles, straighten up the trellises, and prune the vines.

In fact, everywhere we looked on our mountain-top farm we could see possibilities for productivity as well as wildlife shelter. Bruce made plans to cut down the brush at the far field and to plant 4,000 pines and spruces. And finally we came to the question of raising steers. Should we feed the expensive creatures for a year and a half in hopes of getting beef for the freezer, or was there another answer? We looked up at the top of the first field and spotted a herd of white-tailed deer grazing. Because they were wild and beautiful, we had never considered hunting them for food. And yet they lived on our land and were overpopulating it. If we killed one each year, we could add a lot of meat to our diet without the time and money needed to raise steers.

We realized, of course, that no matter how self-sufficient in food we might become in time and no matter how much we might conserve fossil fuels, our small efforts and sacrifices would not save the world. But we couldn't help believing that if everyone would make a start somewhere and be productive rather than wasteful, the world would have at least an equal chance to recover from the rapacious rampages of human beings. At first the idea of saving, making do, using up, and doing for ourselves seemed distasteful and impracticable. And yet, surprisingly, once we started on a do-for-ourselves campaign we discovered more and more what a joyful, interesting life it led to. Whole unprocessed foods now make up a good part of our diet, giving us all glowing health and boundless energy. Kneading bread, churning an eggbeater, and beating batter with a large wooden spoon help keep my arms slender. Hauling water for the chickens, weeding the garden, and hiking on the trails keep me vigorous. And best of all, when I read still another scare article about shortages, I don't panic or feel helpless. Instead, I begin to think—what can we do to alleviate the problem? Almost always we have at least a partial solution.

We originally bought our home on the mountain as a refuge from the materialistic urban world. We have derived joy and peace of mind here, and now we hope to derive a living as well. But while a mountain is as secluded as an island, the problems of the world are inescapable. Perhaps the independent attitudes which our isolated mountain living have engendered in all of us will help us to cope with our rapidly changing world.

Each morning, when I look out on a new day, I find it difficult to believe that humans could do anything to destroy the timeless beauty of the Pennsylvania mountains. The hills should remain eternal. We hope they will.

Epilogue

Farewell to Pop
June 1978

THE GUEST HOUSE stands empty this year, and the wildlife has already moved in. Mice are reclaiming the remodeled kitchen and newly-painted bathroom. A woodchuck family lives under the foundations, phoebes raise their nestlings beneath the porch portico, and chipmunks have returned to the stone wall.

My father-in-law died suddenly in March, and all that is left here are memories. Strange how much of him is still visible and how often we talk of him as if he is just away and will be back again from the South in a few weeks.

The other day I went into his work area in the tool shed to search for some equipment. Each implement hung neatly in its appointed place, but it was covered with a thick layer of dust. This year each tool will not be cleaned and the shed swept with meticulous care. No noisy hammering will greet me when I go down to feed the chickens.

I stood and looked at the desolate sight—tools without their user—and wondered at the irony that leaves the tools and takes the toolmaker away. I left without the tool I was seeking.

We still enter the guest house as little as possible, and then only the kitchen, which was not Pop's domain. Nothing has been cleared out yet. That melancholy job is still to be done when Mom comes north alone. In the living room, near Pop's old beige chair, his footstool lies on the floor with a leg broken off. The desk dominates one corner, the television another. He was liable to be either writing letters at the one or watching the other when we came down to visit, but he would stop whatever he was doing to chat.

Talking was as essential as breathing to him, and we were always asked to sit down and share the day. With Bruce, he discussed the jobs he had done, for he had to feel useful. With me it was usually the boys, or world affairs or, most important of all, the garden.

"I must tell Pop the peas are blossoming," I think, only there is no Pop to tell anymore.

"The flea beetles are bad this year," but Pop is not there to commiserate with.

"I saw a wild turkey on my walk today. A deer leaped right in front of me. The mountain laurel is absolutely beautiful. Look, Pop, at all the iris. Did you hear the whippoorwill last night?" Only silence now and no Pop to share the little joys with.

Or the cookies and lemonade. Pop loved my cookies and usually managed to find an excuse to drop in at mid-morning when I was baking. Often he had gone to town to pick up the mail and to shop at his favorite place, the hardware store. He would sit and eat and chat, then jump up and clump off to do a little job.

He kept my bread board repaired and the kitchen chairs glued. He spent hours servicing the lawn mowers, the rototiller, and the tractor. Whenever any motor gave up, Pop took it apart, whistling happily as he worked, because he was an excellent mechanic. Before he retired, he was an electrical engineer, and when he and Mom moved here, he began to wire buildings that had never been wired before. First the shed with switches at every door. Then the top floor of the barn. He installed lights in the barnyard and overlooking the pig pasture. Finally, he and Bruce together tackled the garage, with Bruce doing the climbing on the roof to erect the mast.

Everywhere we go on the farm we are reminded of things he did, and I know that is how he would like to be remembered. He hated to feel old and useless. How he complained last summer after his operation when he was forced to sit and watch the world go by. David grew a garden for him, but it was not the same. Steve cut his lawns and visited with him on the porch swing.

"It's awful to get old," he told Steve during a dark hour.

But gradually his strength returned and by the end of September, when he left for the South, he looked well.

"Goodbye, Pop," I waved cheerfully. "See you next May."

"If I make it," he answered.

"Oh, Pop," I said impatiently, "you know you will."

He didn't, though. March, that killer of the old and weak, took its toll. In the end, he struggled valiantly but in vain. He almost made his seventy-second birthday.

"Never again will I assist him in repairing a chair or painting a television antenna or sit on the porch swing with him on summer afternoons and talk," Steve wrote in his journal. "It is hard to let him go for I know that he will always, as long as I live, have a place in my heart."

In all of our hearts, Pop. Farewell!

2008

Thirty years have passed since I wrote those words. All of our parents are gone now, and we are the ones who are old.

Much has changed here and yet much remains the same. Bruce and I still live in the old farmhouse, but Bruce retired from Penn State eight years ago. David, who prefers to be called Dave, now lives and works in the guesthouse as a writer, photographer, and environmentalist. Steve teaches Spanish at Penn State Altoona and lives nearby, along with his wife Karylee and their three-year-old daughter Elanor. Already, coming up to the mountain to hike and play in the stream is a big part of her life. Mark, along with his wife Luz and their twelve-year-old daughter Eva, are residents of Cleveland, Mississippi, where Mark teaches cultural geography at Delta State University. Eva, too, has spent many happy hours on the mountain and often calls to ask if I've seen any exciting animals lately. All three sons and our granddaughters have an abiding interest in nature and the outdoors.

We continued our homesteading until the late 1980s when we had a chimney fire. It was either rebuild a large portion of the house or give up our wood burning stove. By then the boys had graduated from Penn State and were off on their own. Without their help in gathering and splitting wood, we decided to close off the chimney and heat with oil. Retrofitting an old farmhouse with a more environmentally sound heating system was not possible given our limited income.

We also had problems with our attempts at animal husbandry and raising all our own food. After more than a decade of warring against the wild animals, I was more interested in watching than killing them. A raccoon raided our barn and wiped out all of our Muscovy ducks and most of our chickens. Deer and woodchucks constantly leaped over or dug under our nine-foot-tall vegetable garden fencing.

At about the time we gave up on gardening, Amish moved into the farming valley below our mountain, and we were happy to leave the gardening up to them. Although I continue to pick and freeze wild berries, cook and bake from scratch, and freeze other fruits for the winter, my canning days are over. Today we try to eat locally as much as possible and have found a local source for organic eggs. Instead of beef, we use venison from our mountain that some of our hunters give us.

I have continued observing and writing about the natural life of our mountain, recording the many new species of wildflowers, birds, reptiles and amphibians and, most of all, the new mammals that have appeared here.

First, black bears arrived and raided our beehives. That was the end of our beekeeping. But encountering bears on our trails and watching sows with their young seem ample compensation for the honey that we now purchase locally.

Then, in the 1990s, eastern coyotes appeared. They raise families in dens they have established on our property and sometimes we hear them howling. I have watched them with their pups, just as I watched a red fox den and their kits for two springs.

Ten years ago, fishers were reintroduced in north central Pennsylvania. These largest members of the weasel family reached our mountain five years ago and my sighting of one male along the stream one September remains an indelible memory.

Over the years, I've identified 162 species of birds here, more than seventy of which breed on our mountain. Several of those are neotropical migrants, such as wood thrushes, worm-eating warblers, black-throated green warblers, scarlet tanagers and Acadian flycatchers, whose numbers are dwindling because of threats on their breeding and wintering grounds. Unfortunately, we have had to become more and more aware of environmental concerns that threaten the existence not only of wildlife but also of humanity.

With the advent of the 1980s, greed settled in, and many of our neighbors had their land unsustainably logged. At the same time, they encouraged the burgeoning of the deer herd by posting their land. The hungry deer ate the understory, which posed a threat to the birds that nest on the ground or in shrubbery. Bruce spent much of that decade and part of the next trying to protect our access road from loggers since we didn't own the land on either side of the first mile of the road. Eventually, we bought the whole end of the mountain—one square mile—saving Laurel Ridge from loggers but not Sapsucker Ridge. One hundred and twenty acres were clearcut, which allowed a host of invasive shrubs and trees to germinate. Even after seventeen years, that section of the property has not recovered.

These forestry issues became a focus of my writing and research and we joined the Pennsylvania Forest Stewardship Program to learn more about the proper ways to manage a forest. Although we were not interested in sustainably harvesting our forest, we wanted to educate others about better ways to treat their properties. We also wanted to do a better job of deer management. As much as I enjoyed watching them, I realized that having a herd of fifty deer grazing in First Field was not healthy for our woods.

We are not hunters ourselves, but we had always kept our land open for hunting. However, very few deer were killed during hunting season. Bruce then decided to post our property for hunting by permission only and we chose a core group of hunters, based on recommendations from friends and neighbors. These same folks have helped us keep our ten miles of trails open, our land posted, and our road drains cleaned. Best of all, they take off between thirty-five and forty-five deer from our property every year. Since our neighbors do not follow a similar program, there are always more deer to harvest.

We can see some improvement in our forest understory. But to educate others, we also built a three-acre deer exclosure in the oldest part of our forest, which includes red and white oak trees that date back to the first cutting here in 1812. Our son Dave and I lead many college students up our road through our intact forest to the exclosure where we point out the differences inside and outside the fence. Even those who are longtime hunters are surprised at the difference. One returning adult student told us that despite hearing about the deer problem from the state game agency, he didn't believe it until he saw our place. We then walk them down the Sapsucker side and talk about and show them hundreds of trees and shrubs that are invasives such as multiflora rose, privet, Japanese barberry, and ailanthus—all of which compete with our natives. Unfortunately, the deer are able to distinguish between the natives and invasives and prefer the former to the latter.

Mountain land used to be the only unfragmented habitat in Pennsylvania. The valleys have filled up, with not only farms but also more and more with development of all kinds. At the base of Sapsucker Ridge, we now have a major interstate that was once a bypass around the town. Pennsylvania has more roads than any other state, and there seems to be no end to the road-building despite protests from local residents. A portion of this same interstate goes up on our mountain farther down the ridge instead of through the valley where the highway it is replacing still runs. We fought and lost that battle. On the other end of the ridge, another portion of the mountain was razed to build still another shopping mall, and we lost that battle too.

Our mountain is part of the Bald Eagle Mountain, the most western of the ridges in the Ridge-and-Valley province of Pennsylvania. Across the town lies the Allegheny Front. Both mountains are now coveted by the wind farm industry, and they are offering fabulous money for the privilege of building on both private and public land. Fortunately, many of the private landowners farther down the ridge, including us, have refused them. The Allegheny Front landowners may be more obliging.

Studies from Europe show that these wind farms will not provide the power that they say they will, especially here where winds are intermittent at best. But our arguments against them are wildlife-related. Both ridges are major flyways for migrating birds and bats. Bat researchers have already documented the deaths of hundreds of bats at a wind farm in southern Pennsylvania.

It is not yet clear how many birds are also affected. Recently, researchers from the Powdermill Avian Research Center and the National Aviary have been catching and radio tagging migrating eastern golden eagles on our ridge. Apparently, our ridge and the Allegheny Front are the major flyways for mature eastern golden eagles as they migrate from northern Quebec, where they breed, to southwestern West Virginia and eastern Kentucky where they winter, according to the travels of two males that they radio tagged in 2007. A female that they radio tagged on our mountain in 2008 is providing still more data about the little known life history of the eastern strain of golden eagles. This ongoing study on our property has been a constant source of inspiration for all of us.

Never Enough of Nature was the title of a book by ornithologist Lawrence Kilham that I read many years ago. Since then, it has been my mantra and will continue to be as we live out our lives here on a mountain that has been bloodied but unbowed. Our sons are similarly inclined, and we will be protecting our land from depredations beyond our lifetimes.

But I fear that most of our hills will not remain eternal and that humans are already finding ways to destroy their timeless beauty. In our rush to grasp at whatever energy straws are offered us, the land will be sacrificed. That is why I continue my record-keeping and writing about what is here now so that future generations will know what the natural world of a Pennsylvania mountain was like from 1971, when we arrived here, until the end of my life.

Index

Map of the Property

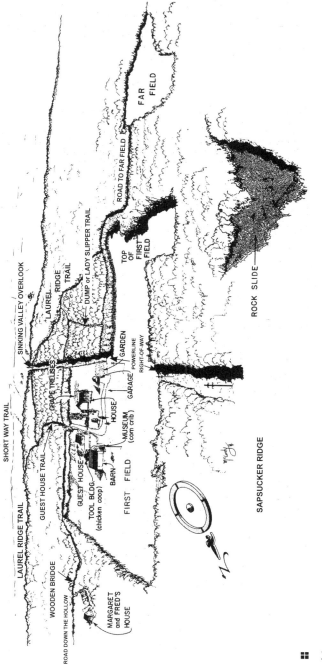